84-7
129-31
*203
208-12
224-9

PHOTOSHOP® ELEMENTS 3

Scott Kelby

PHOTOSHOP® ELEMENTS 3 DOWN & DIRTY TRICKS

The Photoshop Elements 3 Down and Dirty Tricks Team

CREATIVE DIRECTOR
Felix Nelson

TECHNICAL EDITOR
Polly Reincheld

COPY EDITOR
Chris Main

PRODUCTION EDITOR
Kim Gabriel

PRODUCTION MANAGER
Dave Damstra

PRODUCTION DESIGNERS
Dave Korman
Taffy Orlowski

COVER DESIGNED BY
Felix Nelson

COVER PHOTOS AND
STOCK IMAGES
The royalty-free stock images
in this book are courtesy of

Published by
New Riders / Peachpit Press

Copyright © 2005 by Scott Kelby

First edition: December 2004

Composed in Cronos, Helvetica, and Apple Garamond Light by NAPP Publishing

Trademarks
All terms mentioned in this book that are known to be trademarks or service marks have been appropriately capitalized. New Riders / Peachpit Press cannot attest to the accuracy of this information. Use of a term in the book should not be regarded as affecting the validity of any trademark or service mark.

Photoshop is a registered trademark of Adobe Systems, Inc.
Windows is a registered trademark of Microsoft Corporation.

Warning and Disclaimer
This book is designed to provide information about Photoshop Elements. Every effort has been made to make this book as complete and as accurate as possible, but no warranty of fitness is implied.

The information is provided on an as-is basis. The authors and New Riders / Peachpit Press shall have neither liability nor responsibility to any person or entity with respect to any loss or damages arising from the information contained in this book or from the use of the discs or programs that may accompany it.

ISBN 0-321-27835-6

9 8 7 6 5 4 3 2 1

Printed and bound in the United States of America

www.peachpit.com
www.scottkelbybooks.com

For my close friend
Rod Harlan

"It's the friends that you can
call up at 4 a.m. that matter."
—Marlene Dietrich

ACKNOWLEDGMENTS

I consider myself very, very blessed. Each day I get to work with such a wonderful group of people, and when I'm not working, I'm surrounded by family and friends whom I dearly love, all of whom come together to help and enrich my life in so many ways. There's not a printed acknowledgment I could write that would honor them in the way they deserve, but one of the benefits of writing a book is that at least you get to try.

Kalebra: My wonderful, beautiful, amazing, hilarious, fun-filled, loving wife. You're the greatest thing that's ever happened to me, and asking you to marry me 15 years ago was clearly the single best decision I've ever made. Your spirit, warmth, beauty, patience, and unconditional love continue to prove what everybody always says—I'm the luckiest guy in the world.

Jordan: Little buddy—you're just the greatest. A father couldn't ask for a more fun, more crazy, more lovable, or more loving son than you. I'm so thrilled and proud of the little man you're becoming, and you're so blessed to have your Mom's heart, compassion, and spirit. You're a very special little boy, and you've already touched so many people that I can't imagine all the wonders, adventure, and happiness life has in store for you.

Jeff: I can't tell you what a blessing it's been having you as a brother, and how thrilled I am that for the past three-and-half years, you've been part of our team (plus, I love getting to sneak out for lunch with you every day). You've had an amazing, wonderful, and important impact on my life, and just hearing your voice puts a smile on my face. I love you, man.

Dave Moser: I truly value our friendship all these many years, and I'm thrilled with all the fun and exciting things we're able to do together. There are few people with your passion, guts, integrity, vision, unflinching dedication to quality, and who always insist on raising the bar. I have to thank you for totally sharing my "what-we-do-next-has-to-be-better-than-what-we-did-before" credo. It sometimes annoys the hell out of everyone around us, but it is who we are, and "it is what it is."

Felix Nelson: I don't know how you do it, but you always do. If you had nothing but your amazing Photoshop talents, you'd be in the top one-quarter of one percent of Photoshop designers in the world, but your creativity, talent, ideas, discipline, and humor put you in a league all by yourself. I remember Jack Davis asking me: "Where in the world did you find Felix?" I can only figure God sent you our way. Thanks for everything you do, here in the book, in leading our creative team, and for your friendship and dedication. You da man!

Chris Main: You were there from just about the very beginning and I'm honored to still have you on our team, and I'm delighted I get to work and hang out with you doing lots of very fun stuff. Plus, you have a really cool home cinema. Well done, Mr. Main!

Dave Damstra: If they ever have a competition for best page layout guy in the business, I'm sending you to steal the show. Having you lay out my books is definitely a strategic advantage, and you set the standard, not only in your work, but in your amazing attitude in life as well.

Polly Reincheld: You've only been working with us a short time, but you've already become such a valued member of our team. Your tech-editing skills are absolutely top-notch, but your attitude, sense of humor, and personality put you over the top. We're very lucky to have found you, and I'm really delighted to have you tech-editing my books.

Kathy Siler: Despite the fact that the Redskins are at the bottom of their division, you seem to keep a great attitude (but I know that it's only because my Bucs are near the bottom of the NFC South, too). Okay, Redskins jokes aside (Hey, where's Champ Bailey?), I can't thank you enough for all the things you do—you make my job so much easier (partially because you do so much of it for me), and you do it with such great ease and such a great attitude, and you really look out for me (and believe me, that's no easy job). In short—you rock, kid!

Jim Workman and Jean A. Kendra: I'm very fortunate to have business partners who understand what it takes to do what we do. I can't thank you enough for your constant support, understanding, freedom, and help in accomplishing my goals.

Kim Gabriel: I don't have to tell you—it ain't easy putting together one of these books, but you keep a lot of plates in the air, you keep the trains running on time, and you do a marvelous job of keeping it all moving ahead. I can't thank you enough.

Nancy Ruenzel: My heartfelt thanks to you for helping me through the transition, and for placing such a high value on integrity and always striving to do "the right thing." It's the core reason why our partnership works so well, and I'm honored to have you as my publisher. My thanks to everyone at Peachpit Publishing who works so hard, who shows such loyalty, who is willing to take chances and try new things, yet remains solely focused on just making great books.

Adobe: Thanks to all my friends at the mother ship, including Addy Roff, Mark Delman, Julieanne Kost, Rye Livingston, Russell Brown, Terry "T-bone" White, Kevin Connor, Karen Gauthier, Deb Whitman, Russell Brady, and John Nack. Also, a special thanks to Mark Dahm for his invaluable help with this book.

My personal thanks go to Jeffrey Burke at Brand X Pictures for enabling me to use some of their wonderful stock images in this book.

Kudos and continued thanks to my home team: Julie Stephenson, Barbara Thompson, Fred Maya, Ronni O'Neil, Melinda Gotelli, Pete Kratzenberg, Dave "Kid Rock" Korman, Margie "From New York" Rosenstein, Dave Gales, Dave Cross, and Daphne Durkee. Gone but not forgotten: Stacy Behan, Barbara Rice, Chris Smith, Steve Weiss, Sarah Hughes, and Jill Nakashima.

Thanks to my mentors whose wisdom and whip-cracking have helped me immeasurably, including: John Graden, Jack Lee, Judy Farmer, Dave Gales, and Douglas Poole.

Most importantly, I want to thank God, and His son Jesus Christ, for leading me to the woman of my dreams, for blessing us with such a special little boy, for allowing me to make a living doing something I truly love, for always being there when I need Him, and for blessing me with a wonderful, fulfilling, and happy life, and such a warm, loving family to share it with.

ABOUT THE AUTHOR

Scott Kelby

Scott is Editor-in-Chief and co-founder of *Photoshop User* magazine, Editor-in-Chief of Nikon's *Capture User* magazine, Executive Editor of the *Photoshop Elements Techniques* newsletter, and Editor-in-Chief of *Mac Design Magazine*.

He is President of the National Association of Photoshop Professionals (NAPP), the trade association for Adobe® Photoshop® users, and he's President of KW Media Group, Inc., a Florida-based software education and publishing firm.

Scott is the author of more than 20 best-selling books, which have been translated into more than a dozen languages, including *The Photoshop Elements 3 Book for Digital Photographers*, *Photoshop CS Down & Dirty Tricks*, *Photoshop Classic Effects*, and *The Photoshop Book for Digital Photographers*, and co-author of *Photoshop CS Killer Tips*, all from New Riders Publishing.

Scott is Training Director for the Adobe Photoshop Seminar Tour, Conference Technical Chair for the Photoshop World Conference & Expo, and a speaker at graphics trade shows and events around the world. He is also featured in a series of Adobe Photoshop and Photoshop Elements training DVDs and has been training Photoshop users since 1993.

For more background info on Scott, visit www.scottkelby.com.

TABLE OF CONTENTS

CHAPTER 1   1
One Hour Photo
Portrait and Studio Effects

Sharp Foreground, Blurred Background   2
Depth-of-Field Effect   4
Creating Gallery Prints   6
Soft-Edged Portrait Background   12
Burning In Portraits   14
Trendy Fashion Blowout Look   17

CHAPTER 2   21
Maximum Exposure
Photographic Effects

Adding Objects Behind Existing Objects   22
Putting an Image in a Monitor   26
Montage from One Image   28
Blending Images for Instant Collages   32
Adding Motion Effects   34
Adding Motion Step By Step   38

CHAPTER 3   43
Dirty Dancing
Focusing Attention

Backscreening   44
Magazine Pop-Up Effect   46
Vignetting Attention   48
Popping Out of an Image   51
Snapshot Focus Effect   54
Magnifying Glass Trick   58

CHAPTER 4   63
In Living Color
Color Effects

Instant Stock Photo Effect   64
Colorizing Black-and-White Images   67
Painting Away Color   70
Visual Color Change   72
Sepia Tone Effect   74
Photo Tinting   76

TABLE OF CONTENTS

CHAPTER 5   79
Ad-Libbing
Advertising Effects

Backlit Photo Backgrounds   80
Quick, Elegant Product Background   84
Quick Product Shot Background   88
Fade-Away Reflection   91
Classified Ad Effect   94
Credit Card from a Photo   98
High-Tech Transparent Info Boxes   100
Turning a Logo into a Brush   104

CHAPTER 6   107
Jealous Type
Cool Type Effects

Instant 3D Type   108
Perspective Type Logo   111
Type on a Circle   114
Putting an Image into Type (Clipping Group)   117
Moving a Background Object in Front of Type   120
Grunge Type   122
Distressed Type   126
Carved in Stone   129
Transparent TV Type   132

CHAPTER 7   135
Saturday Night Special
Special Effects

Digital Pixel Effect   136
Attaching a Note to a Photo   139
Mapping a Texture to a Person   144
Dividing a Photo into Puzzle Pieces   148
Brushed Metal   152
TV Scan Lines   154
Reflective Chrome Gradient   156
Building a Video Wall   161
Lightning Effect   166
Gettin' "Gelly" with Buttons   169
Yummy Metal Web Buttons   174

CHAPTER 8   179
Shadows of the Night
Glints, Reflections, and Shadows

Perspective Cast Shadow   180
Reverse Cast Shadow   184
Glassy Reflections   188
The Fastest Logo Job in Town   192
Oscar Starbrights   195
Adding a Lens Flare   198
Instant Star Field   200

CHAPTER 9   203
Show Me the Money
3D and Packaging Effects

3D Magazine Effect   204
3D Hardcover Book Effect   208
Creating 3D Packaging   213
Creating a DVD Effect   218
3D Photo Cubes   224

CHAPTER 10   231
Photo Finish
Edge Effects

Filmstrip Templates   232
Photo Mount Effect   238
Quick Slide Mounts   244
Painted Edges Technique   247
Distressed Edge Effect   250
Ripped Edge Technique   254

CHAPTER 11   259
Different Strokes
Artistic Effects

Faking Hand-Drawn Silhouette Illustrations   260
Colorizing Line Art   263
From Photo to Oil Painting   266
Instant Woodcut Effect   270
Photo to Line Art Morph   272

INDEX   276

2005 SUNCOAST GOLF CLASSIC

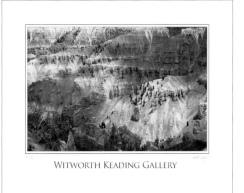

WITWORTH KEADING GALLERY

THIS IS NOT THE INTRODUCTION

Every book has an introduction, and virtually nobody reads it. That's why, instead of including a boring introduction that nobody will read anyway, this is actually the "preamble" to the book. That's right, baby—a preamble. This is more important than it may sound at first, because as you're probably aware, not many printed documents these days have a preamble (though this could certainly start a trend). In fact, the only document I can think of that has a preamble is the U.S. Constitution (and it's done pretty well thus far). So I'm following in the footsteps of our forefathers by trying to create a piece that will endure for more than 200 years (or until the next version of Elements is released—whichever comes first).

When you break it down, the word "preamble" is really ideal because, as you know, the prefix "pre" means "before the fix" (which in layman's terms means "this all occurred before something was broken"), and the word "amble" is the root of the Latin word "ambulance," which is what you'd need if you were to break your foot while reading this book. So, in short, this preamble is what to read before you break your foot. Ah, it all makes perfect sense now, doesn't it?

So now that we've established that this is clearly NOT an introduction, what will reading this do for you (you being the wonderful, multifaceted, truly unique, genius-type person who bought this book)? Reading this will help you "get inside my head." (Don't worry. I've got a huge bobble-head with more than 120,000 square feet of contiguous air-conditioned warehouse space, so climb right in.)

All kidding aside, taking a quick moment to read this preamble will make using this book much easier and much more enjoyable for you. Primarily because you'll then understand how and why it was written, why I did certain things the way I did, and then how to get the most from this book. Plus, it says something about you and the kind of person you are (the kind of person who will continue reading this preamble, knowing full well that it's really the introduction, simply because you don't want to hurt my feelings. I dig you, man). Now, on to how to use this book.

...you'll be able to re-create every single effect in this book, regardless of your previous Photoshop Elements experience.

How to use this book

Think of this as a "Photoshop Elements special effects cookbook." Need to apply a depth-of-field effect to a photo? No sweat. It's in here. Want to make it look like you took your shot in a studio with a full lighting setup? It's in here, too. Need to do cool stuff right now, for a project that's due tomorrow? Just turn to the page that has the effect you need, and follow the step-by-step instructions.

You'll be able to re-create every technique in this book, regardless of your level of Photoshop Elements experience, and you'll unlock the secrets for creating today's hottest photographic effects—the same ones used by the top pros—and the same ones you see every day in magazines, on TV, in Hollywood, and on the Web. Techniques that would otherwise have taken years to learn, but are easy—once you know the secrets. You'll be absolutely amazed at how simple these tricks really are, and they're all here, including those closely guarded, insider, "down-and-dirty" tricks of the trade. It doesn't require years of study—there are no complex mathematical concepts to master—in short, there's no baloney. It's (as we say) "just the funk and not the junk!"

Okay, so now you know what the book is all about—special photographic effects and cool tricks—but you probably have some other questions. Probing, lingering personal questions whose answers may be too uncomfortable for our studio audience, so instead I thought I'd do something safer—a simple Q&A (Quebec & Albatross) section where I make up the questions I'd like to have answered if I were the person buying this book, and then I answer them, as if I'd written this book (which coincidentally, I did). If this sounds at all confusing, it should. Here we go:

Q. Where should I start in the book?

A. Honestly, it doesn't matter. This book isn't designed to be read like a novel, starting with Chapter 1, then Chapter 2, etc. This is a "jump-in-anywhere" book, so jump in at the technique that interests you most. Wherever you start, you'll be able to do the technique right on the spot, because everything is spelled out.

Q. Do I have to be really good at Photoshop Elements?

A. When I wrote this book, I wrote it so any user, at any level of Photoshop Elements experience, could jump right in and create these effects. For most people this is a blessing, but if you've been using Photoshop Elements since version 1.0, there's something you should know: I spell everything out (at least the first time, in every tutorial). And just because I do that (making the book accessible to everyone), you shouldn't let it "get to you." For example, in a tutorial, the first time I have you make a new blank layer, I write: "Create a new blank layer by clicking on the Create a New Layer icon at the top of the Layers palette." If you've been creating layers since *Roseanne* was a top-rated TV show, you're going to be like, "Oh, this is for beginners." I had to do it that way. Since this isn't a "Start at Chapter 1 and read it cover to cover" book (you can jump in anywhere), someone who's new to Photoshop Elements (like a professional photographer who's now shooting digital) might not know how to create a new layer. There is no "Here's how Photoshop Elements 3 works" chapter at the beginning, like you get in every other Photoshop Elements book. Because of that, the first time a command appears in a technique, I write the whole darn thing out. Again, it's just a few extra words, and you can bounce right by it if you already know how to do it, so don't let it slow you down.

...I wrote this book so any user, at any level of Photoshop Elements experience, could jump right in and create these same effects.

Q. So is this book full of advanced techniques?

A. Well, in a way, yes, in a way, no. Here's the thing: The techniques you're going to learn in this book are the very same techniques used by today's leading digital photographers, Web wizards, and designers. They use these effects on a daily basis, and you can be sure that if they're working for some major TV network, a Hollywood studio, or a worldwide ad agency, these people are definitely advanced. But although these techniques were created and are used daily by advanced users, that doesn't mean they're hard or overly complicated. In fact, my goal was to make these advanced techniques as easy as humanly possible. That's because I want every reader of this book to be able to easily pull off every single technique in the book. That's my goal. It's supposed to *look* like it was hard to create; it's not supposed to *be* hard to create. That's the beauty of it, and that's why I call the book *Down & Dirty Tricks*. There is nothing I love more than finding out that the effect that I thought would be so complex is actually a 60-second quick trick. I love that, and sharing those secrets is what I love even more, and that's exactly, precisely, what this book is all about.

Think of it this way: This book is packed cover to cover with stuff that makes it look like you really broke a sweat. Like you spent weeks crafting the effect (because after all, you're going to charge your client like you worked on it for weeks, right?), but most of it requires you to just follow the simple steps. That's it.

Here's an example: In this book, I'm going to show you what is probably the most popular technique used in Hollywood movie posters today. You know, and I know, that the Hollywood studio hired some big muckety-muck designer to do its posters, but absolutely, without a doubt, if you follow the instructions, you'll be able to create the exact same effect. Does that make it a beginner's book—because a beginner can "pull off" the same technique used by the top pros? Or does this make it an advanced book, because you're learning techniques used by some very advanced users? So basically, you're going to learn advanced techniques that are so easy to pull off, it's going to make you look advanced (even if you're not). If you're already an advanced user, the benefit to you is you'll be able to pull these mini-miracles off even faster, by skipping the extra descriptive copy and jumping right in and getting your hands dirty. It's all how you look at it.

Q. Can I get the photos used in the book?

A. You're kind of pushy. I like that. Actually, thanks to the wonderful people at Brand X Pictures (www.brandxpictures.com), you can download low-res versions of all the photos used in the book, so you can practice right along using the same photos.

Q. Okay, where do I download the photos from the book?
A. Go to the book's companion website at www.scottkelbybooks.com/ddelements3.

Q. So why Brand X?
A. Because, in my humble opinion, they've got the best, coolest, most relevant royalty-free stock images in the market today. I came across them when their catalog came in the mail. I looked at it for about 30 seconds and I knew right then: "These are the images I want in my next book." We called them out of the blue, and convinced (okay, we begged) them to let us (and you) use their amazing stock imagery for the book, and I am absolutely thrilled that they did. They offer more than 20,000 images, and best of all, they're totally not the schlocky "two-men-shaking-hands" standard stock photos that permeate the stock agencies. Their stuff rocks because it's so usable, so "non-stock," and I encourage you to visit their site at www.brandxpictures.com and see for yourself. I know this sounds like a big plug for Brand X (and it is, and they deserve it), but I can assure you that outside of their graciously letting me (and you) use their photos, it's not a paid plug. I don't get a kickback—not a nickel, whether you buy 1 or 1,000 of their images (and CDs, did I mention they sell collections?), but I am indebted to them, especially since they didn't know me from Adam (apparently, they know Adam). I just wanted to let them (and you) know how much better this book is because of their generous contribution. Okay, now I'm "un-plugging."

Q. Is this book for Windows users or Macintosh users?
A. It's really just for Windows users. Here's why: When Adobe created Photoshop Elements 3, they left quite a few major (and minor) features out of the Mac version. In fact, the entire Organizer (which is one of the most compelling features of Photoshop Elements 3) isn't in the Mac version at all. When I looked at how much the two versions differed (feature-wise, interface-wise, etc.), I realized I had to make a decision. I could either make a really confusing, disjointed book that lamely attempted to cover both versions, or I could make a kick-ass version that only covered the PC side, and enabled me to add more pages and more content. The fact that the overwhelming majority of existing Photoshop Elements users are PC-based made the decision a bit easier, but I'm still disappointed that I couldn't do both. So, will the book work at all for Mac users? Yup. Every time you see the keyboard shortcut "Alt," as a Mac user you press the Option key; when you see the shortcut "Control," just press the Mac's Command key; and when you see me say "hit Backspace," it's just the Mac's Delete key. Knowing that, you'll still run into a feature here and there that you just don't have, and sometimes an item is under a different menu, but much of it will be the same.

Q. What's the volumetric conversion of 7 cubic yards to liters?
A. Glad you asked. Seven cubic yards equals 5351.99 liters. Other Photoshop Elements books just don't give you this kind of in-depth, seemingly useless information. See, I care.

Q. I noticed you mentioned Felix in the book. Who's Felix?
A. Felix is Felix Nelson (yes, that Felix Nelson), and he's about the best, most creative, most talented Photoshop artist in the known universe, and I'm about the luckiest guy in the world to get to work with him every day. He's the Creative Director for *Photoshop User* magazine, he co-authored my *Photoshop Killer Tips* books, and honestly, I learn more from Felix than any other person on the planet. He's just brilliant at taking techniques to the next level, and coming up with inventive and creative new ideas.

For example, I'd ask him to look at a new technique I'd come up with for the book, and he'd look at it and say, "Hey, that looks slick. Ya know, if you added a..." and then he'd mention that one little thing that

There is nothing I love more than finding out that the effect that I thought would be so complex is actually a 60-second trick.

takes the tutorial from a pretty cool technique to a totally awesome technique. I can't thank him enough for his many tweaks, ideas, and insights that have made this book much better than it would have been.

Q. What's the capital of South Dakota?
A. Pierre.

Q. What if I'm still using Photoshop Elements 2?
A. Dude. That's just wrong. Photoshop Elements 3 is far and away the best version of Photoshop Elements there's ever been. You'll work faster, have more fun, and you'll be able to do more cool things with it than ever before, so in short—it's upgrade time. Although most of the effects in this book will still work in Photoshop Elements 2, you're missing out on much more than special effects if you don't upgrade to Photoshop Elements 3, so…get on it.

Q. How many fingers am I holding up?
A. Three. No, four!

This book is packed cover-to-cover with stuff that makes it look like you really broke a sweat. Like you spent weeks crafting the effect…

Q. Is the rest of the book as down-to-earth and straight-to-the-point as this introduction (I mean, preamble)?
A. Sadly, no. The rest of the book is pretty much written like this: Step One: Go under the Filter menu, under Blur, and choose Gaussian Blur. It's all step-by-step from here, giving the exact steps necessary to complete the effect, so there's not much interference, uh, I mean, ancillary instruction, from me. Well, except I am able to share some carefully crafted insights during the intro of each chapter, so please take a moment to read them if you want the full Zen-like experience that comes from reading chapter intros that are as meaningful and thought-provoking as those found in the opening paragraphs of this preamble.

Q. Hey, I just realized something.
A. What's that?

Q. If this is the preamble, the rest of the book must then be the "Amble," right?
A. That's right, my friend. You are indeed worthy of this book. I mean, this "Amble."

Q. So, is it safe to continue on to the "Amble" now?
A. Wow, you've really bought into that whole Amble thing—I'm proud of you. Well, you've done your duty. You've read the preamble, you know what the book's about, how it was written, what to look for (what you're in for), and how to make the most of it. Armed with that knowledge, go forth and follow in the footsteps of our forefathers, who once wrote, "We, the Village People…"—no, that's not it. Anyway….

Turn the page, my young apprentice. It's time for you to "effect" the world.

Don't let the title of this chapter fool you; the photographic special effects here don't take one hour.

One Hour Photo
Portrait and Studio Effects

Most take like 3 minutes. Well, 4 if you're editing images with one hand and eating a sandwich with the other. If you charge by the hour, this is the last thing you want to hear, but there's a way around that: If the photo effect you want to use has 12 steps, do only the first 10 steps. Then, drive to your client's office and present it as your "initial proof." Then, drop off your dry cleaning, go to a museum, have some dinner, catch a movie, etc. Then, go back to your office, complete Steps 11 and 12, and return to your client with your "second round of proofs." The effect will look like you worked on it for weeks. Give the client your invoice (include the movie and dinner receipts) and you're a hero—you delivered the effect that knocked his socks off in just one day (but it only took you $3^1/2$ minutes to create it). Ahh, now you have a moral dilemma. You feel bad. Guilty even. So you go back to your client and refund everything but a pro-rated $3^1/2$ minutes of your hourly charge. Ya know, looking back, if you charge by the hour, you should probably skip this chapter altogether.

Sharp Foreground, Blurred Background

This is a technique that's usually done with a camera, but it doesn't have to be. Basically, you're blurring a copy of the photo, then erasing the blurred areas where you want to retain detail, giving a simple depth-of-field effect that focuses on an object.

STEP ONE: Open the photo that you want to apply the effect to. Go under the Layer menu, under New, and choose Layer via Copy (or press Control-J) to duplicate the Background layer in the Layers palette.

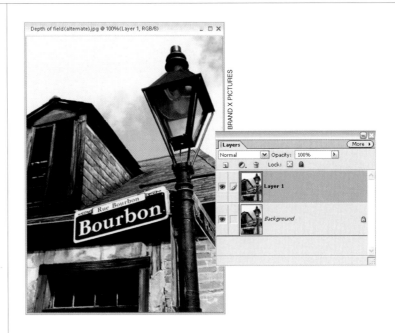

STEP TWO: Go under the Filter menu, under Blur, and choose Gaussian Blur. When the dialog appears, increase the Radius to 4 pixels and click OK to put a blur over the entire image.

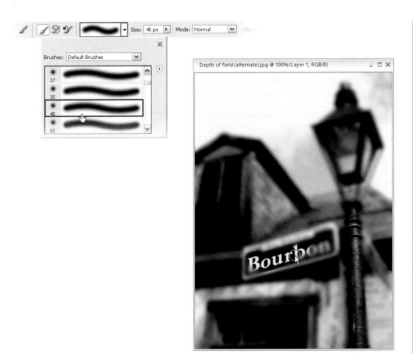

STEP THREE: Press the letter E to switch to the Eraser tool. In the Options Bar, click on the down-facing arrow next to the brush thumbnail and choose a medium, soft-edged brush from the Brush Picker. Start erasing over the parts of the image that you want to appear in focus in the foreground. Erasing on this blurred layer reveals the original, unblurred image on the Background layer. By making these areas sharp and leaving the background areas blurry, it creates a simple depth-of-field effect that focuses on an object.

TIP: Press the Left Bracket key ([) to decrease your brush size to erase over any smaller details in the foreground of the photo. You can also lower the Opacity of your duplicate layer to help you see these smaller areas as you erase.

Before

After

Depth-of-Field Effect

As in the previous tutorial, this effect imitates a shot taken with a camera very close to the subject, where the area closest to the lens is in very sharp focus. But with this technique, the image gradually goes out of focus as the depth of field changes.

STEP ONE: Open the image you want to apply the effect to.

STEP TWO: Go to the Layers palette and choose Levels from the Create Adjustment Layer pop-up menu. When the Levels dialog appears, don't do anything, just click OK. This will create a layer mask that we can use for this effect. Press the G key to switch to the Gradient tool, and in the Options Bar, click on the down-facing arrow next to the gradient swatch and choose the Black to White gradient (the third one in the Picker).

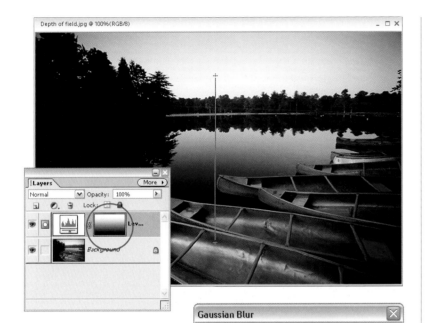

STEP THREE: Click on the layer mask thumbnail of the Levels adjustment layer in the Layers palette to make it active. Now with the Gradient tool active, click on the area that you want to be in focus and drag toward the area that you want to be out of focus. When you do this, a black-to-white gradient will appear in the layer mask thumbnail.

STEP FOUR: Press-and-hold the Control key and click on the layer mask thumbnail. This will put a selection around the gradient you just created. In the Layers palette, click on the Background layer to make it active, then go under the Filter menu, under Blur, and choose Gaussian Blur. As you drag the Radius slider to the right, you'll see your selected area starts to blur. Choose the amount of blur that looks good to you and click OK. Deselect by pressing Control-D, to complete the effect.

Before

After

Creating Gallery Prints

This is a really slick technique for turning a regular photograph into what looks like a gallery print. In the project shown here, you'll start by transforming a color photograph into an Ansel Adams–like black-and-white photo, but we're only doing that because the photo is a mountainous landscape. You can use a regular, less "contrasty" conversion to grayscale for other photos you'll apply this effect to.

STEP ONE: Open the photo you want to turn into a gallery print. Go under the Select menu and choose All. Then, go under the Layer menu, under New, and choose Layer via Cut (or press Shift-Control-J) to put your image on its own layer (Layer 1).

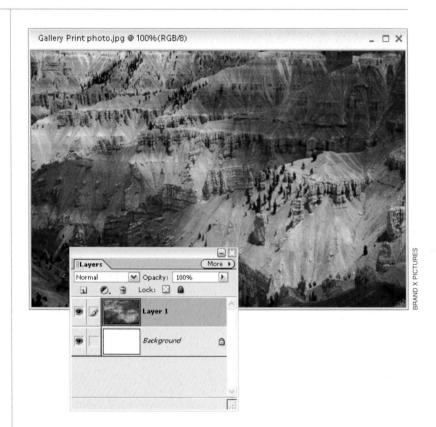

STEP TWO: Rather than just going under the Image menu, under Mode, and choosing Grayscale, choose Levels from the Create Adjustment Layer pop-up menu at the top of the Layers palette. When the Levels dialog appears, just click OK.

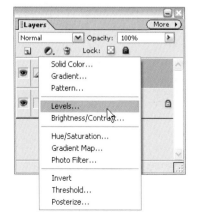

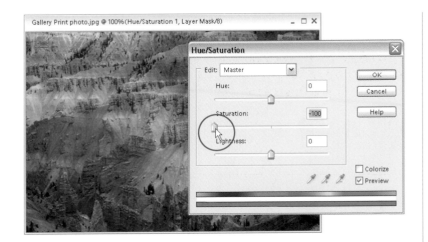

STEP THREE: Then, choose Hue/Saturation from the Create Adjustment Layer pop-up menu at the top of the Layers palette. When the dialog appears, drag the Saturation slider all the way to the left, and you'll see your photo turn black and white. Click OK.

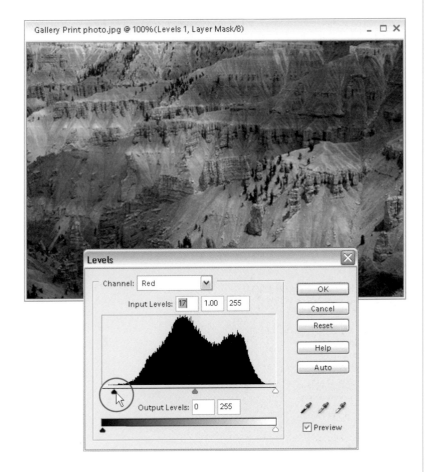

STEP FOUR: We're going for that Ansel Adams effect, so in the Layers palette, double-click on the Levels thumbnail (it's the one on the left) and in the resulting dialog, change the Channel pop-up menu to Red. Now you can adjust the Red channel, and because of the Hue/Saturation adjustment layer above the Levels layer, it appears as a black-and-white photo. You can drag the shadow Input Levels slider to the right slightly to increase the shadows in the Red channel. Don't click OK yet.

Continued

STEP FIVE: Change the Channel pop-up menu to Green, and drag the highlight Input Levels slider to the left to increase the highlights. Then, choose Blue in the pop-up menu. Drag the highlight Input Levels slider to the left to intensify the highlights, and then drag the shadow Input Levels slider slightly to the right to darken the shadows. (What you're doing here is similar to using Photoshop's Channel Mixer, which sadly, is missing in Photoshop Elements 3.) These settings are not standards for every photo; I just experimented with the sliders until the photo looked better.

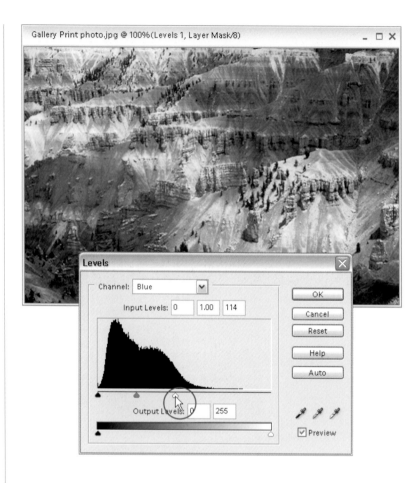

STEP SIX: Now you'll need to add some white space around your photo, so click on the Background layer to make it active, then go under the Image menu, under Resize, and choose Canvas Size. In the Canvas Size dialog, ensure the Relative checkbox is on, then enter 2 inches for Width and 2 inches for Height.

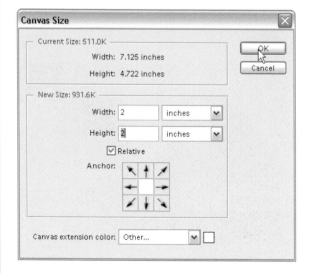

STEP SEVEN: When you click OK, 2 inches of white space is added around your photo. Click on the image layer (Layer 1) in the Layers palette to make it active, then press-and-hold the Control key and click on the image layer's thumbnail, which puts a selection around your photo. Next, click on the Create a New Layer icon at the top of the Layers palette.

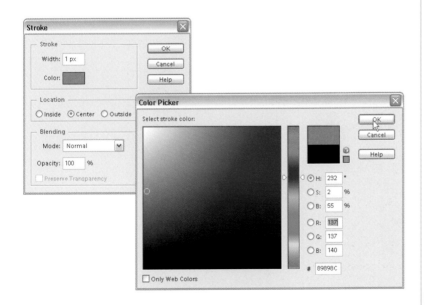

STEP EIGHT: On this new layer, you're going to put a very thin stroke around your photo to create a subtle border. Go under the Edit menu and choose Stroke (Outline) Selection. When the Stroke dialog appears, for Width enter 1 pixel, for Color click on the swatch and choose a light gray in the Color Picker, and for Location choose Center.

Continued

STEP NINE: Click OK and the thin gray stroke is applied around your photo. Press Control-D to deselect. Since you applied this stroke on its own layer, if the stroke seems too bold or calls too much attention to itself, you can simply lower the Opacity of the layer in the Layers palette until it looks right to you.

STEP TEN: Press the M key to switch to the Rectangular Marquee tool. Click near the top-left corner of the image and drag out a selection border that's slightly larger than the image. If needed, press-and-hold the Spacebar to reposition your selection as you drag.

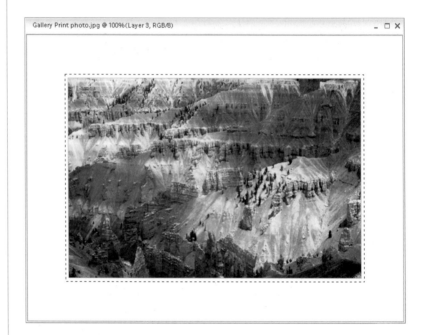

STEP ELEVEN: With your selection in place, click the Create a New Layer icon, then go under the Edit menu and choose Stroke (Outline) Selection. Leave the Width at 1 pixel, but change your stroke color to black by clicking on the gray Color swatch and choosing black in the Color Picker. Leave the Location set to Center.

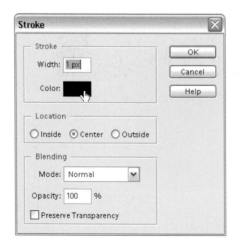

Gallery Print photo.jpg @ 100% (Witworth Keading Gallery, RGB/8)

STEP TWELVE: Click OK to stroke this outer border with a thin black stroke and press Control-D to deselect. Now, press T to switch to the Type tool, click the Color swatch in the Options Bar, and choose gray in the Color Picker, then "sign" the print (if you indeed took the shot, of course) using a font that looks like handwriting (I used DearJoeItalic set at 22 points). Use the Move tool to position it under the bottom-right corner. Under the left corner, I used the same font to give it that "numbered print" look.

WITWORTH KEADING GALLERY

STEP THIRTEEN: I added the name of a fictitious gallery, using the font Trajan Pro in all caps at 24-point size. However, once I added the type, I left the first letter of each word of the gallery name at 24 points, but I highlighted the rest of the letters and lowered their size to 21 points in the Options Bar, to give a "small caps" feel.

Soft-Edged Portrait Background

This is a technique that I started showing in my live seminars as a 30-second portrait or product-shot background. Basically, it adds a quick "burned in" effect around the edges of your image, and although the background looks pretty bland when complete, as soon as you put an object or person on it, it instantly "makes sense."

STEP ONE: Create a new document in RGB mode by going under the File menu, under New, and choosing Blank File (I created a 4x6" document at 72 ppi). Click the Foreground color swatch in the Toolbox, and when the Color Picker appears, choose the color that you want to appear in the center of your background. Press Alt-Backspace to fill your Background layer with this color.

STEP TWO: Click on the Create a New Layer icon at the top of the Layers palette. Click on the Foreground color swatch again and choose a darker shade of the color you just used (in other words, if you started with a light blue, now pick a dark blue). Then, press Alt-Backspace to fill this new layer with the darker color. Press M to switch to the Rectangular Marquee tool and draw a rectangular selection about 1/2" to 1" inside the edges of your image.

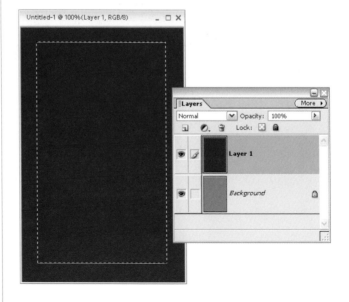

STEP THREE: Go under the Select menu and choose Feather. When the Feather Selection dialog appears, enter 25 pixels for low-res, 72-ppi images (or 60 pixels for 300-ppi, high-res images). Click OK and the feathering will soften the edges of your selection (you'll see the corners of your selection round onscreen). Press the Backspace key to knock out a soft-edged hole in your top (darker) layer.

STEP FOUR: Open the headshot of the person you want to place on this background. Select just the person with no background. (Since my person was on a white background, I clicked the Magic Wand tool [W] on the background and then went under the Select menu and chose Inverse. You could also use the Lasso tool [L] to draw a selection around the person.) Press the V key to switch to the Move tool, and click-and-drag the selected person on top of the new background document to give a studio backdrop look to your headshot, completing the effect.

BRAND X PICTURES

Burning In Portraits

This burned-in edge effect adds an amazing amount of warmth to your portraits, and it's used by professionals everywhere on everything from magazine covers to print ads to the Web. In fact, once you've learned this simple technique, you'll use it again and again. (By the way—once you apply this technique, turn the layer with the effect on/off a couple of times and you'll see what a huge difference it makes.)

STEP ONE: Open the portrait that you want to "burn in."

STEP TWO: Create a new blank layer by clicking on the Create a New Layer icon at the top of the Layers palette. Press the letter D to set your Foreground color to black, and then fill this new layer with black by pressing Alt-Backspace. Press the letter M to switch to the Rectangular Marquee tool and click-and-drag to create a rectangular selection just inside the edges of your image.

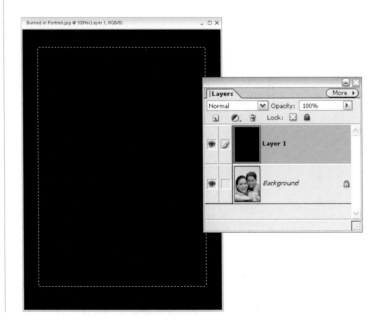

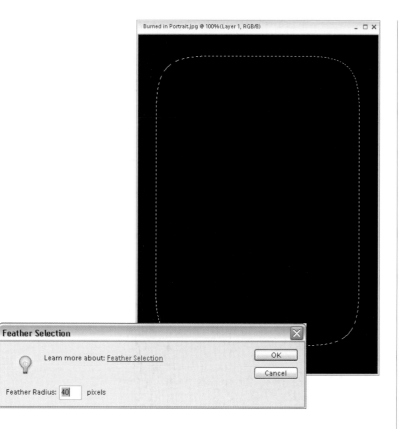

STEP THREE: To soften the edges of your selection, go under the Select menu and choose Feather. When the Feather Selection dialog appears, enter 40 pixels (for high-res, 300-ppi images, try 150 pixels), then click OK.

STEP FOUR: Press the Backspace key to knock out a soft-edged hole in this black layer, revealing the photo on the layer beneath. The only problem is the edges are too dark, but you'll fix that in the next step.

Continued

STEP FIVE: Press Control-D to deselect. Then, go to the Layers palette and lower the Opacity of the black layer to around 40% to complete the burned-in effect. To see how effective this technique is, click on the Eye icon to the left of your black frame layer to hide it, revealing just your original image. Now click again in the box where the Eye icon had been. Notice the difference?

Before

After

Trendy Fashion Blowout Look

This is probably the hottest trend in fashion portrait retouching right now, and you see it everywhere from CD covers (like Madonna's *American Life*), to print ads, to movie posters (like Jet Li's movie *Cradle 2 the Grave*), and everything in between. The effect you're going for is one where the skin tone turns completely white, leaving subtle shadow areas to reveal just the eyes, nostrils, lips, and outline of the face. Here's the trick:

STEP ONE: Open the photo you want to apply the effect to. This technique works best on images with a very light (or white) background (because it usually blows out whatever background is present) and on images of men or women with darker hair. Press Control-J to duplicate the Background layer.

STEP TWO: Press A to switch to the Selection Brush tool. With the duplicate layer active, paint over any areas that have shadow detail, such as the eyes, nostrils, and lips, to select them. (*Note:* To decrease the size of your brush as you paint, press the Left Bracket key on your keyboard, or to increase the size, press the Right Bracket key.) Now, press Control-J again to copy your selection to its own layer. Lower the Opacity of this layer to 40% and change the layer blend mode from Normal to Luminosity.

Continued

STEP THREE: In the Layers palette, click on Layer 1 to make it active. Press D to set your Background color to white, then go under the Filter menu, under Distort, and choose Diffuse Glow. Set the Graininess to 0, the Glow Amount to 10, and the Clear Amount to 15. Click OK to apply the filter. Now, go to the Layers palette and lower the Opacity of this layer to around 80% so you can see some of the original detail from the Background layer.

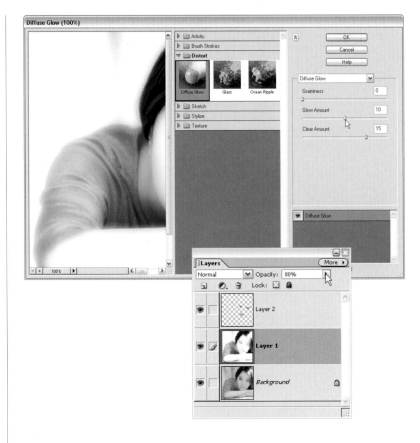

STEP FOUR: You can see that her skin is considerably lighter, but so is everything else. Press the letter E to switch to the Eraser tool, and in the Options Bar, lower the Opacity of the brush to around 40%. With the duplicate layer active, paint over the eyes, eyebrows, nostrils, and lips (which will reveal the color from the Background layer below). Then, lower the brush Opacity again to around 10% and paint over any shadow detail, such as the side of the nose, around the top of the forehead, and sides of the neck.

STEP FIVE: Return to the Options Bar, change the Opacity of the Eraser tool back to 100%, and paint over the rest of the photo (hair, shirt—everything but the skin) to complete the effect.

Before

After

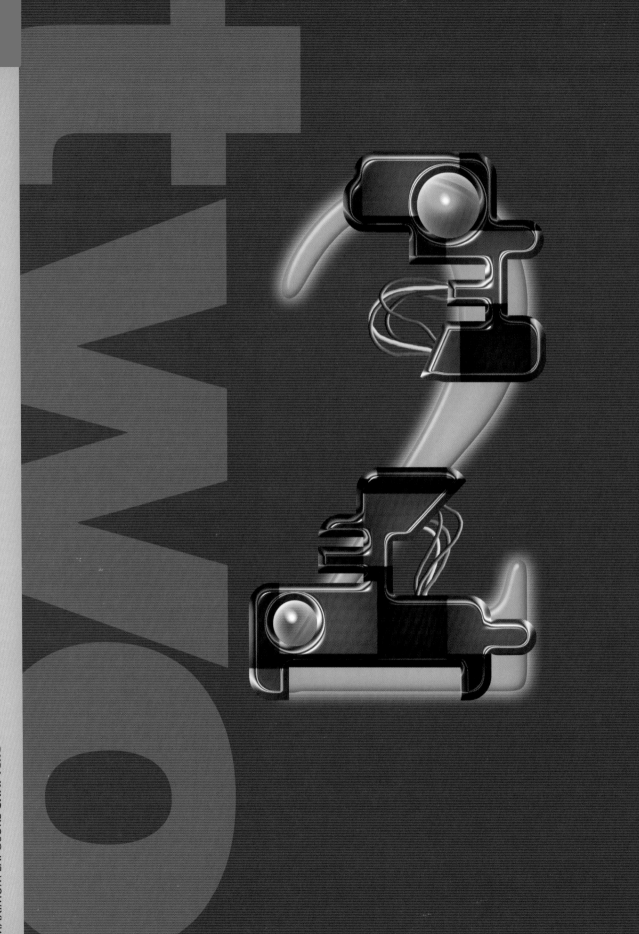

MAXIMUM EXPOSURE CHAPTER 2

This chapter is a nice change because you generally get to start each project with a photograph, and then you just

Maximum Exposure
Photographic Effects

add cool effects to it. This is a bigger advantage than it might first seem. I mean, think about it—if you don't start with a photo, you're starting off with a blank canvas. There's nothing more terrifying than staring at a blank page and trying to come up with an awesome effect entirely from scratch. So, in essence, this chapter is kind of like cheating, and that's good. Unless, of course, you live in Las Vegas, where apparently cheating is frowned upon. In fact, if you're caught cheating in a Vegas casino, I've heard they make you use Elements 1 as punishment; so if you live out that way, you don't want to chance it. In fact, in the interest of personal safety, I'd recommend that all Nevada residents skip this chapter entirely, and always start each Photoshop Elements project with a blank page. Hey, the last thing you want is some angry pit boss chasing you around threatening you with outdated products. It's just not worth it.

Adding Objects Behind Existing Objects

Over the years, I've had question after question on how to add a person into an existing image so that it looks as if that person's standing behind other people in that image. Here's a very flexible and visual way to do just that.

STEP ONE: Open the image you want to add another person (or object) into.

STEP TWO: Use the selection tool of your choice (Lasso tool, Magic Wand tool, etc.) to select the area where you want the additional person to appear in your image. *Note:* When using either of these tools, just press-and-hold the Shift key to add to your selection or press-and-hold the Alt key to subtract from your selection.

STEP THREE: Open the image you want to add into your original photo. Again, use the selection tool of your choice to select the person (or object). After you make your selection, go under the Edit menu and choose Copy.

STEP FOUR: Switch back to the main document, go under the Edit menu, and choose Paste Into Selection. This will place your copied selection (in our example, a headshot of a person) into the selection in your main document. Press the letter V to switch to the Move tool. You can now reposition your pasted person within the selected area. Don't deselect yet.

Continued

STEP FIVE: After you've repositioned the pasted image, chances are good that the size won't be correct (it'll either be too large, as in this case, or too small). We'll adjust the size by pressing Control-T to bring up Free Transform. Hold the Shift key, grab one of the top-corner handles, and drag downward (or upward if your image is too small) to resize the object to match the others in the image. You can also reposition the image as you resize: Just click-and-drag inside the Free Transform bounding box. Don't press Enter just yet.

STEP SIX: You'll also notice in our particular image that the light appears on the opposite side of the woman's head than it does on the other subjects in the image. While your Free Transform box is still active, go to the Image window, under Rotate, and choose Flip Horizontal (reposition your image again if necessary). Press Enter to complete the change, and then press Control-D to deselect.

STEP SEVEN: The edges of the pasted image are too sharp and crisp in comparison with the other subjects in the photo. Press the R key to switch to the Blur tool, and in the Options Bar, lower the Strength to around 50%. Using a small, soft-edged brush, paint a slight blur along the edge of the woman's hair and in the space between the two women. This blends the woman into the image.

STEP EIGHT: Next, we'll have to deal with the contrast of the pasted image. In this example, she looks too saturated in comparison with the other people. A quick trick for matching contrast is to use the Dodge tool with the Exposure set to around 40% in the Options Bar. When you paint, you'll lighten the dark areas of your pasted image to match more closely with the rest of the image (on areas where your object is too light, paint with the Burn tool using the same low settings), which completes the effect.

Before   After

Putting an Image in a Monitor

In this technique, we're going to use Free Transform to put an image into a monitor. Now I don't want you to think, "Oh, how often will I need that?" because this technique works just as well for fitting any image into other spaces—a window of a house, a TV screen, a billboard, etc. So it's really a handy one to know.

STEP ONE: Open the image that contains the monitor (TV, etc.) in which you want to place another image.

STEP TWO: Then, open the image you want to place inside the monitor. Press V to switch to the Move tool, and drag this image onto your monitor image. It will appear on its own layer above your Background layer. In the Layers palette, lower the Opacity of this layer to 50%. This will be a big help when you try to position the image within the monitor area—you'll be able to see the monitor through your photo.

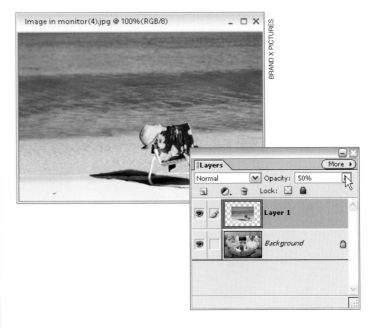

STEP THREE: Press Control-T to bring up Free Transform. Click within the bounding box to move the image on top of the monitor, and then press-and-hold the Shift key, grab one of the corner points, and drag inward to scale the image down to a size that's close to the size of the monitor (it doesn't have to be exact, but get it in the ballpark). While still in Free Transform, release the Shift key, press-and-hold the Control key, grab one of the corner points, and drag it to the corresponding corner of the monitor. Pressing the Control key allows you to distort just that one corner. You'll have to do this for all four corners.

STEP FOUR: When you have a perfect fit, press Enter to lock in your transformation, then in the Layers palette, raise the Opacity of this layer back to 100% to complete the effect.

Montage from One Image

This is a technique I saw a few years ago in a print ad in *Entertainment Weekly* for the VH1® original movie *The Way She Moves*. It's very slick, because it lets you create a montage effect using only one image. To get the effect, we need to create an outer glow, and even though Photoshop Elements 3 has an Outer Glow option, you're stuck with a yellow glow that simply won't work for the look we're going for. So here's how to add some quick visual interest to an otherwise static photo:

STEP ONE: Open an image that you want to apply this effect to. Go to the Select menu and choose All (or press Control-A) to put a selection around the Background layer. Then, go to the Layer menu, under New, and choose Layer via Cut (or press Shift-Control-J) to cut your image from the Background layer, and copy it onto its own layer (Layer 1).

STEP TWO: Click on your Background layer in the Layers palette to make it active. Go under the Image menu, under Resize, and choose Canvas Size. When the Canvas Size dialog appears, enter a dimension that's about 25% larger than your current image size for both Width and Height. Choose Black in the Canvas Extension Color pop-up menu, ensure the Relative checkbox is on, and then click OK to add a black canvas area around your image.

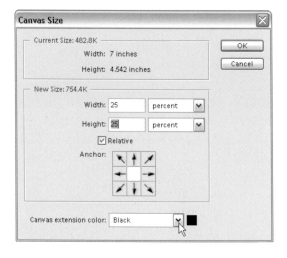

STEP THREE: In the Layers palette, click on your image layer (Layer 1). Press the M key to switch to the Rectangular Marquee tool, and draw a small rectangular selection in one part of your image, but don't select the main focus of the image—choose outer areas for the most part. Copy this selected area from Layer 1 and put it on its own layer by going to the Layer menu, under New, and choosing Layer via Copy (or by pressing Control-J).

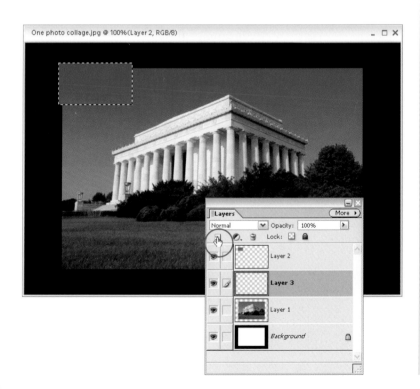

STEP FOUR: Press V to switch to the Move tool, and move this new layer either slightly up, down, to the left, or to the right (your choice) about a half inch. When it's where you want it, Control-click on the layer's thumbnail in the Layers palette to load a selection around the rectangle, and then Control-click on the Create a New Layer icon to add a new layer below the rectangle layer.

Continued

STEP FIVE: Go to the Select menu, under Modify, and choose Border. In the Border Selection dialog, enter 4–5 pixels and click OK (use a higher number for high-res, 300-ppi images). Press D to set your Foreground color to black, then press Alt-Backspace to fill your selection with black. Press Control-D to deselect.

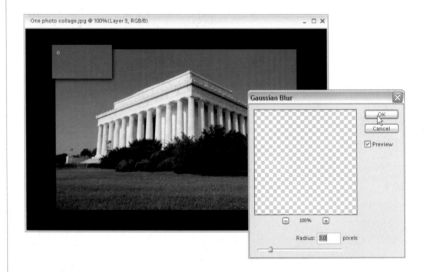

STEP SIX: You're going to use this black border for your outer glow, so we need to soften the edges of the border with a Gaussian Blur. With the rectangular border layer still active, go under the Filter menu, under Blur, and choose Gaussian Blur. Enter 2–3 pixels and click OK. In the Layers palette, click on the rectangle layer above the outer glow layer and press Control-E to merge the two layers together.

STEP SEVEN: You'll continue to repeat Steps 3–6 until you've created multiple rectangles with outer glows. Remember to click on your image layer (Layer 1) each time before you create a new rectangular selection, and don't forget to slightly move the rectangle each time.

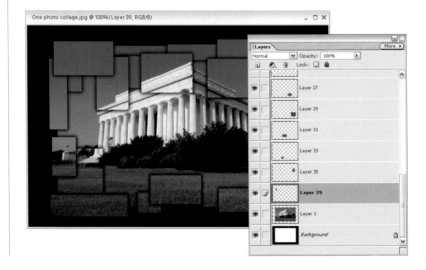

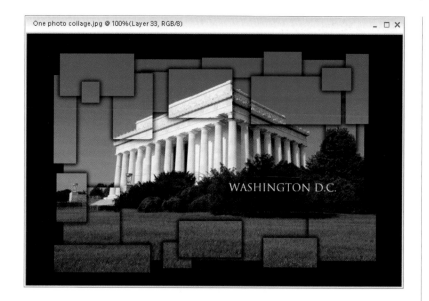

One photo collage.jpg @ 100%(Layer 33, RGB/8)

WASHINGTON D.C.

STEP EIGHT: Once you've applied the glows to all your layers, you can use the Move tool to drag-and-drop your rectangular layers in the Layers palette, shuffling them into a layout that looks good to you. If you choose, you can then add any type using the Type tool (T) to complete the effect (I used Trajan Pro at 17 points). For more fun, once you've created a rectangular layer, try using the Outer Glow option from the Layer Styles category of the Styles and Effects palette, and you'll see why this method (though it takes longer) looks much better.

Before

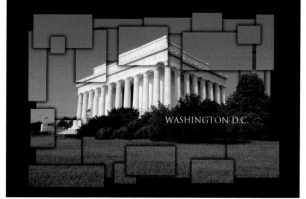

After

Blending Images for Instant Collages

This is one of the fastest and most fun ways to blend (or collage) two or more images together. This is so easy to do, yet so effective, that it opens up a whole new way for many people to collage multiple images.

STEP ONE: Open an image that you want to use as the main image in your collage.

STEP TWO: Open a second image that you want to use in your collage. Press the letter V to switch to the Move tool, and drag this image on top of the image in your original document. Make sure this dragged layer (Layer 1) covers or at least significantly overlaps the Background layer in the Layers palette.

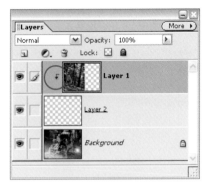

STEP THREE: At the top of the Layers palette, Control-click on the Create a New Layer icon. This creates a new layer (Layer 2) directly below the second image layer (Layer 1). Now click on the top image layer (Layer 1), and from the Layer menu, choose Group with Previous (or just press Control-G). Your top image will disappear, and a tiny arrow will appear to the left of the layer letting you know that you just created a layer clipping group.

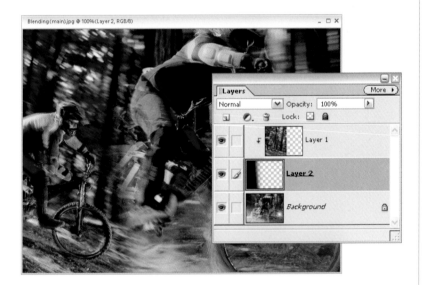

STEP FOUR: Press the letter D to set your Foreground color to black, then press the G key to switch to the Gradient tool. Press Enter and the Gradient Picker will appear onscreen. Make sure the selected gradient is Foreground to Transparent (the second one in the Picker), and then in the Layers palette, click on the empty layer (Layer 2) to make it active. Click-and-drag the Gradient tool through the layer, stopping before you reach the edge of the top image in the layer stack. You'll notice that the images blend together. To add more images, just start again from Step 2. That's all there is to it.

TIP: If you see the edge of your top image after you draw your gradient, you've dragged too close to the edge or past it. Try pressing Control-Z to undo the gradient, and then click-and-drag again, stopping about 1" before the edge of your image.

Adding Motion Effects

The first technique shown here is very popular for photos taken for editorial purposes (for example, if you're shooting a CEO for a magazine or newspaper article about his company). It's also popular in portraits, because the effect leaves the subject totally in focus but adds movement through the rest of the photo. In the second technique, I'll show you another motion effect that you see everywhere—a massive zoom blur. Both effects are so simple to apply that you're going to wonder, "Is that all there is to it?" Yup, that's all there is to it.

MOTION BLUR

STEP ONE: Open a photo that you want to add movement to. Duplicate the Background layer by going under the Layer menu, under New, and choosing Layer via Copy (or by pressing Control-J).

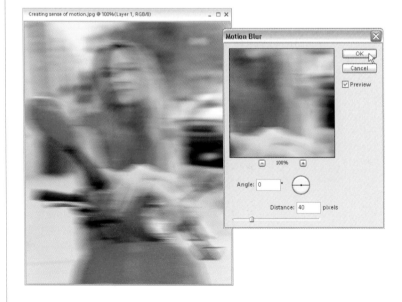

STEP TWO: Go under the Filter menu, under Blur, and choose Motion Blur. In the Motion Blur dialog, set the Angle to the direction you want to have motion applied (I usually use a horizontal setting, but you can set it so it matches the direction of the object). Use the Distance setting to control the amount of effect (choose between 40–50 for low-res, 72-ppi photos, or try 100 for high-res, 300-ppi images), and click OK.

STEP THREE: Press the letter E to switch to the Eraser tool. Then, go to the Options Bar, click on the down-facing arrow next to the brush thumbnail to get the Brush Picker, and choose a soft-edged brush.

STEP FOUR: Now for the fun part—just erase over the areas that you want to retain detail. As you erase, the original Background layer beneath your motion layer will be revealed. I generally erase the person's face, clothes, etc., but I stop right before the edges.

Continued

Before

After

ANOTHER OPTION: You can use this Motion Blur technique to create a different feel, especially if you use the effect on an action shot like the one shown here. I changed the Angle in the Motion Blur dialog to around −11° and set the Distance to 45.

Adding Motion Effects POLLY.tif @ 100%(Layer 1, RGB/8)   _ □ ✕

BRAND X PICTURES

BRAND X PICTURES

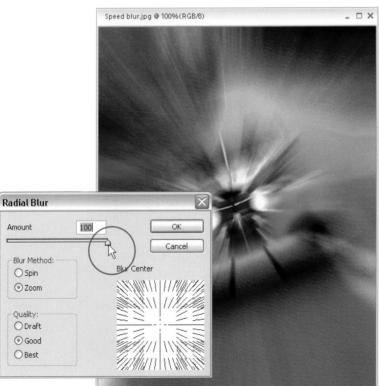

ZOOM BLUR

STEP ONE: To create a zoom effect, first open the photo you want to apply the blur effect to.

STEP TWO: Go under the Filter menu, under Blur, and choose Radial Blur. Set the Amount to 100 and the Blur Method to Zoom. Click OK and the classic speed blur effect is applied to your photo.

Adding Motion Step By Step

This is an old trick that I've used for years to make an object look like it's in motion. This is often used for making an object look as if it's coming out of another object, such as an arm moving from off the screen, an object coming out of a box, etc.

STEP ONE: Open the object that you want to give the effect of movement to. Make a loose selection with the Lasso tool (L) (here I selected the man's forearms along with the bat), and go to the Layer menu, under New, and choose Layer via Copy (or press Control-J) to copy the selection onto its own layer.

STEP TWO: Press Control-T to bring up the Free Transform function. Click within the bounding box and drag the layer to move it to the left slightly. Then, move your cursor outside the bounding box to the right and click-and-drag downward to rotate your image just a little. Now, press-and-hold the Shift key, grab a corner point, and drag inward to scale the image down a bit. Press Enter to lock in your transformation.

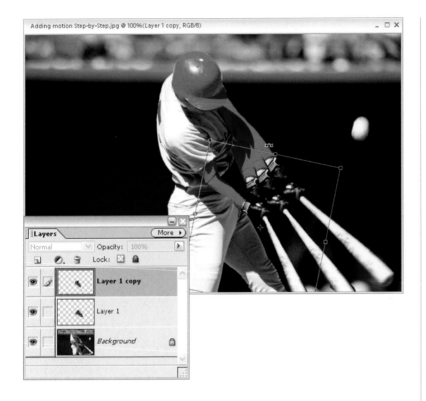

STEP THREE: Drag this rotated layer to the Create a New Layer icon at the top of the Layers palette to duplicate it. Repeat the same process you did in Step 2: bringing up Free Transform, dragging the object to the left, rotating it, making it smaller, and pressing Enter to lock in your transformation.

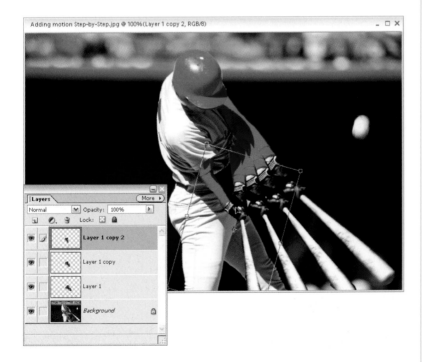

STEP FOUR: Repeat the process one more time (making a copy, bringing up Free Transform, moving it, scaling it, etc.) until your Layers palette looks like the one shown here.

Continued

STEP FIVE: In the Layers palette, click on Layer 1 (it should be above the Background layer). Lower the Opacity of this layer to around 50%. Press Alt-Right Bracket to switch to the next layer above it, then lower the Opacity of this layer to around 30%. Press Alt-Right Bracket again and lower the Opacity of the top layer to around 20%.

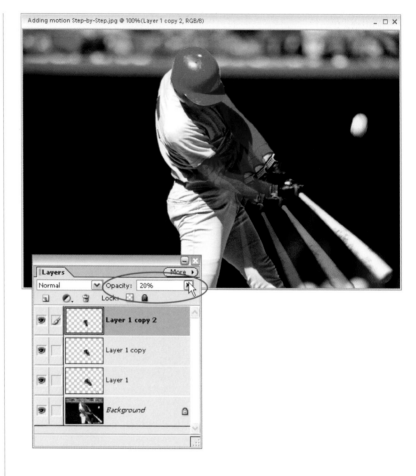

STEP SIX: In the Layers palette, click on Layer 1 again. Go under the Filter menu, under Blur, and choose Motion Blur. For Distance use 7 pixels or less, leave the Angle set at 0°, and click OK. Press Alt-Right Bracket to switch to the next layer above, then press Control-F to run the same Motion Blur on this layer. Repeat this process again for the remaining layers to complete the effect.

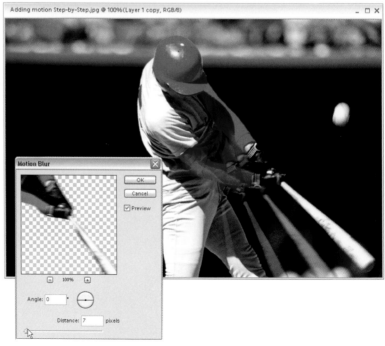

Before   After

3

Remember that scene in the movie *Dirty Dancing*—the big dance at the end of the movie? At one point,

Dirty Dancing
Focusing Attention

Patrick Swayze comes dancing down the center aisle toward the stage where Baby (yes, parents can be so cruel) stands there waiting for him, while swaying the hem of her skirt to and fro? Do you remember that part? Seriously, did she look incredibly gawky and awkward? I think it was the moment when the director decided to change her name in the movie from Angela to "Baby," as a way of publicly shaming her for not having a cool dance move of her own. Now, you're probably wondering what all this has to do with Photoshop Elements? Plenty—because before you read this chapter, I strongly urge you to go out and rent the *Dirty Dancing* video and tell me if you, as a Photoshop Elements user, would freeze up the way Baby did at one of those "all-eyes-on-you" moments. If you see this movie and feel certain that you could come up with a more compelling "come hither" dance than Baby did, then and only then should you read this chapter.

Backscreening

This is a popular effect in print and multimedia, and it's used when the background image is very busy or very dark (or both) and you want to place ad type over your image that can be read easily. Although we're using the technique with a white-screened effect here, it's just as popular using a dark-screened effect.

STEP ONE: Open a background image that you want to put type over.

STEP TWO: Press M to switch to the Rectangular Marquee tool, and make a selection where you want your type to appear. While this area is still selected, create a new layer by clicking on the Create a New Layer icon at the top of the Layers palette.

STEP THREE: Press the letter D and then the letter X to set your Foreground color to white. Fill your selection with white by pressing Alt-Backspace, and then deselect by pressing Control-D.

STEP FOUR: Lower the Opacity of this layer to create the amount of back-screen effect you'd like. A 20% screen is a very popular choice for backscreening, so to achieve a 20% screen, you lower the Opacity in the Layers palette to 80% on this layer. In this example, I actually lowered the Opacity to 70%. This lets a bit more of the background show through, as we're going to add very large, black text.

STEP FIVE: Press the T key to switch to the Type tool, and enter your text. The headline and body copy in this example are set in Minion Pro at 50 points and 12 points, respectively. The title of the medication is set at 14 points in Myriad Pro, while the tagline for the medicine is set at 11 points in Gill Sans. Because the black text is so large, it's still very read-able over our white backscreened layer.

Magazine Pop-Up Effect

This effect is inspired by *Sports Illustrated* magazine. It's a technique for focusing attention on one object in an image. Basically, you select an object from the background, put that object on its own layer, lighten the background layer, and add a drop shadow to the object to create depth and focus.

STEP ONE: Open an image that has an element in it that you want to stand out from the background. Press the L key until you have the Magnetic Lasso tool. Click once on the edge of the object to create an anchor point, and slowly drag the tool around the object. The Magnetic Lasso tool will automatically add other anchor points along the edge of the object as you drag. When you get back to where you started, just click on the original anchor point to create the selection. If you need to add to your initial selection, press L again to switch to the regular Lasso tool, press-and-hold the Shift key, and select any additional areas; to subtract from your selection, press-and-hold the Alt key and select any areas you want to remove.

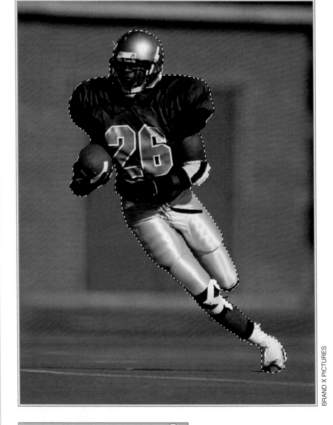

STEP TWO: With your selection in place, go under the Layer menu, under New, and choose Layer via Copy (or just press Control-J) to copy your selection onto its own layer (Layer 1). Now, click on the Background layer in the Layers palette to make it active.

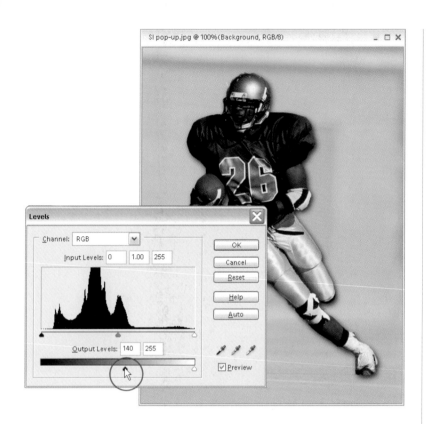

STEP THREE: Press Control-L to bring up the Levels dialog. When it appears, drag the shadow Output Levels slider to the right to lighten the Background layer. Drag the slider until the shadow Output Levels field reads at least 140 (move farther to the right to lighten even more). Click OK when it looks good to you.

STEP FOUR: To help the object stand off the background even more, you'll add a drop shadow. First, click on Layer 1 in the Layers palette, then go to the Styles and Effects palette (found under the Window menu) and choose Layer Styles in the top-left pop-up menu. In the top-right pop-up menu, choose Drop Shadows, and then click on the Soft Edge shadow, which completes the effect.

Vignetting Attention

I saw this technique used very effectively on a menu cover for the Olive Garden® restaurant. It's a takeoff on the classic vignette effect, but rather than just softening the edges to focus the attention on the subjects of the image, it adds a soft border technique at the same time.

STEP ONE: Open the image you want to apply the effect to. Press the M key to switch to the Rectangular Marquee tool, and make a selection around the area you want as the focal point of your effect.

STEP TWO: Go under the Select menu and choose Feather. Enter 5 for the Feather Radius and click OK. (*Note:* For high-res, 300-ppi images, use a Feather Radius of 15 instead.)

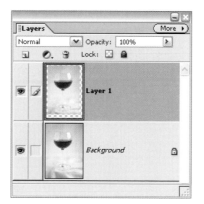

STEP THREE: While your selection is still in place, go under the Layer menu, under New, and choose Layer via Copy (or press Control-J) to put the selected area on its own layer above your Background layer.

STEP FOUR: In the Layers palette, click on the Background layer to make it active. Press Control-L to bring up the Levels dialog. Click on the shadow Output Levels slider at the bottom of the dialog and drag it to the right about two-thirds of the way (somewhere around 175) to lighten the background image.

Continued

STEP FIVE: To enhance the vignette, click on the Create a New Layer icon in the Layers palette. Now, get the Rectangular Marquee tool again and draw a frame inside the middle of the vignetted border. Go to the Edit menu and choose Stroke (Outline) Selection. In the Stroke dialog, enter 1 pixel for Width, click on the Color swatch and choose black in the Color Picker, choose Inside for Location, and click OK. Press Control-D to deselect. Now, go to the Layers palette and lower the Opacity to around 35%.

STEP SIX: For the final step, you can add type to finish off the design. (The typeface I used for "Ristorante" was Zapfino, and for "BELLA NOTTE" and "WINE LIST" I used Trajan Pro.)

Popping Out of an Image

This is one of those techniques for which I've had so many requests that I wanted to include it here in the book. It's primarily seen in print ads where a person, a body part, a car, etc., extends out from part of the photo and into white space where body copy usually resides. It's kind of as if the object is popping out of the photo, and it not only adds visual interest and movement but it also gives you something to wrap type around.

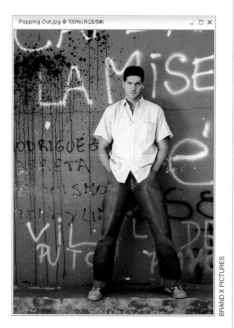

STEP ONE: Open the photo that has the object or person that you want to extend from part of the image.

STEP TWO: Press the L key to switch to the Lasso tool and draw a selection around the part of the object you want to extend from the photo. If needed, you can hold the Shift key to add to your selection or the Alt key to subtract from your selection. (In this example, we held the Alt key to deselect the area of wall between his right arm and his body.) Once your selection is in place, go under the Layer menu, under New, and choose Layer via Copy (or press Control-J) to put the selected area on its own layer (Layer 1).

Continued

STEP THREE: In the Layers palette, click on the Background layer. Press M to switch to the Rectangular Marquee tool, and draw a selection around the entire left side of your document window, starting near the right edge of where you made your original selection on the object. Press Backspace to erase that part of the background.

STEP FOUR: Press Control-D to deselect. In the Layers palette, click back on Layer 1 and then go to the Styles and Effects palette (found under the Window menu). With the Layer Styles category selected, choose Drop Shadows from the palette's top-right pop-up menu. Click on the Soft Edge drop shadow. Go under the Layer menu, under Layer Style, and choose Style Settings. When the dialog appears, enter 10 pixels for Shadow Distance and click OK. (*Note:* If the drop shadow creates a visible seam anywhere inside your object, adjust the Lighting Angle in the Style Settings dialog.)

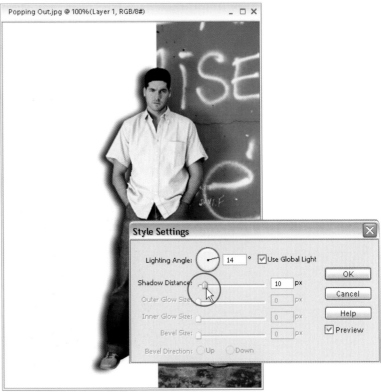

STEP FIVE: Press the T key to switch to the Type tool, and add any additional text. (In my example, I used the typeface Helvetica Condensed for the company name and Helvetica Light for the body copy.)

STEP SIX: To complete the effect, you can add a logo as I did here. Draw a square with the Rectangular Marquee tool, choose a dark blue as your Foreground color, and press Alt-Backspace to fill your square selection with blue. Go under the Edit menu, choose Stroke (Outline) Selection, and in the resulting dialog, choose a 5-point black stroke. Then, draw a small rectangular selection inside the square and fill it with red. Add type using the Type tool (I used the typeface Machine for the logo and Helvetica Italic for the tagline under the logo).

Snapshot Focus Effect

I first saw this clever, yet amazingly simple technique used in a brochure for the SeaWorld theme park in Orlando, Florida. It focuses the viewer's eye on one area of the photo by using a snapshot effect, but rather than cropping the photo to fit inside the "Polaroid" snapshot frame, they left the rest of the photo visible and applied a filter to it, creating a very appealing photographic effect. Here's how it's done:

STEP ONE: Open the photo in which you want to have the snapshot focus effect. Press the letter L until you have the Polygonal Lasso tool. You're going to draw a tilted rectangular selection around the area you want to use as the focal point of your photo.

STEP TWO: Start by clicking the Polygonal Lasso tool once where you want the top-left corner of your frame to be, then move your cursor up and to the right and click where you want the top-right corner to be. Continue this until you've created a tilted rectangular selection that has the same basic proportions as a Polaroid photo (like the selection shown here). Then, go under the Layer menu, under New, and choose Layer via Copy (or press Control-J) to copy this selected area onto its own layer above your Background layer in the Layers palette.

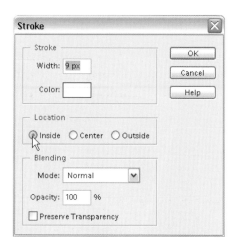

STEP THREE: Choose Stroke (Outline) Selection from the Edit menu. In the Stroke dialog, increase the Width to 9 pixels, and then click on the Color swatch and choose white when the Color Picker appears. Change the Location to Inside (which prevents the stroke from having rounded corners by placing it inside the copied photo layer, rather than extending out from it), and click OK.

STEP FOUR: Go to the Styles and Effects palette (found under the Window menu), and in the Layer Styles category, choose Drop Shadows from the top-right pop-up menu in the palette. Click directly on the High shadow to give the photo layer a drop shadow. Now, the rest of the tutorial is about adjusting the background to focus more attention on the snapshot you just created.

Continued

OPTION ONE: Here's one way of focusing more attention on the snapshot: In the Layers palette, click on the Background layer to make it active. Press Control-L to bring up Levels, then drag the highlight Output Levels slider at the bottom of the dialog to the left to darken the background. Read on for more options....

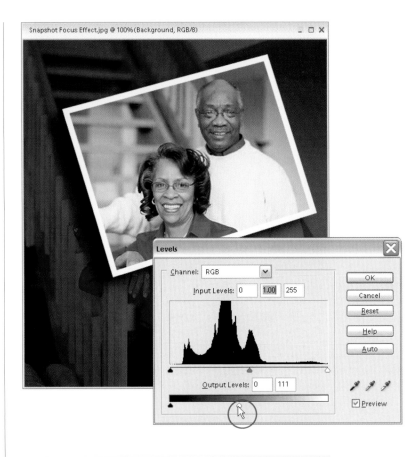

OPTION TWO: Another option is to lighten the background using Levels. Just press Control-Z to undo the darkening of the background from the previous step. Press Control-L to bring up Levels again, but this time, drag the shadow Output Levels slider to the right to lighten the background.

OPTION THREE: Press Control-Z to undo the background lightening. This is the effect SeaWorld's designers used on the background—a zoom blur. To apply a zoom blur, go under the Filter menu, under Blur, and choose Radial Blur. When the dialog appears, choose Zoom under Blur Method, increase the Amount to 35, and click OK.

OPTION FOUR: Press Control-Z to undo the zoom blur effect, and try this simple technique that focuses the viewer's eye on the snapshot by removing all color from the Background layer. Just go under the Enhance menu, under Adjust Color, and choose Remove Color.

Magnifying Glass Trick

It's amazing how many times I've seen this particular effect in ads. In this effect, we select and enlarge part of the background, copy it into memory, and then paste it into the circle of a magnifying glass. This makes it look like the magnifying glass is really magnifying what's beneath it.

STEP ONE: Open your background image and open an image of a magnifying glass.

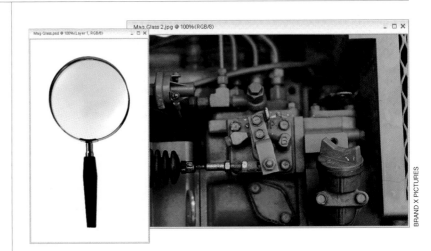

BRAND X PICTURES

STEP TWO: With the magnifying glass document active, press W to switch to the Magic Wand tool, and click on the white background surrounding the object. Then, go under the Select menu and choose Inverse. With the magnifying glass selected, press V to switch to the Move tool, and drag it onto your background image (it will appear on its own layer in the Layers palette).

STEP THREE: Press Control-T to bring up the Free Transform function. Press-and-hold the Shift key, grab a corner point, and drag inward to resize the magnifying glass. Click-and-drag outside the bounding box to rotate the magnifying glass, and then click within the bounding box to position it over the part of the image you want to magnify. Press Enter to lock in your transformation.

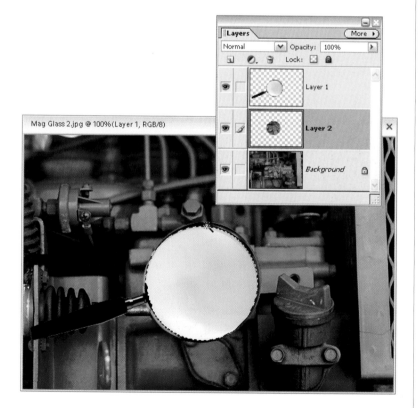

STEP FOUR: Press the letter W to switch to the Magic Wand tool. Click once inside the round glass area to select it. (*Note:* If the tool doesn't select all of the white space in the glass, go to the Options Bar, increase the Tolerance to around 80, and try again.) In the Layers palette, click on the Background layer, then go under the Layer menu, under New, and choose Layer via Copy (or press Control-J) to put your selection onto its own layer.

Continued

STEP FIVE: Press Control-T to bring up the Free Transform function again. When the bounding box appears, press-and-hold the Shift key, click on a corner point, and drag outward until it gives you the amount of magnification you want. (*Note:* You may want to drag this layer above your magnifying glass layer in the Layers palette as I did here to better see your transformation.) You can reposition the image as you like by clicking-and-dragging within the bounding box. When it looks right, press Enter.

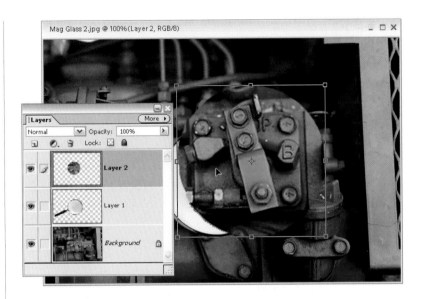

STEP SIX: Press-and-hold the Control key, and in the Layers palette, click on your circular image layer (Layer 2) to select it. Then, press Control-X to cut your selection and save it into memory. Now, delete your current layer by dragging it to the Trash icon at the top of the Layers palette.

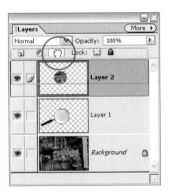

STEP SEVEN: In the Layers palette, click on the magnifying glass layer to make it active. Get the Magic Wand tool again and click once inside the round glass area of your magnifying glass to select that area. Go under the Edit menu and choose Paste Into Selection. Your enlarged image will now appear within your magnifying glass.

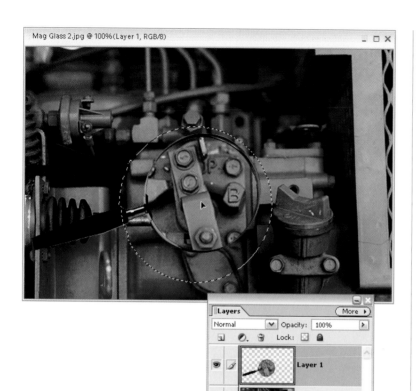

STEP EIGHT: You can switch to the Move tool to reposition this enlarged piece. When it looks good to you, press Control-D to deselect, completing the effect.

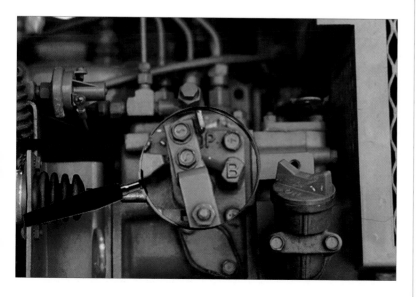

4

PRODUCT

Do you have any idea how hard it is for a color effect to be included in this chapter? Sure, by the time a

In Living Color
Color Effects

color effect winds up here, with all the glitz and glamour, it looks like a lot of fun, but believe me, it's a lot of hard work. It starts with an open audition for color effects, which takes place in Houston, L.A., New York, and Atlanta. In each city, a panel of judges then views each aspiring color effect, and from that group they choose only 30 color effects to go compete in the regional semifinals. At the semis, the judges then narrow the color effects down to just 10, who will be vying for the title "Coolest American Color Effect." *Cool American Color Effects*, which airs Wednesday nights on FAUX, is hosted by Ryan Seabiscuit, and…. (Do I even have to keep this up? Seriously, I was pretty sure that you would've stopped reading a hundred words or so ago, and since I was kind of counting on that, I never really developed an ending for this intro. So I'm just kinda going to end it right here. If you don't tell anyone I didn't have an ending, I won't tell anyone you read this far. Deal? Deal.)

Instant Stock Photo Effect

This "wild color" effect is incredibly popular right now. In fact, there are entire collections of royalty-free stock photos that use this technique, and you often see it used in print ads, in magazines, and on the Web. It's ideal for taking an otherwise boring image and using wild colors to make it trendy and interesting.

STEP ONE: Open the photo you want to apply the effect to. In this case, it's a regular RGB photo that looks kinda, well…boring.

STEP TWO: Go to the Layers palette, and from the Create Adjustment Layer pop-up menu, choose Gradient Map. This will bring up the Gradient Map dialog (seen in the next step).

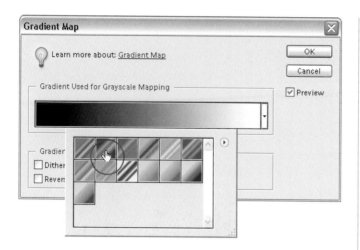

STEP THREE: Click on the little down-facing triangle to the right of the current gradient swatch to bring up the Gradient Picker. From the Picker's flyout menu (the right-facing arrow), choose Color Harmonies 2 to load this set of gradients; when they appear, choose the "Purple, Green, Gold" gradient (the second one in the Picker).

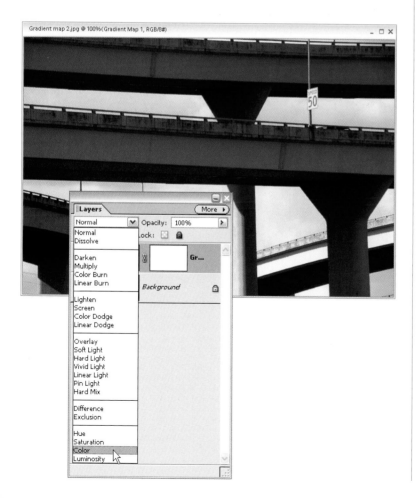

STEP FOUR: Click OK and this applies a Gradient Map adjustment layer over your photo. This gradient map is usually too intense, and pretty much trashes your photo. To fix that, go to the Layers palette and change the layer blend mode of this layer from Normal to Color. Now the color of the Gradient Map layer blends in more smoothly, and also replicates the wild color effect that's so popular with stock photo collections.

Continued

STEP FIVE: To fine-tune the effect, press the X key until you've set your Foreground color to black, and then press B to switch to the Brush tool. Up in the Options Bar, lower the Opacity for your brush to 50%, then click on the brush thumbnail and choose a large, soft-edged brush from the Brush Picker. Now, paint over areas where you want to have more detail. You're actually painting on the layer mask of the Gradient Map adjustment layer, and as you paint in black, some of the original color will start to reappear.

Before

After

Colorizing Black-and-White Images

This technique for colorizing grayscale images is great for getting that hand-tinted effect. This particular version uses Photoshop Elements 3's Hue/Saturation command to add color to selected areas.

STEP ONE: Open a grayscale image that you want to colorize. You have to be in a color mode to colorize a grayscale image, so go under the Image menu, under Mode, and choose RGB Color.

STEP TWO: Using one of the selection tools, select the first area that you'd like to colorize (try pressing A to switch to the Selection Brush tool and painting in your selection). If needed after you make your initial selection, press L to switch to the Lasso tool, press-and-hold the Shift key, and click-and-drag around areas that you want to add to your selection (or press-and-hold Alt as you drag to deselect areas).

Continued

STEP THREE: Now, you'll want to copy your selection to its own layer (in case you want to change colors later), so go under the Layer menu, under New, and choose Layer via Copy (or press Control-J).

STEP FOUR: Go under the Enhance menu, under Adjust Color, and choose Adjust Hue/Saturation (or press Control-U). When the dialog appears, turn on the Colorize checkbox. Now, you can move the Hue slider to choose the color you'd like. If the color seems too intense, drag the Saturation slider to the left.

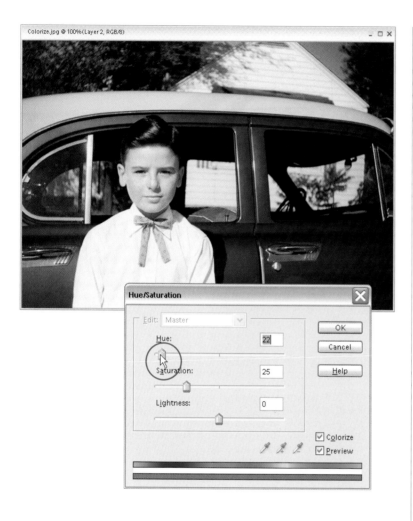

STEP FIVE: Continue this process of selecting areas, pressing Control-J to copy your selection to its own layer, going to Hue/Saturation, checking the Colorize box, and moving the Hue slider to add color to your image. As I mentioned before, if you change your mind and want to alter the color of an object, just click on its layer in the Layers palette and open Hue/Saturation to select the new color.

Before

After

Painting Away Color

You see this technique widely used in print ads and on TV. It was used very effectively in a print campaign for the Las Vegas nightclub Studio 54 (in the MGM Grand), where everyone in the image was in black and white, but one person appeared in full color, totally drawing the eye to that one person. Here's how it's done:

STEP ONE: Open a color image that you want to apply this effect to. Press the letter D to set your Foreground color to black.

STEP TWO: Press the B key to switch to the Brush tool. Go to the Options Bar and change the Mode pop-up menu from Normal to Color, then click on the brush thumbnail and choose a large, soft-edged brush from the Brush Picker.

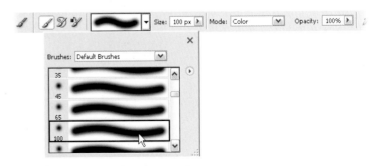

STEP THREE: Start painting. As you paint, the color will disappear, leaving just grayscale in its wake. Paint everything except for the object(s) that you want to remain in color.

Before

After

Visual Color Change

If there's one thing clients love to do, it's change the color of the products in their product shots. Luckily for you, (a) it's easy, and (b) it creates billable work. Here's one of the easiest ways to change the color of just about anything.

STEP ONE: Open a color image that contains an object or part of an object whose color you want to change.

STEP TWO: Use any selection tool (Lasso, Selection Brush, etc.) to select the object you want to apply a quick color change to. (In this example, I pressed L to switch to the Lasso tool and selected the woman's blouse. If you use the Lasso tool, after you make your initial selection you can press-and-hold Shift to add to your selection or press-and-hold Alt to deselect areas.)

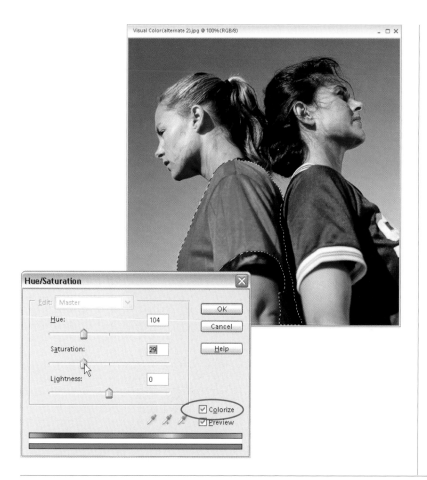

STEP THREE: Go under the Image menu, under Adjust Color, and choose Adjust Hue/Saturation. When the Hue/Saturation dialog appears, check the Colorize box in the lower-right corner. Now, simply grab the Hue slider and drag it until your image changes to a color you like. To soften your color, drag the Saturation slider to the left. When it looks good, click OK.

Before   After

Sepia Tone Effect

The sepia tone effect (popularized many decades ago) has been a staple of many photographers for years. In the project you're going to do here, you get an added twist by using a gradient map to convert your image to grayscale, which gives you a more "contrasty" grayscale conversion.

STEP ONE: Open the image you want to apply the sepia tone effect to.

STEP TWO: We're going to convert the photo to black and white (okay, grayscale), but we're going to do that using a gradient map so that the conversion has more contrast. Set your Foreground color to black by pressing the letter D. Choose Gradient Map from the Create Adjustment Layer pop-up menu at the top of the Layers palette. When the dialog appears, it immediately makes the photo look black and white, so just click OK. Next, you'll add the sepia tone color over your black-and-white image.

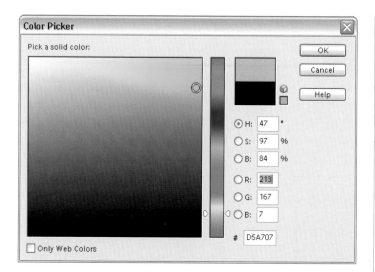

STEP THREE: Go under the Create Adjustment Layer pop-up menu again, but this time choose Solid Color. When the Color Picker appears, click on the color you want for your sepia tone and click OK.

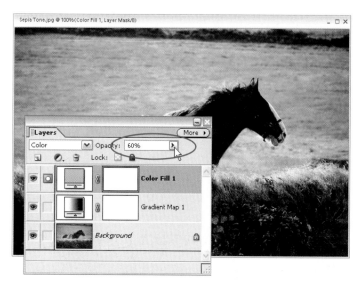

STEP FOUR: Once you click OK, you'll have just a solid block of color, so in the Layers palette, change the layer blend mode of the Solid Color adjustment layer from Normal to Color, and you'll see the sepia tone effect appear. If the color seems too intense, just lower the Opacity in the Layers palette.

Before

After

Photo Tinting

Tinting a color photo with a solid color is very popular and fairly easy—once you know how. What I really like about this technique is that it lets you take a fairly boring photo and turn it into something artistic quickly and easily.

STEP ONE: Open the photo you want to apply a tint effect to.

STEP TWO: Go to the top of the Layers palette and choose Hue/Saturation from the Create Adjustment Layer pop-up menu (it's the second icon from the left). When the dialog appears, click on the Colorize checkbox. Then, move the Hue slider to choose your tint, and if needed, drag the Saturation slider to the left to decrease the color saturation. When it looks good to you, click OK and a tint is applied to the image. Easy enough, eh?

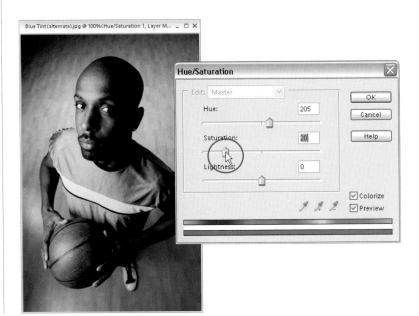

Before

After

This chapter is where you learn to create the effects that will subconsciously force people to purchase products and

Ad-Libbing
Advertising Effects

services they neither want nor need, at prices they can't afford—increasing their personal debt, thereby putting them, and perhaps the entire country, on the verge of a financial collapse that can only be compared to "Black Saturday," when the market *didn't* drop, because it was closed for trading, but had it been open, surely something would've happened, which I would then feel compelled to chronicle here; and that would've made this perhaps the longest run-on sentence in the history of modern literature, rather than the concise, straight-to-the-point introduction that you've come to expect from writers like me, who value your time, yet don't mind using a comma or two (but only when absolutely, positively necessary), like now. Okay, keep breathing, keep breathing. In through the nose, out through the mouth. Or why not try Nasatrin, which provides 12-hour nondrowsy relief from common allergy symptoms, such as....

Backlit Photo Backgrounds

I got the idea for this technique after seeing ABSOLUT VODKA's very slick print ad campaign, and I figured out how to create a similar background in Photoshop Elements—plus, it's easy to do!

STEP ONE: Create a new document in RGB mode (the one shown here is 6x8"). Press the G key to switch to the Gradient tool. In the Options Bar, ensure that the Linear Gradient icon is selected, then click on the Edit button to bring up the Gradient Editor. Click on the third gradient from the left in the top row (Black to White). Double-click on the bottom-left black color stop under the gradient ramp and choose a dark blue in the resulting Color Picker. Then, double-click the bottom-right color stop and choose a light blue in the Picker. Type "Blue" in the Name field, click the New button to save the gradient, and then click OK.

STEP TWO: Click-and-drag the Gradient tool from the top of your image window to the bottom so the lighter shade is on the bottom. Press M until you have the Elliptical Marquee tool, and draw a circular selection in the center of your background. With the selection in place, press Control-L to bring up the Levels dialog. At the bottom of the dialog, drag the shadow Output Levels slider to the right (to around 200), and a soft spotlight effect will appear on your gradient background. Click OK in the dialog, and press Control-D to deselect.

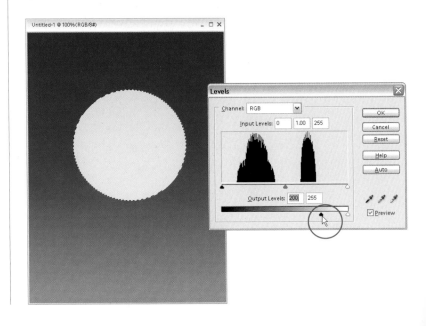

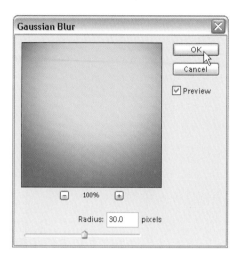

STEP THREE: Go under the Filter menu, under Blur, and choose Gaussian Blur. Enter 30 pixels (65 pixels for high-res, 300-ppi images) and click OK to blur the edges of your spotlight in the gradient layer.

TIP: If you want to change the color of your gradient, press Control-U to bring up the Hue/Saturation dialog while the Background layer is active. Turn on the Colorize checkbox in the lower right-hand corner, and then adjust the Hue slider until you've found the color you like. You can also drag the Saturation slider to the left if your gradient color looks too intense.

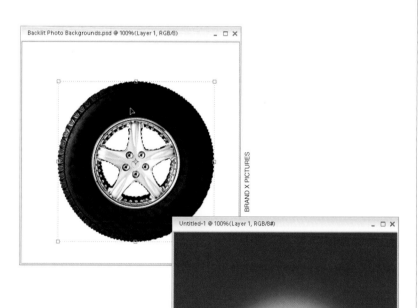

STEP FOUR: Open your object image (in this case, a tire). Use any selection tool to select the tire (here I Shift-clicked on the Magic Wand tool [W] in all the white background areas and then went under the Select menu and chose Inverse). With your selection in place, press the letter V to switch to the Move tool, drag this object onto your spotlight document, and position it over your spotlight. Next, go under the Layer menu, under New, and choose Layer via Copy (or press Control-J) to duplicate your object layer.

Continued

STEP FIVE: With your duplicate layer active, go under the Image menu, under Rotate, and choose Flip Layer Vertical. With the Move tool, hold the Shift key, click on the flipped image, and drag straight down (the Shift key will keep the flipped object in the same vertical position as you drag). Keep dragging straight down below the original object so their bottoms are just overlapping. In the Layers palette, lower the Opacity to around 40%, then drag this copied layer below your original object layer (Layer 1).

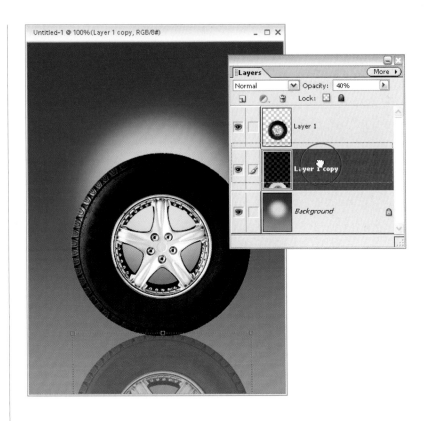

STEP SIX: Go under the Filter menu, under Blur, and choose Motion Blur. For Angle enter 0°, for Distance enter 13 (try 30 for high-res images), and click OK to blur the reflection a bit and put the focus back on the main object. Press D to set your Foreground color to black, and then click the Create a New Layer icon. With this layer active, press B to get the Brush tool, and in the Options Bar, click on the down-facing arrow next to the brush thumbnail to open the Brush Picker and choose a medium, soft-edged brush. Change the Mode pop-up menu in the Options Bar to Behind and lower the Opacity of the Brush tool to 60%. Press-and-hold the Shift key and draw a straight line under the object to add a soft shadow. If the shadow seems too intense, lower the Opacity of the layer in the Layers palette.

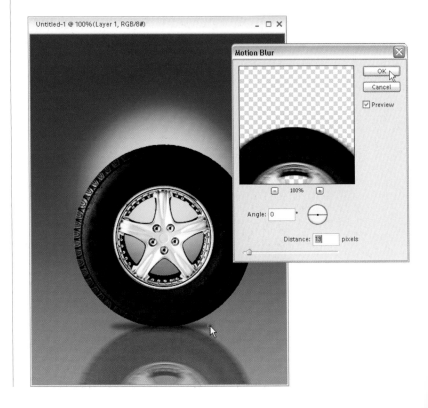

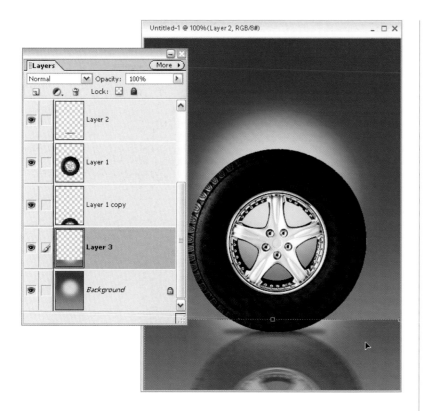

STEP SEVEN: Press M until you have the Rectangular Marquee tool. In the Layers palette, click on the Background layer, and then make a selection around the bottom half of the background. Go under the Layer menu, under New, and choose Layer via Copy (or press Control-J) to copy this selected area onto its own layer. Switch to the Move tool again, hold the Shift key, and drag this layer straight down until the edge of it appears just above the bottom edge of your object.

STEP EIGHT: To complete the effect, press T to switch to the Type tool and add some copy. (In this example, for the headline "Now in Stock!" I used the font MS Serif, and for the body copy I used Helvetica Neue.)

Quick, Elegant Product Background

This is a nice way to showcase an elegant product, such as jewelry, watches, etc. It really gives that "shot-in-the-studio" look because it appears as though the red area is created by a soft spotlight. Best of all, this is one of those "create-it-from-scratch-in-60-seconds" effects that appear to have taken hours.

STEP ONE: Create a new document in the size you'd like for your background (the one shown here is a 6x8" document in RGB mode). Press D to set your Foreground color to black, then press Alt-Backspace to fill the Background layer with black. Now, add a new blank layer by clicking on the Create a New Layer icon at the top of the Layers palette.

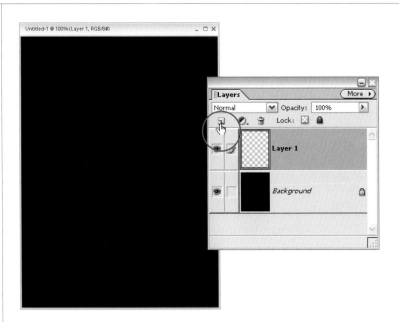

STEP TWO: Press M until you get the Elliptical Marquee tool, and draw a horizontal, oval-shaped selection that extends near the document's left and right edges. If you have to center your selection once you've drawn it, just click the Elliptical Marquee tool within the oval selection area and drag to reposition it.

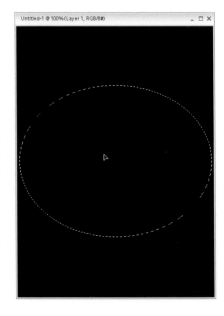

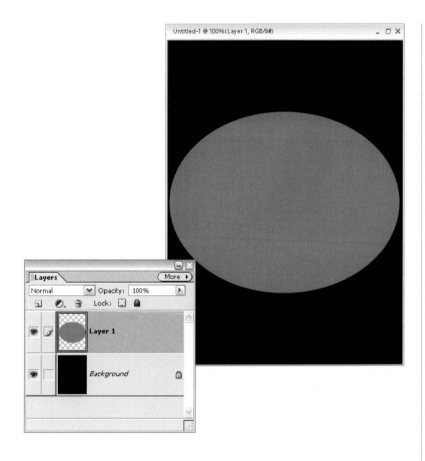

STEP THREE: In the Toolbox, click on the Foreground color swatch to bring up the Color Picker, and then choose red for your Foreground color. Press Alt-Backspace to fill your oval selection with red. Now you can deselect by pressing Control-D.

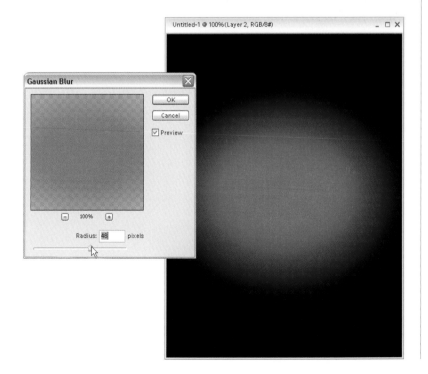

STEP FOUR: To soften the edges of our red oval (and make it look more like a soft, red spotlight), go under the Filter menu, under Blur, and choose Gaussian Blur. When the Gaussian Blur dialog appears, enter 48 pixels (for high-res, 300-ppi images, enter 230 pixels). When you click OK, the edges of your red circle will be softened, creating the effect of a spotlight (this will look more realistic once you add a product to your image, as you'll soon see).

Continued

STEP FIVE: Open an image of the product you want to place on your red spotlight background (in this case, it's a watch). Use any of the selection tools you're comfortable with to put a selection around your product. (In this example, the product is on a white background, so the Magic Wand tool [W] will probably do the trick—just click the Wand on the background, go under the Select menu, and choose Inverse to select just the watch.)

STEP SIX: Once the object is selected, press the letter V to switch to the Move tool, click on the object, and drag it over into your red spotlight document. The watch automatically appears on its own layer in the Layers palette.

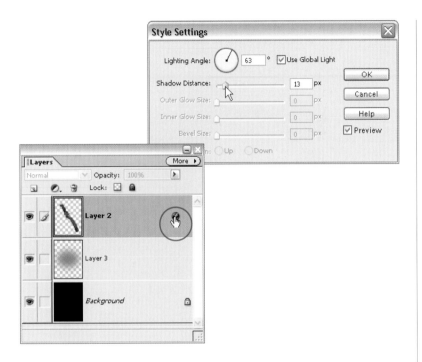

STEP SEVEN: To add some depth and to make it look as if the watch is above the background, go to the Styles and Effects palette (found under the Window menu), and with the Layer Styles category selected, choose Drop Shadows from the top-right pop-up menu in the palette. Click on the Soft Edge drop shadow, and then go to the Layers palette and double-click on the Layer Styles icon (it looks like an "*f*") to the right of the layer's name. When the Style Settings dialog appears, increase the Shadow Distance to 13, change the Lighting Angle to 63°, and click OK.

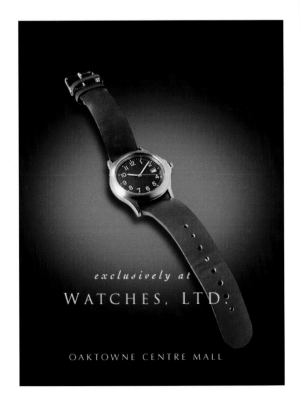

STEP EIGHT: The effect is now complete. To finish things off, you can add some type by pressing T to switch to the Type tool. In the example shown here, the words "exclusively at" are set in the font Cochin Italic. The words "WATCHES, LTD." are set in Trajan Pro, and at the bottom, the words "OAKTOWNE CENTRE MALL" are set in Optima Regular.

Quick Product Shot Background

Here's a very useful photographic background technique that not only looks great, but takes only seconds to create—perfect for catalog shots, magazine ads, and product shots of all kinds. You can even use it as a background for portraits (though you might want to use a less warm combination than yellow and brown).

STEP ONE: Create a new document (the example here is a 6x8" document in RGB mode). Click on the Foreground color swatch at the bottom of the Toolbox and choose a bright yellow in the Color Picker (the build shown here is R: 252, G: 252, and B: 2). Fill your Background layer with this yellow color by pressing Alt-Backspace.

STEP TWO: Click on the Create a New Layer icon at the top of the Layers palette. Change your Foreground color to a very dark brown and fill your new layer with this color by pressing Alt-Backspace. Press the letter M to get the Rectangular Marquee tool, and draw a vertical, rectangular selection in the center of your image area. Then, go under the Select menu and choose Feather. When the Feather Selection dialog appears, enter 50 pixels and click OK. You'll see the edges of your rectangular selection become rounded.

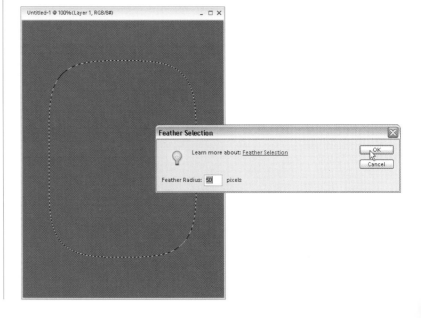

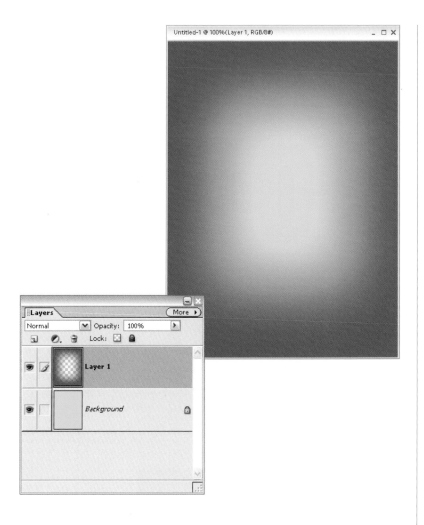

STEP THREE: Now, press Backspace to knock a large, soft-edged hole out of your brown-filled layer, revealing part of your yellow Background layer. Deselect by pressing Control-D.

BRAND X PICTURES

STEP FOUR: Open an image of the product you want to appear on this background and put a selection around the product. (In my example, I switched to the Magic Wand tool [W], clicked on the white background, went under the Select menu, and chose Inverse to select just the makeup cases.) Then, press V to switch to the Move tool, and click-and-drag the product over to your brown/yellow background document. (*Note:* If needed, press Control-T for Free Transform, press-and-hold the Shift key, grab a corner point, and drag to resize your image.) In the Layers palette, drag this layer below your brown-filled layer to soften the effect on the makeup cases.

Continued

STEP FIVE: To add some depth to the image, go to the Styles and Effects palette (found under the Window menu), and with the Layer Styles category selected, choose Drop Shadows from the top-right pop-up menu in the palette. Click on the Soft Edge shadow, and in the Layers palette, double-click on the Layer Styles icon (it looks like an "ƒ") to the right of the layer's name. In the resulting dialog, choose a Lighting Angle of 122°, increase the Shadow Distance to 9, and click OK.

STEP SIX: Finish off your image by pressing the T key to switch to the Type tool, and enter some text. In the example shown here, I entered the word "beautyscape" set in the font Cochin. The store name is set in Gill Sans MT Condensed, and the cities are set in Perpetua.

Fade-Away Reflection

This is a popular technique for products that are displayed on a white background. It makes the product look as if it were shot on a reflective surface, and the reflection just fades away underneath it. Here, we're going to create an ad for a fictitious tennis racket company, and we'll apply the fade-away reflection to the racket.

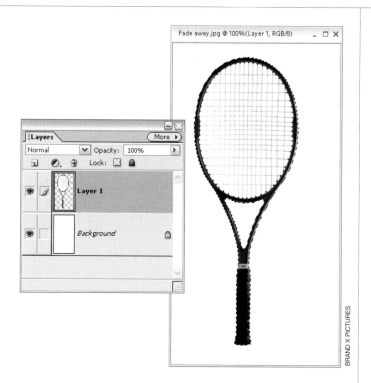

BRAND X PICTURES

STEP ONE: Open an image of an object that you want to add a fade-away reflection to. Put a selection around the object using any selection tool. In this example, we need to select the racket, so press the letter W to switch to the Magic Wand tool. In the Options Bar, set the Tolerance to 10 and make sure the Contiguous checkbox is on. Shift-click on the white background areas in the image and then choose Inverse from the Select menu to select the racket. Go under the Layer menu, under New, and choose Layer via Cut (or press Shift-Control-J) to cut the object from the Background layer, and copy it onto its own layer.

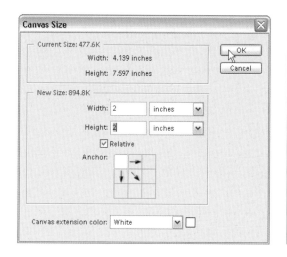

STEP TWO: In the Layers palette, click on the Background layer to make it active, and then go to the Image menu, under Resize, and choose Canvas Size. In the Canvas Size dialog, enter 2 inches for both Width and Height, ensure the Relative checkbox is on, and click on the top-left square in the Anchor grid. Set the Canvas Extension Color pop-up menu to White and click OK to add white space below and to the right of the racket.

Continued

STEP THREE: Click on the object layer in the Layers palette, then go under the Layer menu, under New, and choose Layer via Copy (or press Control-J) to duplicate the layer. Then, from the Image menu, under Rotate, choose Flip Layer Vertical. Press the letter V to switch to the Move tool, press-and-hold the Shift key, then click on the flipped object and drag it straight down until the bottoms of the two objects meet, creating a mirror reflection.

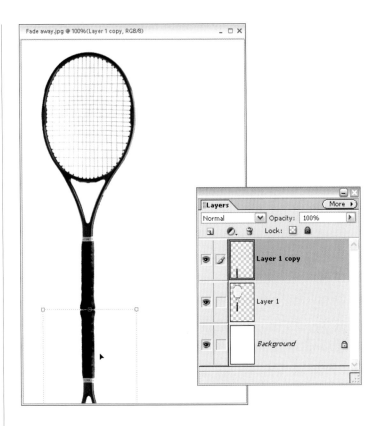

STEP FOUR: With the duplicate layer active, Control-click on the Create a New Layer icon at the top of the Layers palette. This creates a new layer directly below the duplicate layer. Then, click on the duplicate layer, and from the Layer menu, choose Group with Previous (or just press Control-G). Your reflected object will disappear because it's hidden by the empty layer below it. Control-click on the duplicate object layer to load a selection around the reflected object, and then click on the empty layer to make it active.

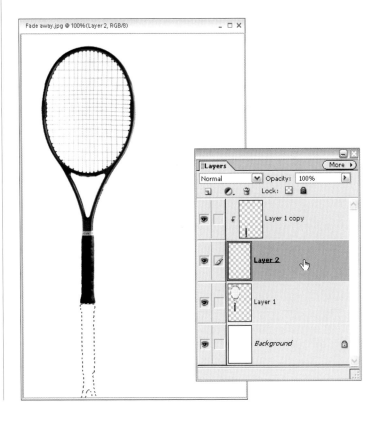

STEP FIVE: Press the G key to switch to the Gradient tool, and then press Enter to open the Gradient Picker (which will appear in the top-left corner of your screen). Select the Foreground to Transparent gradient (the second one in the Picker), and then click-and-drag from the top of your selection down toward the bottom of the document. Your reflected object will fade away. Press Control-D to deselect, then in the Layers palette, lower the Opacity of the gradient object layer to around 50%.

STEP SIX: To finish off the project, just press the T key to switch to the Type tool, and add some type. (The headline and body copy are set in HelveticaNeue and the name of the fictitious company is set in the typeface Mata. For the red block logo, I created a square selection with the Rectangular Marquee tool (M), set my Foreground color to red, pressed Alt-Backspace to fill the square with the Foreground color, and entered white type set in Mata.)

Classified Ad Effect

You've probably seen this effect used in print ads and on TV a dozen times. It's designed to look like someone tore a classified ad out of a newspaper and highlighted the important points. The effect is easy to pull off—the only thing that takes any time is creating the fake classified ad (but I give you a sample one to download from this book's website, in case you don't feel like doing it yourself).

STEP ONE: This technique starts with a fake classified ad. You can either create your own (as I did here) so that you can customize the text in the center ad (where the focus of the effect will be), or you can download this one from the book's website (check it out at scottkelbybooks.com/ddelements3).

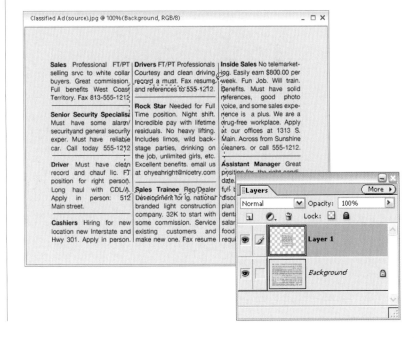

STEP TWO: Press the letter L to get the Lasso tool and draw a loose, rip-like selection around the classified ad that you want the viewer to focus on. This selection should look a little jaggy, as if the section were torn from a newspaper by hand. Then, go under the Layer menu, under New, and choose Layer via Copy (or press Control-J) to copy the selected area up onto its own layer. Press the letter D to set your Background color to white.

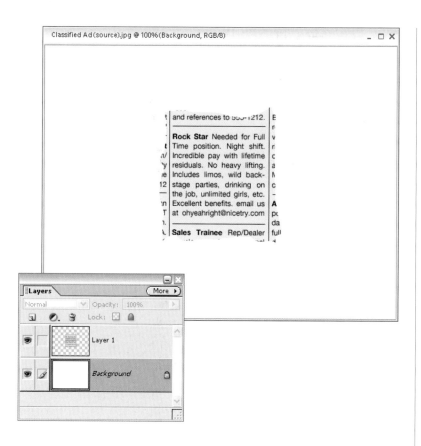

STEP THREE: Go to the Layers palette and click on the Background layer. Go under the Select menu and choose All (or press Control-A) to select the entire background, then press Backspace to delete the excess classifieds, leaving just your ad on the layer above. Deselect by pressing Control-D.

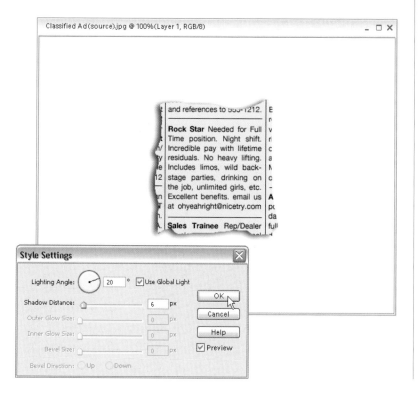

STEP FOUR: Click back on the torn classified layer in the Layers palette to make it active. Go to the Styles and Effects palette (found under the Window menu), and with the Layer Styles selected, choose Drop Shadows from the top-right pop-up menu in the palette. Click on the Soft Edge drop shadow, then go to the Layers palette and double-click on the Layer Styles icon (it looks like an "*f*") to the right of the layer's name. In the resulting dialog, set the Lighting Angle to 20, set the Shadow Distance to 6 pixels (try 40 for high-res, 300-ppi images), and click OK to apply a soft drop shadow to your torn classified ad.

Continued

STEP FIVE: Press-and-hold the Control key and click on the torn newspaper layer to put a selection around it. Then, go under the Select menu, under Modify, and choose Contract. When the dialog appears, enter 3 pixels and then click OK to shrink your selection. Go under the Select menu and choose Inverse, which leaves only the outside edge of your newspaper selected. You'll lighten those edges to help make them look more like they really were torn, so press Control-L to bring up Levels. At the bottom of the dialog, drag the shadow Output Levels slider to the right until the edges look good to you, and then click OK. Deselect by pressing Control-D.

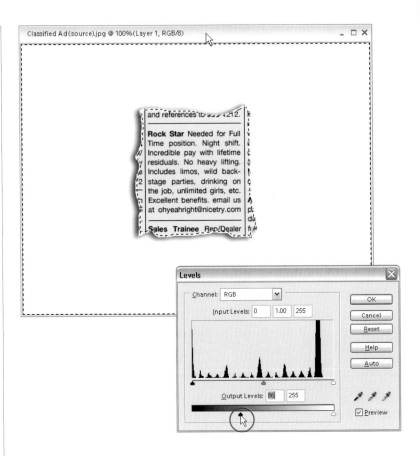

STEP SIX: Next, click on the Create a New Layer icon at the top of the Layers palette. Press B to switch to the Brush tool, then Right-click in the document to bring up the Brush Picker. From the Picker's flyout menu, choose Load Brushes. Navigate to the Photoshop Elements 3.0 folder, then open the Brushes folder inside the Presets folder. From the list that appears, choose the brush set named Wet Media Brushes and click the Load button. The brushes will appear at the bottom of the Picker. Click on the 19-pixel Light Oil Flat Tip brush, and then press the Left or Right Bracket key until the brush is the same height as a line of your type in the classified. Click on the Foreground color swatch in the Toolbox and set your Foreground color to a highlighter yellow in the Color Picker (I used R: 216, G: 209, and B: 0). Now paint strokes over the lines you want the reader to focus on.

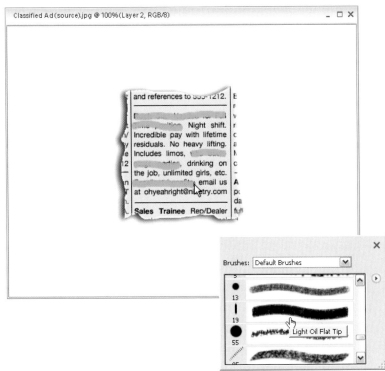

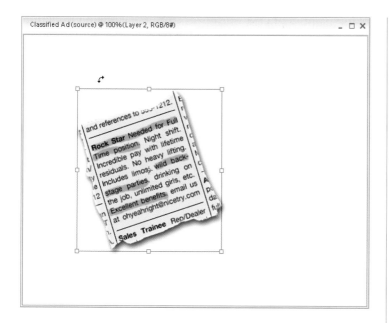

STEP SEVEN: To complete the effect, change the layer blend mode of this layer from Normal to Multiply in the Layers palette, and then you'll be able to see the words through the highlighting. In the ad here, I clicked on the highlight layer and then clicked in the empty box to the left of the classified layer to link them. Then, I pressed Control-T bring up Free Transform to rotate and adjust those layers just a bit.

STEP EIGHT: Finally, I pressed T to switch to the Type tool and added text (in the example here, I used the typeface Minion Pro for the headline and body copy, and for the company name I used Helvetica Compressed). *Note:* Make sure you keep a copy of the original with all its layers, because then you can easily update the text for any classified you'll need in the future.

Credit Card from a Photo

In the old days, unless you worked for Visa, MasterCard, or American Express, your chance of designing a credit card was fairly slim, but now there are phone cards, frequent flyer cards, frequent shopper cards, slot club cards, convention badges, and about a hundred other reasons why you may need this effect, primarily as a mockup to show clients.

STEP ONE: Create a new document that's roughly 7x5" set at 72 ppi in RGB. Press D to set your Foreground color to black, and then click on the Create a New Layer icon at the top of the Layers palette. Press the U key until the Rounded Rectangle tool appears in the Toolbox, and then press Control-R to show the rulers in your document. In the Options Bar, set the Radius for the Rounded Rectangle tool to 10 pixels, then draw your rounded-corner box at the size of a credit card (approximately 3¼ x 2⅛ ", but I'm going to draw mine slightly larger to show the effect better).

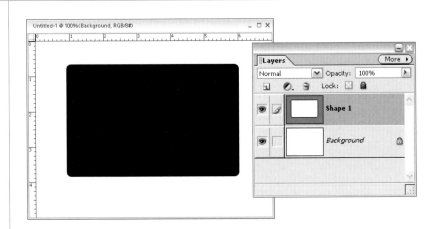

STEP TWO: Open the image you want to use in your credit card. Press V to get the Move tool, and drag it into your credit card document. (In the example here, I wanted only the package in the gift card, so I clicked the Magic Wand tool [W] in the white background, went under the Select menu, chose Inverse, and then moved only the package into the card document.) In the Layers palette, lower the image layer's Opacity to 50% to help you see the credit card shape layer when resizing the image. Press Control-T to bring up Free Transform. Press-and-hold the Shift key, grab a corner point, and drag inward to size down your image. Move your cursor outside the bounding box and click-and-drag to rotate the package slightly; then click-and-drag inside the bounding box to position the image.

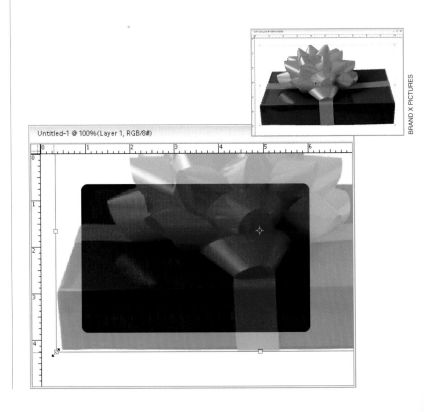

BRAND X PICTURES

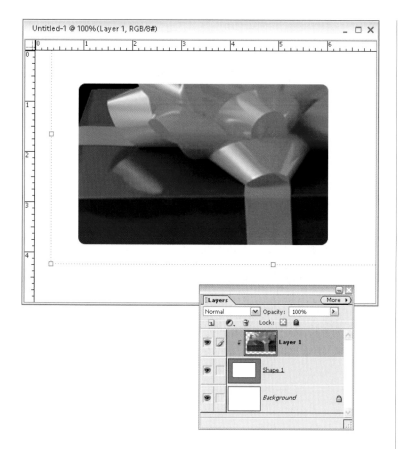

TIP: If you can't see the corner points of the Free Transform bounding box, press Control-0 [zero] to zoom out; when finished, double-click the Zoom tool in the Toolbox to return to 100% zoom.

STEP THREE: Press Enter to lock in your changes, and in the Layers palette, raise the Opacity of this layer back up to 100%. Now, under the Image menu, choose Group with Previous (or press Control-G) to place your photo inside the black credit card shape on the layer below it. The grouping you just created is temporary, so press Control-E to permanently merge your photo layer with the credit card shape layer, leaving just a Background layer and your rounded-corner photo layer.

STEP FOUR: Press T to switch to the Type tool, and add some "credit card type" to your image. Press the letter X to change your Foreground color to white and then add your text, completing the effect. (In this example, I used the font Helvetica Neue Light for "SEFINA" and for the word "card," and I used Helvetica Neue Condensed Bold for the word "gift.")

High-Tech Transparent Info Boxes

I wanted to include an effect that was similar to the high-tech transparent info boxes you see used on nationally televised sports events on ESPN, FOX Sports, etc., for displaying scores, stats, and team info during games. I've used this effect myself when creating the interface for Photoshop training CD-ROMs, but it works just as well over video, as a DVD interface, or even simply in print.

STEP ONE: Open the photo you want to use as your interface background. Then, create a new document at the size you want for your interface (the example here is 8x6"). Create a new blank layer by clicking on the Create a New Layer icon at the top of the Layers palette.

STEP TWO: Press the L key until you have the Polygonal Lasso tool, and draw a selection on the left of the blank document that will later become the navigation area (like the one shown here). To build a selection, press-and-hold the Shift key, click once, move to the next spot, then click again. (The Shift key creates perfectly vertical or horizontal lines and exact 45° angles.) Keep clicking to make these straight-line sections until you have the shape you want. Click on your original starting point to complete the selection.

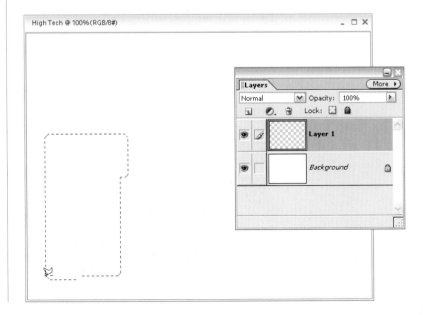

STEP THREE: Press D to set your Foreground color to black, then press Alt-Backspace to fill the selection with black. Deselect by pressing Control-D.

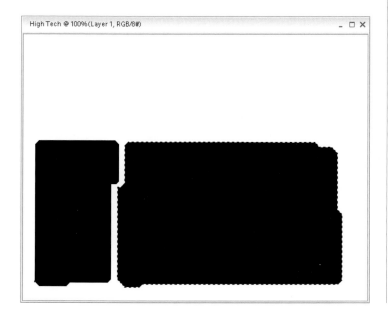

STEP FOUR: On this same layer, draw another shape using the Polygonal Lasso tool. Again, press-and-hold the Shift key to create perfectly vertical or horizontal lines and exact 45° angles. When the selection is complete, press Alt-Backspace to fill it with black. Deselect by pressing Control-D.

Continued

STEP FIVE: Use the Polygonal Lasso tool to draw another shape selection at the top, fill it with black as well, and deselect by pressing Control-D.

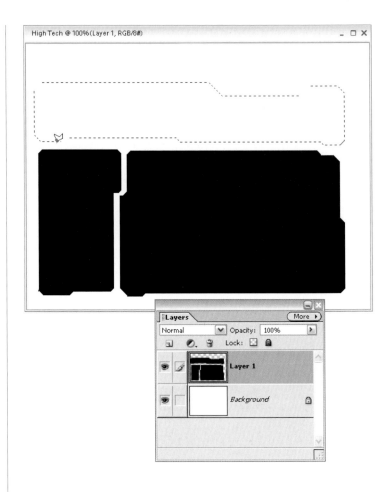

STEP SIX: Press the letter V to switch to the Move tool, press-and-hold the Shift key, and drag-and-drop this shape layer into the photo that you opened in Step One. (The Shift key will center the shapes in the photo.) Now that the main areas of your interface are in place, all you have to do is a little tweaking.

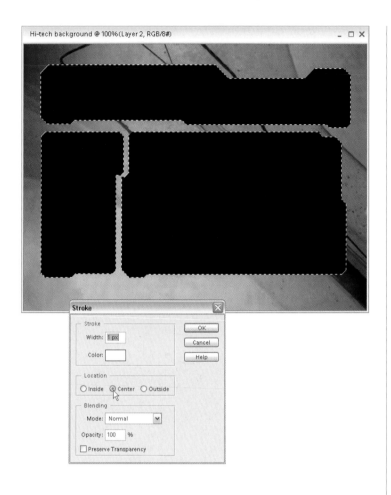

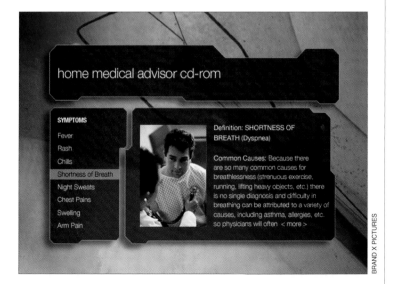

BRAND X PICTURES

STEP SEVEN: Go to the Layers palette and click on the Create a New Layer icon. Press-and-hold the Control key and click on your shape layer (Layer 1) to put a selection around your shapes. Go under the Edit menu and choose Stroke (Outline) Selection. Set the Width to 1 pixel, click on the Color swatch and choose white in the Color Picker, set the Location to Center, and click OK to put a white stroke around your shape selection. Deselect by pressing Control-D. In the Layers palette, lower the Opacity setting of this white stroke layer to 50%. This makes the stroke appear thinner than its 1-pixel width.

STEP EIGHT: In the Layers palette, click on your shape layer (Layer 1) to make it active. Go to the Styles and Effects palette (found under the Window menu), and with Layer Styles selected, choose Drop Shadows in the palette's top-right pop-up menu. Click on the Soft Edge shadow. Return to the Layers palette and double-click on the Layer Styles icon to the right of the layer. In the resulting dialog, increase the Shadow Distance to 13 pixels and click OK. In the Layers palette, lower the Opacity setting for this layer to 60% to let the image show through your shapes. Now press the letter T to switch to the Type tool, and create the text. (All the type shown here is in the font Helvetica Light.) To highlight any of your interface's menu items, simply select the text with the Type tool, change its color to black, and then draw a selection around it using the Rectangular Marquee tool (M). Create a new layer, and then fill your selection with white. Lower the Opacity of this layer to around 20% and press Control-D to deselect. You can also drag-and-drop an image into the interface as I did here, which completes the effect.

Turning a Logo into a Brush

Tired of importing your client's logo into every little project you do for him? Well, here's a trick for turning his logo into a brush so you can choose it directly from the Brush Picker in the Options Bar and simply paint it into any document.

STEP ONE: Open the document that contains your client's logo.

STEP TWO: Press the letter M to switch to the Rectangular Marquee tool, press-and-hold the Shift key, and draw a square selection around the logo. Go under the Edit menu and choose Define Brush from Selection. Name your brush in the New Brush dialog and click OK. As soon as you do, that logo is added as a new brush (with a tiny thumbnail) at the bottom of the Brush Picker.

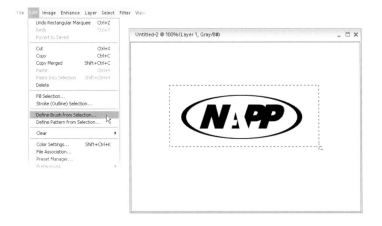

STEP THREE: To use the brush, press the letter B to switch to the Brush tool, then up in the Options Bar, click on the brush thumbnail to open the Brush Picker, and scroll to the bottom to select your new "logo" brush. Click once on a new document to make the logo appear, or click-and-drag for multiple logos. And if you need the logo in a different color, just change your Foreground color before you paint.

I know what you're thinking: "Are the techniques in this chapter really 'cool' effects, or is this just marketing hype?"

Jealous Type
Cool Type Effects

First, I want to point out that there are strict guidelines set in place by a large, scary-sounding government agency to make sure that when a claim is made about a particular product, the claim is true. So, to substantiate the claim that these type effects are indeed worthy of the glitzy marketing term "cool," I formed a blue-ribbon panel that was charged with putting together a crack team of addicts to find Arthur Fonzarelli and get his full endorsement of these effects. Sadly, the panel was not able to locate Mr. Fonzarelli within the allotted time. However, a woman identified only as Pinky Tuscadero, with whom he was once romantically linked, did render her expert opinion in his stead. Her opinion proved beyond reasonable doubt that the effects in this chapter would be considered by Mr. Fonzarelli, or any of the *Happy Days* cast (with the notable exception of Chachi), to be "cool" effects. I think that pretty much settles it.

Instant 3D Type

This technique is so easy and so versatile that I wanted to include it first. The initial few steps of this technique show you how to apply a perspective transformation to your type, while the last few steps show you how to create depth by adding 5,000 type layers (kidding—it's more like 40 or so layers).

STEP ONE: Create a document in RGB mode (the one here is 8x6"). Click on the Foreground color swatch at the bottom of the Toolbox, and in the Color Picker that appears, choose a bright blue. Then, press Alt-Backspace to fill the Background layer with this color. Click on the Foreground color swatch again and choose a bright red in the Picker. Press the T key to switch to the Type tool, and enter your type (the font used here is called Impact).

STEP TWO: You're going to use Free Transform to add a perspective effect to your type, but first let's go under the Layer menu and choose Simplify Layer to change your Type layer into an image layer. Now, press Control-T to bring up Free Transform. Press-and-hold Shift-Alt-Control, grab the top-right Free Transform control point, and drag upward to create a perspective effect. When the perspective looks good to you, press Enter to lock in your transformation.

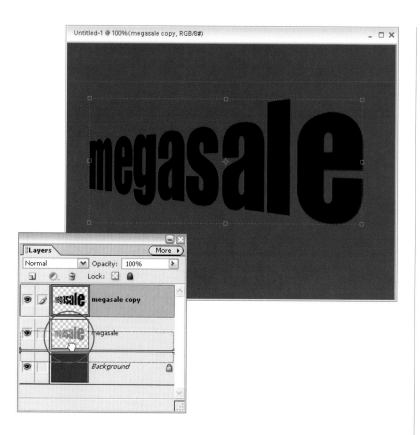

STEP THREE: In the Layers palette, make a copy of your text layer by dragging it to the Create a New Layer icon at the top of the Layers palette. Press D to set your Foreground color to black, then press Shift-Alt-Backspace to fill your type with black (holding the Shift key fills just the object on the layer instead of the entire layer). Next, in the Layers palette, drag this new black text layer beneath your original text layer.

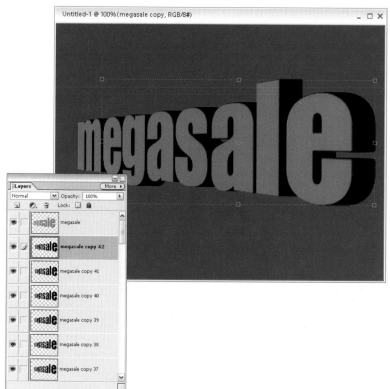

STEP FOUR: Here's where you create the 3D effect. Press-and-hold Alt-Control and press-and-hold the Right Arrow key on your keyboard. As you do this, you'll see the 3D effect emerge. What you're doing is duplicating and simultaneously nudging to the right the black text layer over and over again very quickly. (In the example shown here, I added 42 layers, yet it only took about 15 seconds.) Don't worry about the extra layers; we'll deal with them in the next step.

Continued

STEP FIVE: In the Layers palette, your original red text layer should be on top of the layer stack. Hide this layer from view by clicking once on the Eye icon in the far-left column beside it. Then, scroll down to the bottom of the layer stack and hide the Background layer from view as well, leaving only the 40+ black text layers still visible.

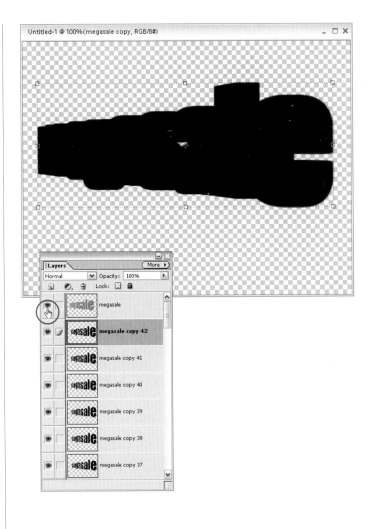

STEP SIX: Go to the Layers palette's flyout menu and choose Merge Visible to combine the 40+ text layers into just one layer. Now, you can make both your Background layer and the top text layer visible again by clicking in the empty box where the Eye icon used to appear, which completes the effect.

Perspective Type Logo

When the UPN TV network first introduced its current logo, I just assumed it was created in a 3D program, but you can pretty much get the same effect (where it looks like the logo is dropping back, like a one-point perspective effect) from right within Photoshop Elements, thanks to the Free Transform tool's Distort feature.

STEP ONE: Create a new document in RGB mode (the one here is 8x6"). Click on the Foreground color swatch in the Toolbox and choose a bright red in the Color Picker. Fill the background with this red color by pressing Alt-Backspace. Next, press D and then X to set your Foreground color to white. Press the T key to switch to the Type tool, and enter your type (the font shown here is Impact).

STEP TWO: Create a new blank layer by clicking on the Create a New Layer icon at the top of the Layers palette. Press M until you get the Elliptical Marquee tool. Press-and-hold the Shift key and drag out a circular selection that's larger than your type. (*Note:* If you need to reposition your selection, press-and-hold the Spacebar while you're still dragging with the Elliptical Marquee tool; release just the Spacebar key when you've repositioned the selection where you want it, and finish drawing your selection.)

Continued

STEP THREE: Go under the Edit menu and choose Stroke (Outline) Selection. When the Stroke dialog appears, choose 16 pixels for your Width, set the Location to Center, click on the Color swatch, choose white in the Color Picker, and then click OK. This puts a white stroke around your circular selection. Press Control-D to deselect.

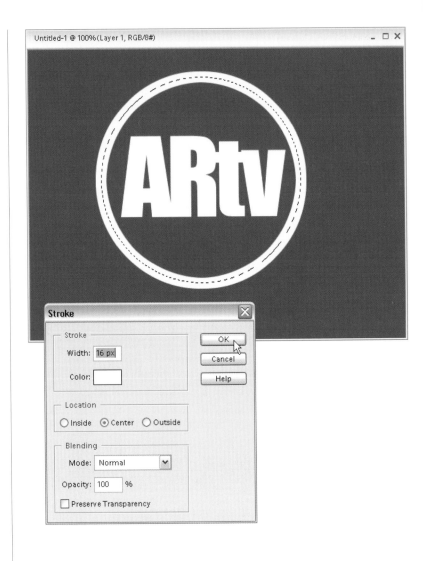

STEP FOUR: In the Layers palette, link your Type layer and your white circle layer together by making sure the white circle layer is active and clicking in the second column to the left of the Type layer (the tiny Link icon will appear). Then, press Control-E to merge the two layers. (*Note:* Whenever you want to merge an image layer down into a Type layer, you have to link the two layers first in the Layers palette.)

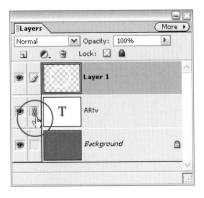

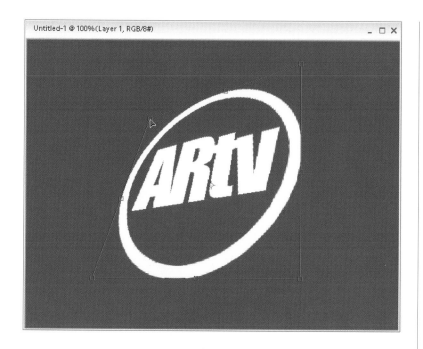

STEP FIVE: Press Control-T to bring up the Free Transform bounding box. Press-and-hold the Control key, click on the top-left corner point of the Free Transform bounding box, and drag down and to the right (you're dragging diagonally inward); the logo will appear to tip backward. Holding the Control key allows you to distort just that one point of the bounding box.

STEP SIX: Press Enter to lock in your transformation and to complete the effect.

Type on a Circle

While this could be a tedious step-by-step technique for wrapping type around a circle, it doesn't have to be. Photoshop Elements' cool Warp Text feature lets you create this effect much faster and easier. Here's how:

STEP ONE: Open the circular image you want to place type around. (*Note:* You can start with a blank document: Just draw a circular selection with the Elliptical Marquee tool; go under the Edit menu, under Stroke [Outline] Selection; and add a 1-pixel black stroke to the selection. You can then use your stroked selection as a guide for the rotation of your text.)

BRAND X PICTURES

STEP TWO: Press the T key to switch to the Type tool, and then enter your type (the typeface I used here is Copperplate Gothic Bold). Use the Spacebar to add a space between each letter you type (we do this because the next step tends to condense the type, so we need to stretch it out a bit).

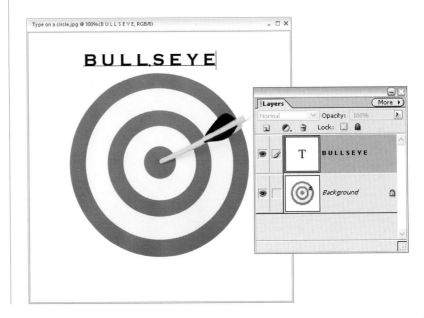

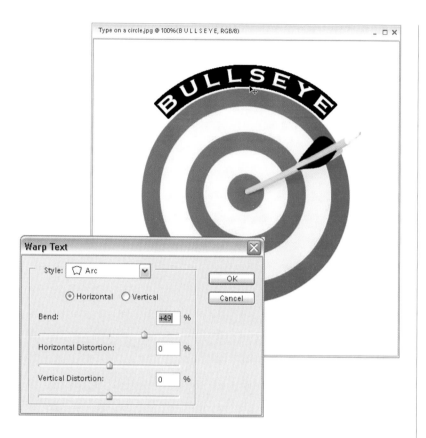

STEP THREE: Next, go to the Layers palette and double-click on the "T" thumbnail to highlight your type. (*Note:* It's not necessary to highlight the type to use Warp Text, but I like to use the highlight to help me align the type around the circle.) Click on the Warped Text icon in the Options Bar (it's the third icon from the right and it has the letter "T" with a bent line beneath it) to bring up the Warp Text dialog. From the dialog's Style pop-up menu, choose Arc. While the dialog is open, move your cursor outside the box, click on your type, and drag it into position in your image. Adjust the amount of Bend (dragging the slider to the right in the dialog) until it looks good to you. Click OK to complete the top arc.

STEP FOUR: Make a duplicate of your arced Type layer by dragging it to the Create a New Layer icon at the top of the Layers palette. Next, go to the Layers palette and double-click on the "T" thumbnail to highlight your duplicated type. Once highlighted, type in the word you want for the bottom of the circle (it will replace the highlighted text). Don't forget to add a space between each letter you type. Click outside your duplicate type to temporarily switch to the Move tool, and position the type near the bottom of the circle.

Continued

STEP FIVE: Double-click the "T" thumbnail for the new Type layer in the Layers palette to highlight the text. Click on the Warped Text icon again in the Options Bar. This time, you'll move the Bend slider to the left to arc your type in the opposite direction to match the bottom of the circle. Move your cursor outside the dialog, click on your type, and drag it into position at the bottom of the circle.

STEP SIX: Click OK to complete the bottom arc. Two things to keep in mind when using Warp Text: (1) Longer words require more Bend amount than shorter words; and (2) if your type appears too condensed after using Warp Text, just add spaces between letters.

Putting an Image into Type (Clipping Group)

This technique lets you take any image and place (clip) it inside type that you've set on the layer directly beneath it. This is a pretty flexible effect because you can reposition your image inside the type once it's grouped, and if for some reason you don't like the results, you can easily undo the effect.

STEP ONE: Create a new document in RGB mode (the one here is 8x6"). Press the letter D to set your Foreground color to black, then press the letter T to switch to the Type tool. Create some large display-sized type (tall, thick type-faces, like the Impact font that I used here, work well for this effect).

STEP TWO: Open the image you want to put inside your type. Switch to the Move tool by pressing the letter V, and then click-and-drag this image into your original text document. This should give you three layers: (1) your Background layer, (2) your Type layer, and (3) a layer with the image that you want clipped into your type.

Continued

STEP THREE: With the image layer active in the Layers palette (it should be at the top of the layer stack), choose Group with Previous from the Layer menu (or press Control-G) and your image will appear inside your type. You can now reposition your image within your type by clicking-and-dragging with the Move tool. (*Note:* To undo this effect, press the keyboard shortcut Shift-Control-G.)

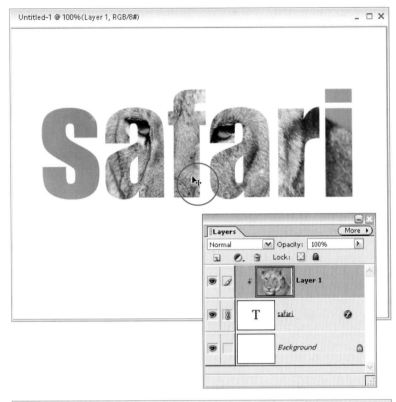

STEP FOUR: In most cases, it helps if you add a drop shadow to your Type layer to better define the edges of your letters (plus it looks cool). Click on the Type layer (in the Layers palette), then go to the Styles and Effects palette, and with Layer Styles selected, choose Drop Shadows from the top-right pop-up menu in the palette. Click on the Soft Edge icon to apply a drop shadow.

BRAND X PICTURES

STEP FIVE: Even though we've already created the type effect, let's take it a step further by adding a backscreened background. Open an image that you want to appear in the background, and with the Move tool, drag-and-drop this image into your text document. In the Layers palette, drag this new image layer below your Type layer.

STEP SIX: Go to the Layers palette and lower the Opacity of this image layer to around 20% or less. Press U until you have the Line tool, and in the Options Bar enter 1 pixel in the Weight field. Then, draw a line underneath the type. Now add any additional type that you'd like below the line (here I used the typeface Litterbox ICG for the words "ADVENTURE PARK") to complete the effect.

Moving a Background Object in Front of Type

You see this technique used a lot on the covers of major magazines. It's where an object (most often a person's head) appears in front of type. That doesn't sound like that big of a challenge, but once you realize that the person is on a flattened background image, with no layers, it becomes a little trickier. Not hard, just a little trickier.

STEP ONE: Open the background photo that has an object you want to appear in front of some type. Press the letter T to switch to the Type tool, click on the Foreground color swatch at the bottom of the Toolbox to select your color, and create the type you want to appear behind the object. In this example, we're going to put the nameplate of a magazine behind the person's head (the font I used is CronosMM250 Light using two different colors). You create the type now so you'll know how much (or how little) of the object you need to select in the next step.

BRAND X PICTURES

STEP TWO: Click on your Background layer in the Layers palette and put a selection around the part of the object you want to appear in front of your type. (You can temporarily hide your Type layer by clicking on the Eye icon to the left of the layer in the Layers palette.) I pressed the L key until I had the Magnetic Lasso tool in the Toolbox, and then I clicked once on the right side of her head, released the mouse button, and traced around the top of her head and arms. Once you've traced around the areas you want to select, return to where you first clicked (your cursor will have a circle beside it) and click to complete your selection.

STEP THREE: Once your object is selected, go under the Layer menu, under New, and choose Layer via Copy (or press Control-J) to copy that selected area up onto its own layer. Then, in the Layers palette, drag this layer above your Type layer. Moving that "top-of-the-head" layer in front of the Type layer makes it appear as though the person is in front of the type. (If you hid your Type layer, make it visible again by clicking on the layer's empty Eye icon box to the left of the layer.)

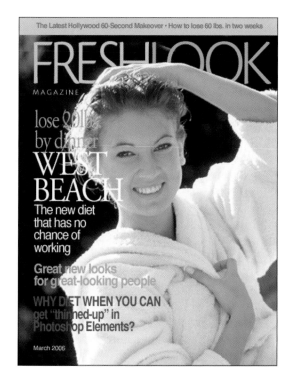

STEP FOUR: To finish this project, add in any other type you want on your cover using the Type tool. You can also use the Rectangle tool to add a colored bar across the top (as I did here), and then enter text over it. (The type at the top is in Helvetica Bold; the main headline, "lose 20 lbs. by dinner," is set in Adobe Garamond Pro; and the rest of the subheads are set in Helvetica Bold.)

Grunge Type

This is probably the most popular effect in Hollywood movie titles, and it's used in a dozen other places as well (in fact, I saw it in a Levi's print ad the evening I was writing this). It uses the technique of "grunging" a photo, but it uses it with type. After you've created the effect, you'll drop it into a movie poster layout (you'll have to do a little work there—mostly formatting type—but it's easy).

STEP ONE: Create a new document in RGB mode (the example here is 8x8"). Press D to set your Foreground color to black, and then fill the background with black by pressing Alt-Backspace. Press X to set your Foreground color to white, and then press the letter T to switch to the Type tool. Now create your white type (the type shown here is in Compacta Bold).

STEP TWO: Open the photo that you'll use to create your grunge. Photos with lots of vertical lines seem to work best; photos that have lots of rounded objects (like palm trees) don't work nearly as well (I know from experience). I had to test the effect on about eight photos before I found this one.

BRAND X PICTURES

STEP THREE: Go under the Filter menu, under Adjustments, and choose Threshold. Your image will turn into what looks like a black-and-white line drawing. Drag the slider nearly all the way to the left to remove some of the black detail, leaving just broken lines, spots, and smudges. This is the step you'll probably have to try on a number of photos until you find one that looks good. Click OK to apply the Threshold.

STEP FOUR: Press W to switch to the Magic Wand tool, then click directly inside one black area of your photo (it will probably only select a tiny section of your photo). Then, go under the Select menu and choose Similar to select all of the black areas in your photo.

Continued

STEP FIVE: Press V to switch to the Move tool, and drag-and-drop these selected black areas (as one unit) into your white text document. When the "grunged" image appears, press Control-T to bring up Free Transform. Press-and-hold the Shift key, grab a corner point, and drag to adjust the size of the photo until it looks good to you inside the text. (*Note:* If you can't see the corner points of the bounding box, press Control-0 [zero] to adjust your image to fit onscreen.) Click-and-drag inside the bounding box to reposition your "grunged" image. Then, press Enter to lock in your transformation.

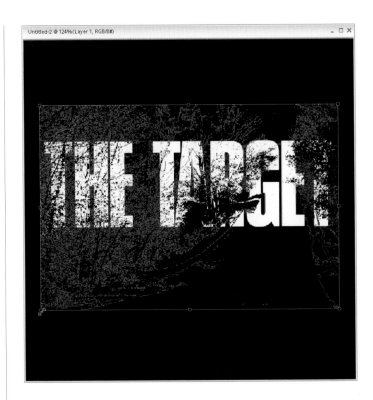

STEP SIX: From the Layer menu, choose Group with Previous (or press Control-G) to clip the black grunge photo inside your white text. You can now use the Move tool if you need to reposition the grunge that's inside the text. At this point the type portion of this effect is now complete.

BRAND X PICTURES

STEP SEVEN: Open the main photo you want to use in your movie poster. (The example here is a shot of a soldier as seen through an infrared scope.) Go back to your grunge text document. You need to merge the grunge layer and Type layer together, but you can't merge an image layer down into a Type layer. The trick is to link the image and grunge layers first, so click on the grunge layer to make it active, and then click in the column to the left of the Type layer to link it to the grunge layer. Press Control-E to permanently merge them together. Switch to the Move tool and drag this white grunge type over onto your poster document. You can scale the text to size using Free Transform (Control-T).

STEP EIGHT: The final step is to add the rest of the movie poster type, along with any logos you'd like, which completes the effect. (The actors' names at the top are set in Trajan Pro; the subhead above the movie and the descriptive type at the very bottom are set in Helvetica Neue; and the words "SUMMER 2006" are set in Impact.)

Distressed Type

It's not grunge type—it's distressed (damaged) type. This classic effect is as popular as ever, and it shows up in everything from store brands to clothing to movie posters—all using a distressed look based on the technique you're going to do here.

STEP ONE: Create a new document that's 9x7" at 72 ppi in RGB mode. Create a new layer by clicking on the Create a New Layer icon at the top of the Layers palette. Press the letter M to switch to the Rectangular Marquee tool, press-and-hold the Shift key, and draw a square selection. Press the letter D to set your Foreground color to black, then fill your square selection with black by pressing Alt-Backspace. Deselect by pressing Control-D.

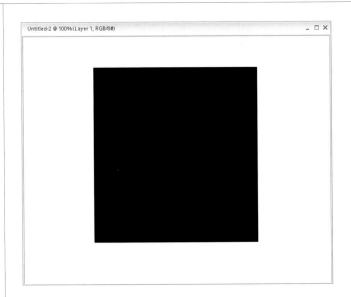

STEP TWO: Press the letter X to set your Foreground color to white, then press the letter T to switch to the Type tool. Click on the black square and enter your white type (I used the font Helvetica Black). Once you've entered your type, with the Type layer active in the Layers palette, press Control-E to merge the Type layer with the black square layer (leaving Layer 1).

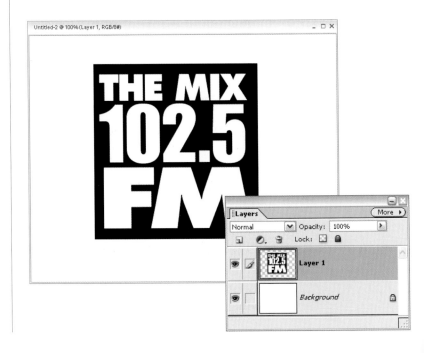

STEP THREE: Now to add the distress: Press the letter B to switch to the Brush tool, and click on the brush thumbnail in the Options Bar to bring up the Brush Picker. In the Brush Picker, scroll down until you find the 39-pixel Dry Brush from the default set of brushes. With your Foreground color still set to white, move this brush over black areas in your image and start clicking your mouse button. Don't paint strokes—just click your mouse button a number of times. Try 10 or 12 clicks in one area, then move your cursor to another area, click seven or eight times, and move to another area, keeping your locations and number of clicks random.

STEP FOUR: Now, go back up to the Brush Picker and choose a different brush size and shape. In this case, try the 48-pixel Oil Heavy Flow Dry Edges brush, and do the same thing you did in the previous step—click multiple times over black areas in your logo. Press the D key to set your Foreground to black and click a few times over the white type in the same fashion. The more distressed, the better.

Continued

STEP FIVE: To enhance the type effect, you can add a photo in the background. Simply open an image you want to add, press V to switch to the Move tool, and drag-and-drop the image onto your type document. In the Layers palette, drag the image layer below the distressed text layer, and lower the image layer's Opacity until it looks good to you.

BRAND X PICTURES

STEP SIX: You may notice some brush strokes splattering over onto your back-screened photo. If that's the case, click on the distressed text layer in the Layers palette to make it active, and with the Rectangular Marquee tool, put a selection around the black square. Go to the Select menu, choose Inverse, and then press the Backspace key to delete the excess brush strokes. Press Control-D to deselect, completing the effect.

Carved in Stone

This "carved in stone" technique is more realistic, has more depth, and is basically "more gooder" (as my son would say) than most "carved" type effects out there. Actually, I just think it's "bester."

STEP ONE: We're going to start by opening an appropriate image (this technique will work with almost any background image, but honestly, carving in stone looks best when the background image is, well…stone). Duplicate the Background layer by dragging it to the Create a New Layer icon at the top of the Layers palette.

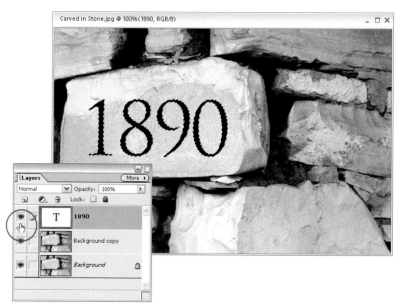

STEP TWO: Press D to set your Foreground color to black. Then press T to switch to the Type tool, and enter your text at a large size (I used the font Trajan Pro). Control-click on your Type layer in the Layers palette to put a selection around your type. Then, click on the Eye icon next to your Type layer to hide the layer from view.

Continued

STEP THREE: Now, click on the Background copy layer in the Layers palette to make it the active layer. Press Shift-Control-I to *inverse* the selection, meaning it selects everything but the part of the photo you want to keep. Press Backspace to remove the excess background from the Background copy layer. You won't see anything happen really, but what you're doing is creating a layer that contains only the stone in the shape of the text. Press Control-D to deselect.

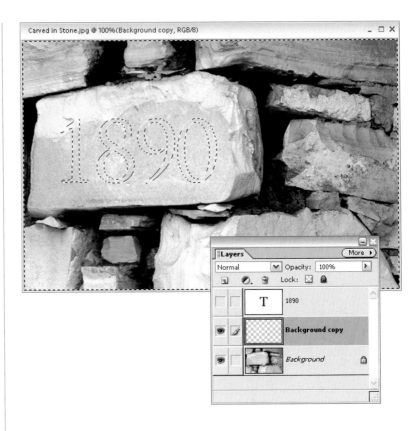

STEP FOUR: From the Edit menu, choose Stroke (Outline) Selection. In the Stroke dialog, set the Width to 1 pixel, click on the Color swatch and choose white in the Color Picker, set the Location to Inside, and then click OK.

STEP FIVE: From the Styles and Effects palette (found under the Window menu), ensure Layer Styles is selected, and then choose Inner Shadows from the palette's top-right pop-up menu. Click the Low icon to apply an inner shadow. Return to the Layers palette and drag the Type layer to the Trash icon to delete it since you no longer need that layer.

STEP SIX: The final step is to darken the inside of the letters to help "sell" the effect that the type is carved into the background. To do this, press Control-L to bring up the Levels dialog (you should still have the Background copy layer active). At the bottom of the dialog, move the highlight Output Levels slider to the left until you reach approximately 210, then click OK to complete the effect.

Transparent TV Type

I call this "TV Type" because you see a similar effect all the time on network logos in the lower right-hand corner of your TV screen. Although it's ubiquitous on television, I've seen this effect used in print and on the Web over and over again, and I like the fact that you can make it as subtle or powerful as you want simply by adjusting the Opacity slider in the Layers palette.

STEP ONE: Open the image to which you want to add the effect. Press D to set your Foreground color to black, and then press T to switch to the Type tool. Create your type (I used the font Trajan Pro here).

STEP TWO: We now want to run a filter on the text, but we can't run a filter on a Type layer, so we'll first have to convert it to an image layer. Go to the Layer menu and choose Simplify Layer to convert it from a Type layer into an image layer. In the Layers palette, click on the Lock Transparent Pixels icon (it's the first icon next to the word "Lock").

STEP THREE: Go under the Filter menu, under Stylize, and choose Emboss. When the Emboss dialog appears, change the Height to 5 (try 9 for high-res, 300-ppi images) and click OK to apply a hard bevel to your type. Your type will turn gray, with highlights and shadows along the edges. In the Layers palette, change the layer blend mode of this layer from Normal to Hard Light to make the gray fill disappear while leaving the highlights and shadows still visible.

STEP FOUR: To round and smooth out the effect, with Lock Transparent Pixels still turned on in the Layers palette, go under the Filter menu, under Blur, and choose Gaussian Blur. Enter 1–2 pixels (try 6 for high-res images), and click OK to apply soft shading inside the letters, completing the effect. If the effect is too intense, try lowering the Opacity of the text layer in the Layers palette.

Here we are—more than half way through the book—at a chapter subtitled "Special Effects," but I don't

Saturday Night Special
Special Effects

want you to think that I've run out of cool things to share. Au contraire (gratuitous use of French in everyday conversation inspired by *Frasier*). I specifically used the term "Special Effects" because that's just what these effects are—special. Oh sure, I toyed with other names, like "Zowie-Wowie Effects," "Turbo-Mondo Spasmatic Effects," and even "Intergalactic Alien Death-Ray Effects," but those names just weren't special enough for the effects I had planned for this chapter. But before you launch into the chapter and begin creating effects with an unbridled zeal heretofore hidden beneath layers of conformity and years of ingrained neo-conservatism (I'm not sure what any of that means, but my publisher told me to use a lot of big words), I just want to thank you for spending these special moments with me. See, how could I call this chapter anything but "Special Effects"?

Digital Pixel Effect

This is one of those classic effects that's used every time the word "digital" appears on a book cover, a billboard, or a magazine cover or spread. It makes the image (in our example, a person) look like he's becoming "digital" because half of the image is turning into pixels.

STEP ONE: Open the photo you want to apply the effect to (it's usually applied to photos of people, but I've seen it used on product shots as well).

STEP TWO: Duplicate the Background layer by going under the Layer menu, under New, and choosing Layer via Copy (or by pressing Control-J). You'll apply the effect to this duplicate layer (Layer 1).

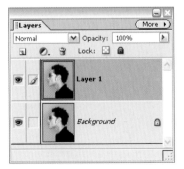

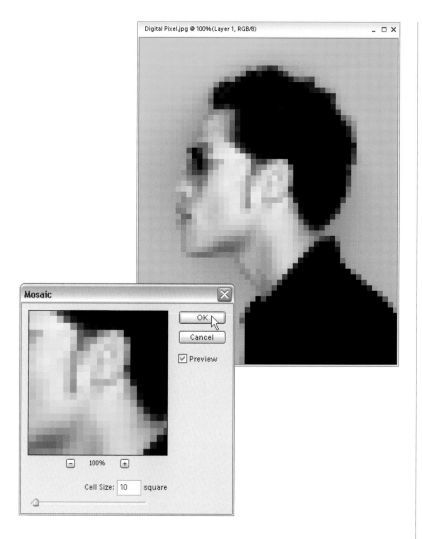

Digital Pixel.jpg @ 100%(Layer 1, RGB/8)

Mosaic

OK

Cancel

☑ Preview

100%

Cell Size: 10 square

STEP THREE: Go under the Filter menu, under Pixelate, and choose Mosaic. When the dialog appears, for Cell Size enter 10 pixels (this isn't an "official" size, so if you'd like smaller or larger pixels, feel free to experiment), then click OK to pixelate the entire layer.

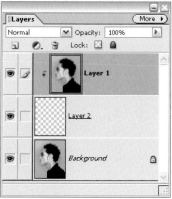

Layers — More ▶

Normal ▾ Opacity: 100% ▶

Lock: ☒ 🔒

Layer 1

Layer 2

Background

STEP FOUR: Press-and-hold the Control key and click on the Create a New Layer icon at the top of the Layers palette. This adds a blank layer (Layer 2) directly beneath your duplicate image layer. In the Layers palette, click on the duplicate image layer to make it active, then under the Layer menu choose Group with Previous (or press Control-G). This creates a clipping group, which hides the pixelated effect on the duplicate image layer.

Continued

STEP FIVE: In the Layers palette, click on the blank Layer 2 to make it active. Press the letter G to switch to the Gradient tool, then press Enter, and the Gradient Picker will appear onscreen. Choose the Foreground to Transparent gradient (it's the second one in the Picker), and then click the Gradient tool on the right side of the document and drag horizontally to the left.

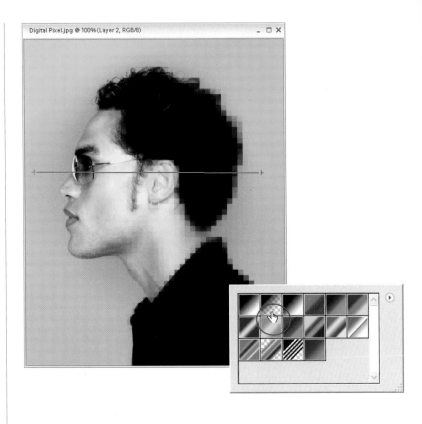

STEP SIX: The photo will then blend gradually from the clean photo on the left to the pixelated photo on the right. What you're really doing here is revealing the clean photo on the Background layer, and then blending to the pixelated image layer at the top of the layer stack, giving the classic pixelated "digital" look.

Attaching a Note to a Photo

If you need to add a caption to a photo, you *could* just backscreen an area or create some reverse type, but with this effect you can create stronger visual interest for your caption, drawing the reader's eye right where you want it to go.

STEP ONE: Open the photo you want to use in the effect. Press Control-A to select the entire photo, then go under the Layer menu, under New, and choose Layer via Cut (or press Shift-Control-J) to cut the photo from the Background layer and copy it onto its own separate layer (Layer 1).

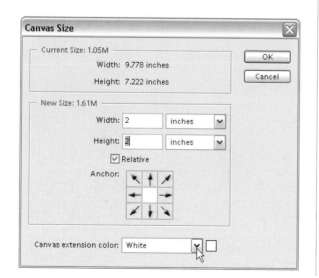

STEP TWO: Go under the Image menu and choose Canvas Size. When the dialog appears, turn on the Relative checkbox, enter 2 inches for both Width and Height, and choose White in the Canvas Extension Color pop-up menu. Click OK to add some white space around your photo.

Continued

STEP THREE: Choose Stroke (Outline) Selection from the Edit menu. Set the Width to 15 pixels (30 pixels for high-res, 300-ppi images), set the Location to Inside (to give your stroke straight corners rather than the default rounded corners), and click on the Color swatch to choose a light gray in the Color Picker. Click OK to apply a gray stroke around your image area.

STEP FOUR: Go to the Styles and Effects palette (found under the Window menu) and with Layer Styles selected, choose Drop Shadows from the palette's top-right pop-up menu. Click on the Soft Edge icon, and then in the Layers palette, double-click on the Layer Styles icon (it looks like an "*f*") to the right of the layer's name. In the Style Settings dialog, increase the Shadow Distance to 10, turn off the Use Global Light checkbox, and click OK.

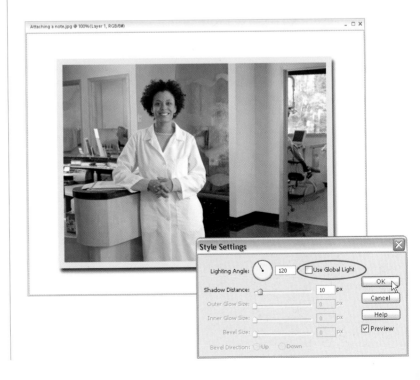

STEP FIVE: Create a new layer by clicking on the Create a New Layer icon at the top of the Layers palette. Press the letter M to switch to the Rectangular Marquee tool, press-and-hold the Shift key, and make a square selection in the area you want your note to appear. In the Toolbox, click on the Foreground color swatch and choose a "Post-it–like" yellow color in the Color Picker (I used R: 255, G: 255, and B: 161). Fill your selection with this yellow by pressing Alt-Backspace, then deselect by pressing Control-D.

STEP SIX: Press U until you get the Custom Shape tool from the Toolbox, and then press the Enter key to bring up the Custom Shape Picker onscreen. From the Picker's flyout menu, choose Objects to load a new set of custom shapes. Scroll down until you find the Paper Clip shape and select it. In the Toolbox, click on the Foreground color swatch and select gray in the Color Picker. Now, click the Custom Shape tool near the top of your yellow note, then press-and-hold the Shift key and drag the tool to create a paper clip. Press the V key to switch to the Move tool and position the paper clip at the top of your yellow note.

Continued

STEP SEVEN: Click on the Foreground color swatch and choose a dark blue in the Color Picker, then press the letter T to get the Type tool. Add your message to the note (the text here is in the font ITC Bradley Hand). Go to the Layers palette and link the paper clip, note, and Type layers together by clicking in the second column of each layer (the Link icon will appear) so you can move all three layers as one group.

STEP EIGHT: Press Control-T to bring up Free Transform. Move your cursor outside the bounding box and click-and-drag to rotate the note slightly. You can click-and-drag inside the bounding box to reposition the note. Press Enter when it looks about right.

STEP NINE: Next, you'll add a metallic look to the paper clip. Click on the paper clip layer in the Layers palette to make it active, then go to the Styles and Effects palette (found under the Window menu), and with Layer Styles selected, choose Wow Chrome from the palette's top-right pop-up menu. Click on the Wow-Chrome Textured icon and your paper clip will get a metallic look. Now, go under the Layer menu and choose Simplify Layer to change your paper clip Shape layer into a regular image layer.

STEP TEN: Press the letter E to switch to the Eraser tool. In the Options Bar, click on the brush thumbnail, and in the resulting Brush Picker, choose a small, soft-edged brush. Erase the inside part of the paper clip (along with some of the shadow areas) to make it appear as if that part of the paperclip is behind the note and photo. Now, click on the yellow note layer, then choose Drop Shadows in the top-right pop-up menu in the Styles and Effects palette and click on the Soft Edge icon. In the Layers palette, double-click the Layer Styles icon, turn off the Use Global Light checkbox in the resulting Style Settings dialog, and click OK to complete the effect.

Mapping a Texture to a Person

You may have heard this effect referred to as a Displacement Map technique because it uses Photoshop Elements' Displace filter to map a texture from one object onto another object. This has become particularly popular in the past couple of years, and fortunately it's quite easy to do, even though it looks as if you worked on the image for hours.

STEP ONE: Open the image that you want to apply a texture to. (In this example, we're using a photograph of a man, and we're going to apply the texture to his skin.)

STEP TWO: Make a duplicate of your image by going under the File menu and choosing Duplicate. Then, go under the Image menu, under Mode, and choose Grayscale. When the warning dialog appears, just click OK to discard the color and convert this duplicate image into a grayscale image.

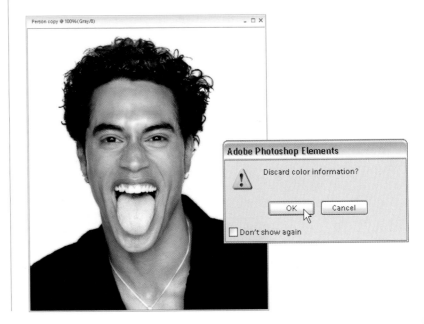

STEP THREE: Go under the Filter menu, under Blur, and choose Gaussian Blur. Apply a 2-pixel blur to your grayscale image and click OK. (*Note:* Two pixels is okay for low-res, 72-ppi images; for high-res, 300-ppi images, try 4 or 5 pixels.) Now, go under the File menu and choose Save. Name this blurry grayscale image file "Map" and save it in Photoshop's native format (making it a PSD file). This is the file we'll use when we apply the Displace filter in Step 6.

BRAND X PICTURES

STEP FOUR: Open the image you want to use as a texture. Press V to switch to the Move tool, press-and-hold the Shift key, and click-and-drag this texture image on top of your original color image. (Pressing-and-holding the Shift key will center the image above the target image of the person.)

Continued

STEP FIVE: Press Control-A to put a selection around the entire image area. Then, go under the Filter menu, under Distort, and choose Displace. When the Displace dialog appears, enter 10 for both Horizontal Scale and Vertical Scale. Under Displacement Map, choose Stretch To Fit, and for Undefined Areas, choose Repeat Edge Pixels. Click OK.

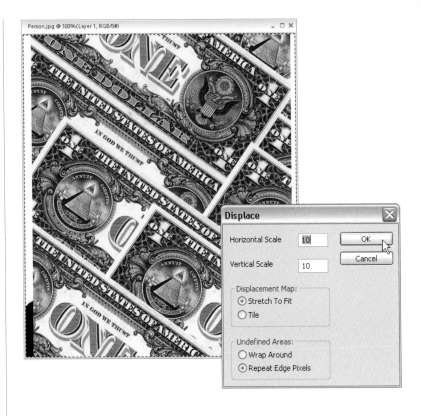

STEP SIX: When you click OK, a dialog appears prompting you to "choose a displacement map." Locate the grayscale file you saved earlier (in Step 3), click the Open button, and the Displace filter will use this map file to "map out" the texture to fit your image. You'll see your image area warp a bit when you apply this filter, but to see the full effect, there's still a little more work to do.

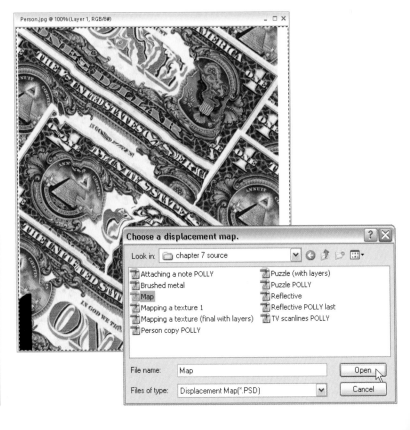

STEP SEVEN: Press Control-D to deselect. In the Layers palette, click on the Eye icon in the far-left column beside the texture layer to hide it. Click on your original image layer (the man) and use your favorite selection tool to select the background area behind him. (*Note:* Since the background behind this man is a solid color and easy to select, I clicked the Magic Wand tool [W] on the background to select it.)

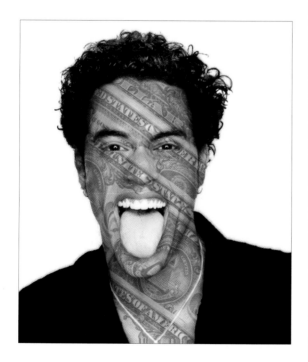

STEP EIGHT: In the Layers palette, click on the texture layer to make it active (your selection should still be in place). Press the Backspace key to leave a silhouette of the texture in the shape of the man's head. Deselect by pressing Control-D. At the top left of the Layers palette, change the layer blend mode of this texture layer to Multiply to make it look as if it were tattooed on his skin. (*Note:* For different effects, try the Overlay or even Soft Light layer blend mode.) Lower the layer's Opacity to around 50%. With the texture layer active, use the Eraser tool (E) with a small, hard-edged brush to erase over his hair, eyes, lips, teeth, tongue, eyebrows, shirt, and chain so that the effect just appears on the skin to complete the effect.

Dividing a Photo into Puzzle Pieces

This effect has been around for a while, but what rekindled my interest was seeing it on Apple's iLife product box. If you had to draw the puzzle pieces, it would be quite a task, but luckily, four puzzle shapes are built right into Photoshop Elements (as custom shapes). The technique can be used to make an editorial statement, a dramatic effect, a fun effect—it's pretty much up to you how you use it.

STEP ONE: Create a new document in RGB mode (for this example, I created an 8x6" document). Press D to set your Foreground color to black, and then press U until you get the Custom Shape tool from the Toolbox. Up in the Options Bar, click on the Shape thumbnail to bring up the Custom Shape Picker. From the Picker's flyout menu, choose Objects to import this set of shapes.

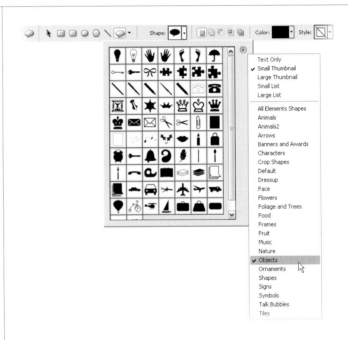

STEP TWO: Once the set is loaded, navigate in the Picker until you see four puzzle shapes. Select the second puzzle shape (Puzzle 2), and then click the Custom Shape tool in the top-left corner of the blank document and start to drag. Now press-and-hold the Shift key after you start dragging. (*Note:* The Shift key constrains the puzzle piece proportionally. But if you press-and-hold the Shift key before you click-and-drag, all of your shapes will be added to the same Shape layer, and we need each puzzle piece on its own layer so we can reposition or resize it as necessary. So make sure you don't press the Shift key until *after* you start dragging.)

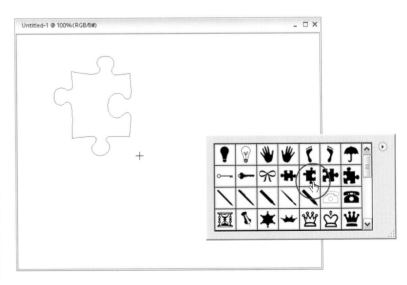

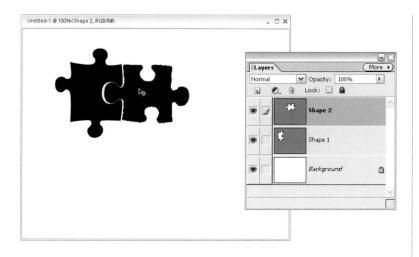

STEP THREE: Return to the Custom Shape Picker in the Options Bar and choose the first of the four puzzle shapes (Puzzle 1). Click the Custom Shape tool to the right of the current shape, then press-and-hold the Shift key once you start dragging out a puzzle piece that is approximately the same size as your first puzzle piece. Press V to switch to the Move tool, then position this piece into the other piece, but make sure you leave a slight gap between the two (let them almost touch, but for this to work correctly, you need a tiny gap—it shouldn't look as if it's one solid piece).

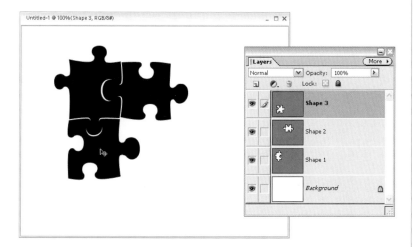

STEP FOUR: Press U until you have the Custom Shape tool again, and from the Custom Shape Picker choose the third of the four puzzle shapes (Puzzle 3). Click below the left puzzle piece, press-and-hold the Shift key once you start dragging out this puzzle shape, which also creates another layer (Shape 3) in the Layers palette. Use the Move tool to position this piece up against the bottom of the left puzzle piece. Again, make them very close, but leave a tiny gap between the pieces.

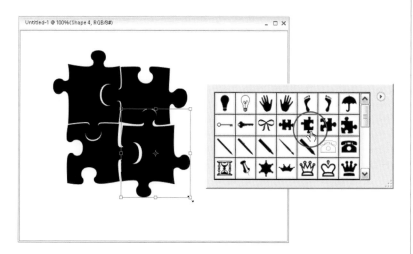

STEP FIVE: Get the Custom Shape tool again. In the Custom Shape Picker, click on the second puzzle piece (Puzzle 2). Click below the far-right puzzle piece and press-and-hold the Shift key after you start to drag out the shape. This shape won't match up without some tweaking: Go under the Image menu, under Rotate, and choose Layer 180°. Switch to the Move tool and press Control-T to bring up Free Transform. Hold the Shift key, grab a corner point, and adjust this puzzle piece so it fits with the others. Press Enter to lock in your transformation.

Continued

STEP SIX: You'll need to save a selection of the bottom-right puzzle piece so you can later pull that piece away from the others, so with the last Shape layer you created still active (Shape 4), go under the Layer menu and choose Simplify Layer to change it into a regular image layer. Now, in the Layers palette, Control-click on this layer to put a selection around the bottom-right puzzle piece. Go to the Select menu and choose Save Selection. Name your selection in the resulting dialog and click OK. Press Control-D to deselect.

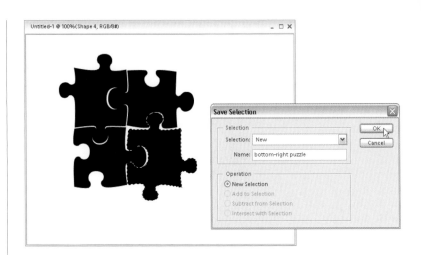

STEP SEVEN: Open the photo you want to apply the puzzle effect to. Using the Move tool, click-and-drag this photo into your puzzle document, positioning the photo at the top of the layer stack in the Layers palette. Hide both the Background and photo layers from view by clicking on the Eye icons to the left of those layers in the Layers palette. Then, with any visible layer active, choose Merge Visible from the palette's flyout menu to merge all the puzzle pieces into one single layer. You can make the Background and photo layers visible again by clicking in the empty boxes where the Eye icons used to be.

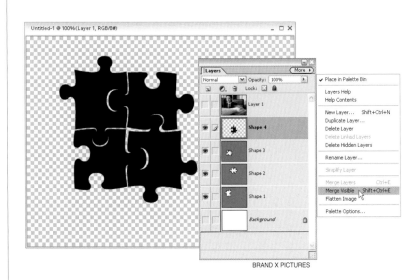

BRAND X PICTURES

STEP EIGHT: In the Layers palette, click on the photo layer to make it active, and choose Group with Previous from the Layer menu (or just press Control-G) to clip the photo into the puzzle pieces. Now you can use the Move tool to reposition your image within the puzzle pieces.

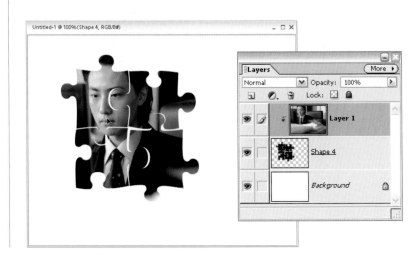

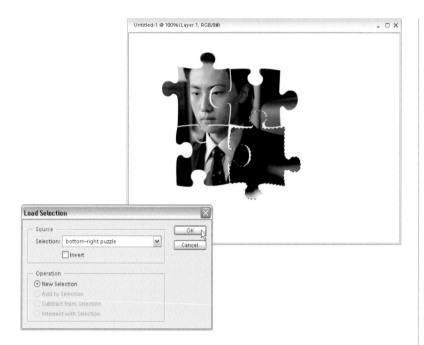

STEP NINE: In the Layers palette, ensure that your image layer is active, and then press Control-E to merge the image and puzzle layers into one layer. Now remember that selection you saved? You're going to need it, so go under the Select menu and choose Load Selection. Your saved selection should appear in the Selection pop-up menu (if not, click on the down-facing arrow to bring up the Selection pop-up menu and choose it from the list). Once your selection loads, go under the Layer menu, under New, and choose Layer via Cut (or press Shift-Control-J) to cut this selection and copy it onto its own layer in the Layers palette.

STEP TEN: With the Move tool, drag your cut puzzle piece to the right. Then, press Control-T to bring up Free Transform, click outside the bounding box, and rotate the puzzle piece slightly to the left. Press Enter when it looks good to you. Now press Control-E to merge this rotated puzzle piece layer with the other puzzle layer. With this puzzle layer active, go to the Styles and Effects palette (found under the Window menu). With the Layer Styles category selected, choose Bevels from the top-right pop-up menu and click on the Simple Emboss icon. Now select Drop Shadows from the palette's top-right pop-up menu and select the Low shadow icon. From the Layer menu, under Layer Style, choose Style Settings and in the resulting dialog, lower the Shadow Distance to 1 pixel and change the Lighting Angle to 30° to complete the effect.

Brushed Metal

If you're creating interfaces, it's just a matter of time before you say to yourself, "Ya know, I could really use some brushed metal." I know it sounds unlikely, but it happens (more often than I care to admit). Here's how to whip up some brushed metal from scratch (just like grandma used to make):

STEP ONE: Create a new document in RGB mode (this example is 8x6"). Press G to switch to the Gradient tool, and then press Enter to bring up the Gradient Picker onscreen. From the default set of gradients, choose the Copper gradient (it's the fifth gradient in the second row). Click the Gradient tool at the top of the image window and drag to the bottom—but you need to do two things when dragging the gradient: (1) Drag at a slight angle to the right, and (2) start at the top but drag about an inch past the bottom of the image window (it's easier than it sounds). Then release the mouse button to create the gradient shown here.

STEP TWO: Go under the Enhance menu, under Adjust Color, and choose Remove Color (or press Shift-Control-U) to remove the copper color from your gradient. Then, go under the Filter menu, under Noise, and choose Add Noise. When the Add Noise dialog appears, enter 20 for Amount, select Gaussian, turn on the Monochromatic checkbox, and click OK.

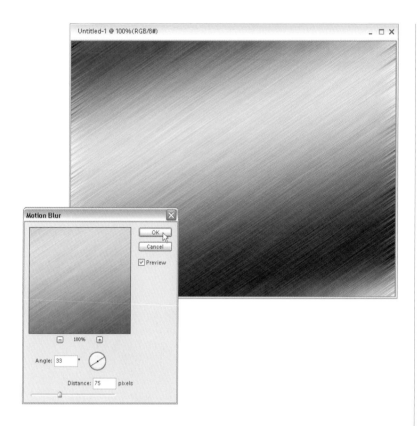

STEP THREE: Return to the Filter menu, under Blur, and choose Motion Blur. When the Motion Blur dialog appears, enter 33° for Angle and 75 for Distance. When you click OK, Photoshop Elements applies the Motion Blur to your image.

Brushed metal after cropping away harsh edges

TIP: Take a look at the left and right edges of the image in the previous step, and you can see that these areas don't look as good as the rest of the image. To get around that, we often make our new document about 1/2" wider than we really need so we can crop it down later to remove those harsh edges.

TV Scan Lines

This technique, which simulates the scan lines that a television produces when photographed with a camera, remains one of the most popular effects in print, on TV, and on the Web.

STEP ONE: Open the image in which you want to apply TV scan lines—either RGB or Grayscale will work. Create a new document that's 1 pixel wide by 4 pixels high in the same resolution and color mode as your open image (e.g., if you want to add scan lines to an RGB image, choose RGB).

STEP TWO: Press Z to switch to the Zoom tool and zoom in on this tiny document until it's easily seen (you might have to zoom in as much as 1600%). Press D to set your Foreground color to black, then press M to switch to the Rectangular Marquee tool and select the top half of the image. Press Alt-Backspace to fill the selected half of your image with black, and then press Control-D to deselect. Go under the Edit menu and choose Define Pattern (this command will save your black-and-white document as a pattern that we'll use in the next step). A dialog will appear in which you can name your new pattern "Scan Lines." You can now close this file without saving it.

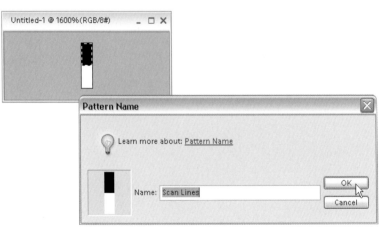

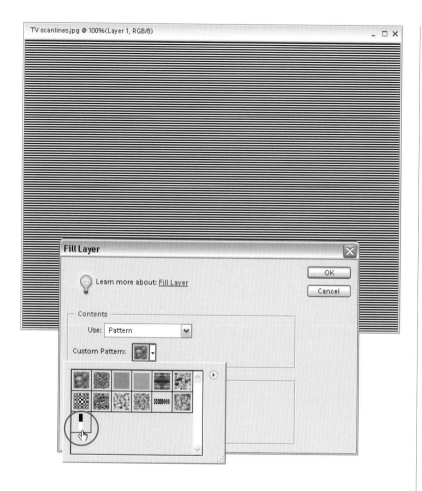

STEP THREE: Go back to your original document and click on the Create a New Layer icon at the top of the Layers palette. Go under the Edit menu and choose Fill Layer. In the Fill Layer dialog, choose Pattern in the Use pop-up menu, then click on the Custom Pattern thumbnail to reveal the Pattern Picker. Click on the last pattern (it will be the Scan Lines pattern you just saved) to choose it. Click OK to fill your new layer with your black-and-white scan lines pattern.

STEP FOUR: In the Layers palette, change the scan lines layer's blend mode from Normal to Overlay. Lower the Opacity so that the effect isn't too strong (in other words, adjust to suit your taste) to complete the effect.

Reflective Chrome Gradient

This technique, a takeoff on the chrome effect created by traditional airbrush artists, uses a gradient that mimics the reflection of the ground and the sky the same way they would be reflected by real chrome. In this example, we'll create a custom gradient to simulate that style of chrome, but the gradient alone isn't enough—it's the other elements you add to it that give the impression of chrome.

STEP ONE: Create a new document in RGB mode at 72 ppi (this example is 8x6"). Press D to choose black as your Foreground color, then press Alt-Backspace to fill the Background layer with black. Add a new blank layer by clicking on the Create a New Layer icon at the top of the Layers palette. Hide the black background by clicking on the Eye icon in the far-left column beside the Background layer.

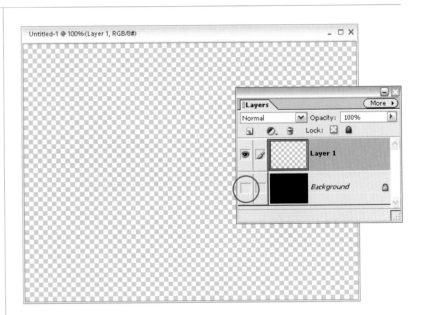

STEP TWO: Create the shape you want for your metal console. In this example, I clicked on the Foreground color swatch and chose gray in the Color Picker. Then I pressed U until I had the Rounded Rectangle tool and created, well...a simple rounded rectangle. In the Options Bar, I clicked on the Simplify button to change this Shape layer into a regular image layer.

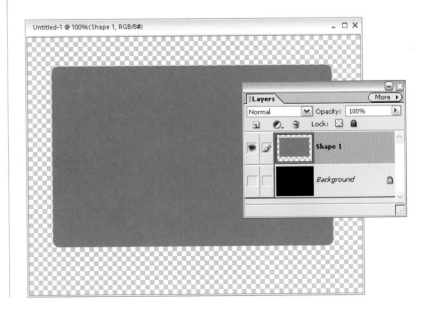

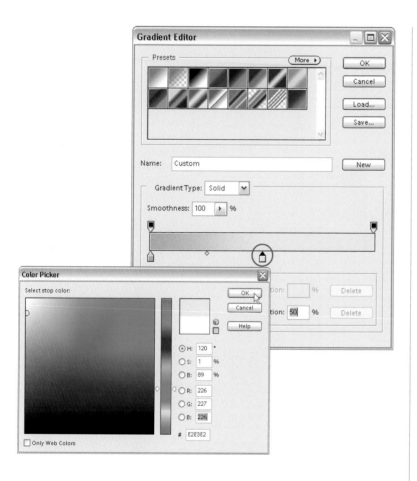

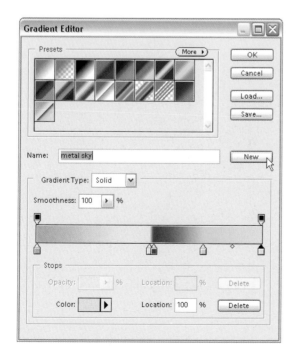

STEP THREE: Next, press G to switch to the Gradient tool, and in the Options Bar, click on the Edit button to bring up the Gradient Editor. When the Gradient Editor appears, click on the Black to White gradient (it's the third gradient in the top row). Using the Black to White gradient as a starting point, double-click on the far-left color stop located directly below the gradient ramp. This brings up the Color Picker. In the RGB fields, enter R: 164, G: 175, and B: 184 to set this first stop to a light "sky" blue. Click OK in the Picker. Next, slide the far-right color stop over to the center of the gradient ramp. Double-click on it to set its color. This time in the RGB fields, enter R: 226, G: 227, and B: 226 to set this middle stop to an almost white color. Click OK in the Picker.

STEP FOUR: Click immediately to the right of your middle color stop under the gradient ramp to add a new color stop. Slide this color stop almost right up against the middle color stop. Double-click on this new color stop, and in the RGB fields of the Color Picker, enter R: 78, G: 73, and B: 67 to set this new stop to a brownish-gray color. We're going to add two more stops: one halfway between the middle and the end (set to R: 224, G: 221, and B: 87 for a dull yellow) and then one at the very right end of the gradient ramp (set to R: 226, G: 225, and B: 198 for a very light, almost white stop). Your gradient should look like the one shown here. Name this gradient "metal sky," click the New button, and then click OK to save it.

Continued

STEP FIVE: Now we add the fluff stuff that helps sell the effect. Press-and-hold the Control key, and in the Layers palette, click on the layer with your rounded rectangle to put a selection around it. Then, go under the Select menu, under Modify, and choose Contract. Enter 6 pixels and click OK to shrink your selection. Hold the Shift key, click the Gradient tool at the top of your selection, and drag it to the bottom. Don't deselect yet.

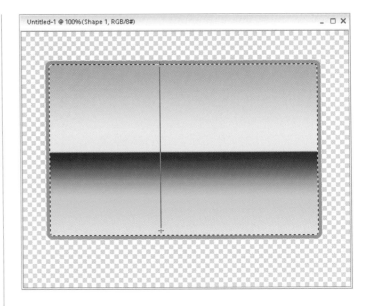

STEP SIX: While your selection is still in place, add a new blank layer above your current layer by clicking on the Create a New Layer icon at the top of the Layers palette. Go under the Edit menu and choose Stroke (Outline) Selection. When the Stroke dialog appears, make sure the stroke color is set to black, and enter 2 pixels for the stroke Width. Set your Location to Center and click OK to apply a 2-pixel stroke around your selection. Don't deselect yet.

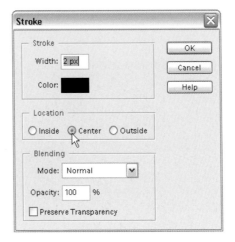

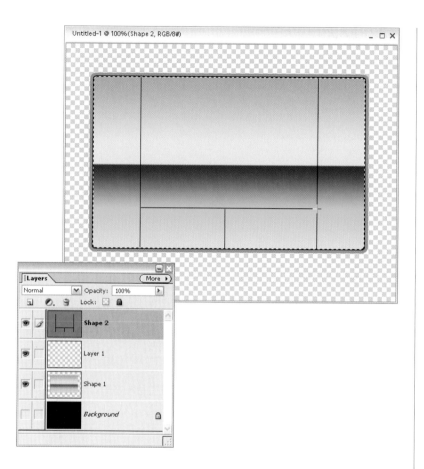

STEP SEVEN: Now press U until you have the Line tool (it's one of the Shape tools in the Toolbox). In the Options Bar, enter 1–2 pixels for Weight. We're going to visually divide our console using lines, so create the lines similar to the ones shown here (make sure to stay within the selected area). Press-and-hold the Shift key, then click-and-drag to create your lines (the Shift key keeps each line perfectly horizontal or vertical and also keeps all the lines on one Shape layer instead of creating a new layer for each line that you draw). Deselect by pressing Control-D.

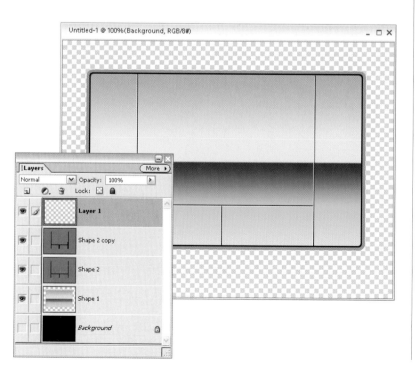

STEP EIGHT: Make a duplicate of this line Shape layer by dragging it to the Create a New Layer icon at the top of the Layers palette. Press D and then X to set white as your Foreground color, then press Shift-Alt-Backspace to fill your lines with white (adding the Shift key fills just the object on the layer instead of filling the entire layer). Press V to switch to the Move tool, then press the Left Arrow key once and the Down Arrow key once to offset your white lines from your black lines, giving the impression of an indentation. Now, drag your stroked rectangle layer (Layer 1) to the top of the layer stack to ensure your lines appear inside the black stroke.

Continued

STEP NINE: Make your black Background layer visible again (click in the far-left empty box where the Eye icon used to be). Click on the gradient layer, and go to the Styles and Effects palette (under the Window menu), and with Layer Styles selected, choose Bevels from the top-right pop-up menu. Click on the Simple Inner bevel to add a bevel effect to your rounded rectangle.

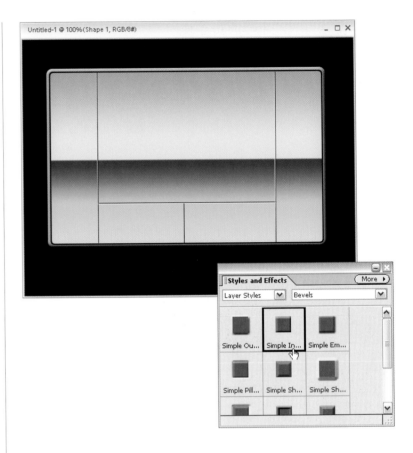

STEP TEN: Now, just create any buttons to complete the effect. Simply press U until you get the Polygon tool, set its Sides to 3 in the Options Bar, and click-and-drag to add navigation buttons. To give the buttons the "sunken-in" look, choose the Simple Sharp Pillow Emboss from the Bevels section of the Styles and Effects palette.

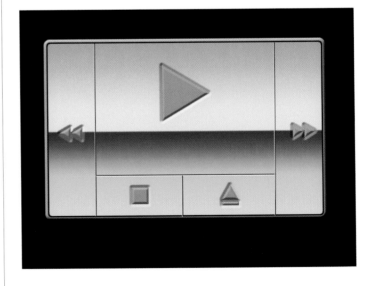

Building a Video Wall

This technique creates a wall made out of TV monitors, with each monitor containing part of a much larger, single image. You start by creating a single screen, duplicating and stacking it, and pasting an image into a selection of each monitor.

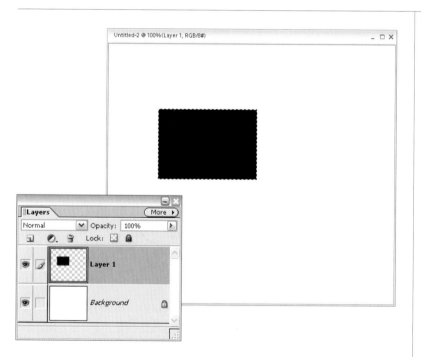

STEP ONE: Create a new document in RGB mode (the one here is 8x7"). Create a new blank layer by clicking on the Create a New Layer icon at the top of the Layers palette. Press M to get the Rectangular Marquee tool, and draw a horizontal rectangular selection. Press D to set your Foreground color to black, and then press Alt-Backspace to fill your selection with black.

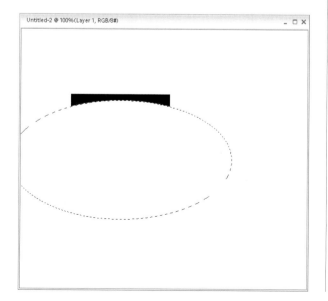

STEP TWO: Press M until you have the Elliptical Marquee tool. Drag out a large oval-shaped selection over the black rectangle. Move your cursor inside the oval, and click-and-drag to position the top edge of the oval near the top of the black rectangle. Press the Backspace key to knock out the bottom section of the black rectangle, then deselect by pressing Control-D. This leaves a narrow rectangle that curves inward on the bottom.

Continued

STEP THREE: Create another new layer by clicking on the Create a New Layer icon. Press M until you have the Rectangular Marquee tool again, and draw a rectangular selection that's wider and a bit higher than the black shape. Press-and-hold the Alt key (which lets you subtract from your selection) and draw a smaller selection that starts at the top-left corner of the thin black shape and extends down and to the right, forming a smaller rectangle. This will become the frame of your video monitor.Click the Foreground color swatch at the bottom of the Toolbox, and in the resulting Color Picker, choose a very dark gray. Fill your selection with gray by pressing Alt-Backspace, and then press Control-D to deselect.

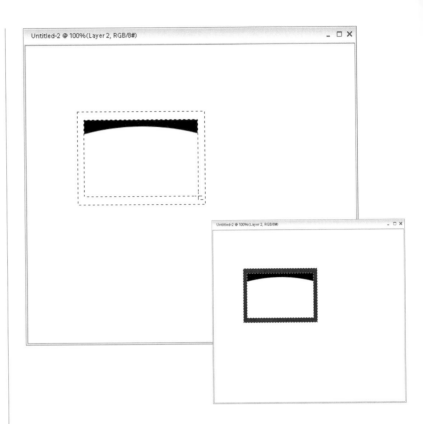

STEP FOUR: Go to the Styles and Effects palette (found under the Window menu), and with Layer Styles selected, choose Bevels from the palette's top-right pop-up menu. Click on the Simple Emboss icon. Now, go to the Layers palette, and with this frame layer active, press Control-E to merge it with the black rectangle layer, creating a white Background layer and your video monitor layer (Layer 1). Although it doesn't look like it at this stage, the first video monitor is complete; but it needs to be resized, so you'll use Free Transform to scale it down in the next step.

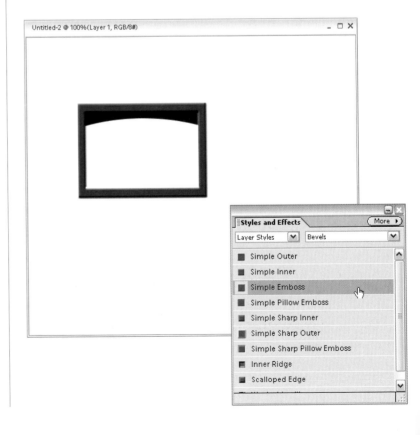

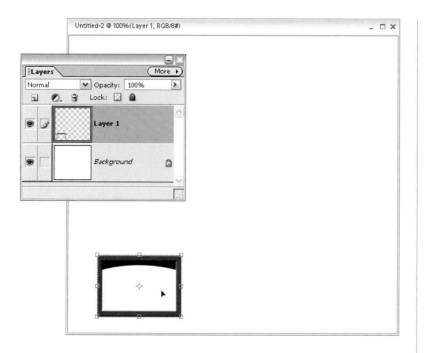

STEP FIVE: Press Control-T to bring up the Free Transform bounding box. Press-and-hold the Shift key, grab a corner point, and drag inward to shrink the size of the video monitor. Once you've scaled it down, move your cursor inside the bounding box and click-and-drag the video monitor down toward the bottom-left corner of the image area. Press Enter to lock in your transformation.

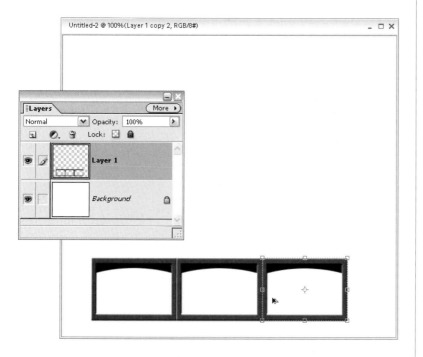

STEP SIX: Press V to switch to the Move tool, then press-and-hold Shift-Alt, click within your monitor, and drag to the right to create a copy of your monitor. Drag the duplicate until its left edge touches the right edge of the original monitor. Release the mouse button. While pressing the same keys, click in the new monitor and drag to the right to create a third image. Now, go to the Layers palette, and with the top monitor layer active, press Control-E two times to merge the three monitor layers into one monitor layer (Layer 1).

Continued

STEP SEVEN: Press-and-hold Shift-Alt again, then click on the monitors and drag upward to create a copy of your three monitors. Repeat this process until you have a stack of monitors four rows high, resembling a video wall. With the top monitor layer active, press Control-E three times to merge all the video monitor layers together into one layer (Layer 1).

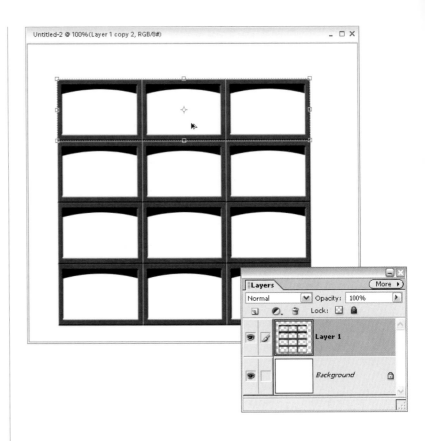

STEP EIGHT: Press W to switch to the Magic Wand tool. Click once inside one of the monitor screens to select it. Hold the Shift key and click in every screen until the inside of each monitor is added to the selection. (We used the Magic Wand, but you can use any selection tool you're comfortable with.) When the inside of each screen is selected, open the image you want to add into your screens.

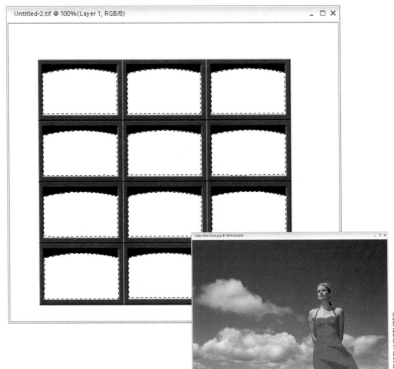

BRAND X PICTURES

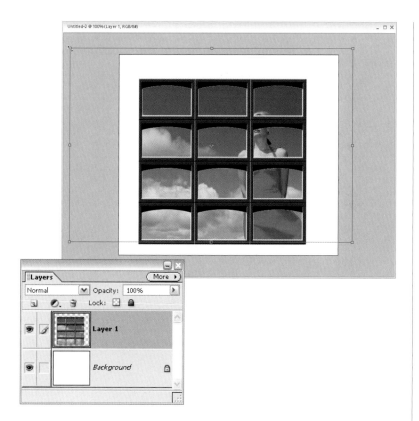

STEP NINE: With the image that you want to add to your video wall active, select the entire image by pressing Control-A, then press Control-C to copy it into memory. Switch back to your video wall image. In the Layers palette, with the video wall layer active, go under the Edit menu and choose Paste Into Selection to put this image into your video wall. Switch to the Move tool and click-and-drag to position your image inside the wall. Press Control-T to bring up Free Transform. (*Note:* If you can't see the bounding box corners, press Control-0 [zero] or just drag out your image window to change your view.) Press-and-hold the Shift key, grab a corner point, and drag to scale your image. When it looks good to you, press Enter, but don't deselect your image just yet.

STEP TEN: Using the Move tool, position your image within the video wall. Press Control-D to deselect, completing the effect. (*Note:* Make sure you have your pasted image where you want it, because once you deselect, your image is "stuck" inside the monitors and you won't be able to move it again.)

Lightning Effect

This is about the quickest, easiest, and most time-tested way to add a lightning effect to your photo without having to draw a bunch of shapes or jump through a lot of time-consuming hoops.

STEP ONE: Open the photo you want to use as your background (in this case, a photo of a creepy house at night). Press D and then X to set your Foreground color to white and your Background color to black. Create a new layer by clicking on the Create a New Layer icon at the top of the Layers palette.

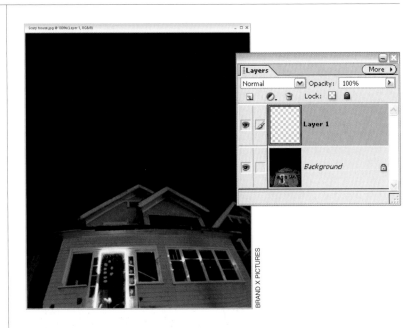

STEP TWO: Press the G key to switch to the Gradient tool and then press Enter to bring up the Gradient Picker. Choose the Foreground to Background gradient (it's the first gradient in the Picker). Click the Gradient tool on the left side of your image area and drag all the way to the right.

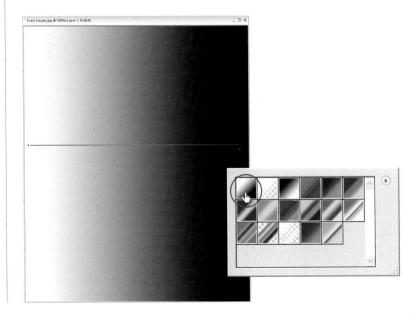

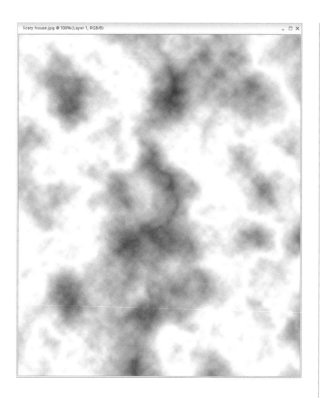

STEP THREE: Now go under the Filter menu, under Render, and choose Difference Clouds to apply a random cloud pattern over your gradient. (*Note:* Each time you apply this filter, you get a different look, so if you don't like the way your lightning appears, just press Control-F to reapply the Difference Clouds, or even try applying it three or four times until you come up with a lightning pattern that looks better.) When the lightning strikes look good to you, press Control-I to invert them.

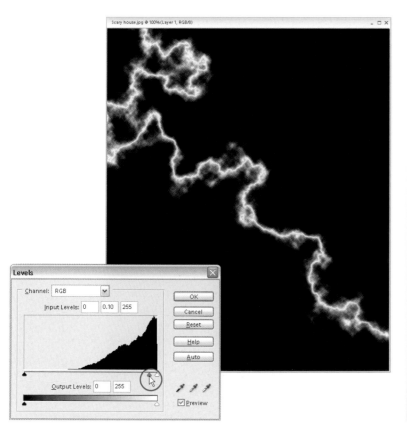

STEP FOUR: Press Control-L to bring up the Levels dialog. Grab the top-center Input Levels slider (the midtones slider) and drag it to the right. When you're almost all the way to the right, you'll see your lightning appear in your image. Click OK.

Continued

STEP FIVE: To make your lightning blend in with your photo, go to the Layers palette and change the layer blend mode of your lightning layer from Normal to Screen.

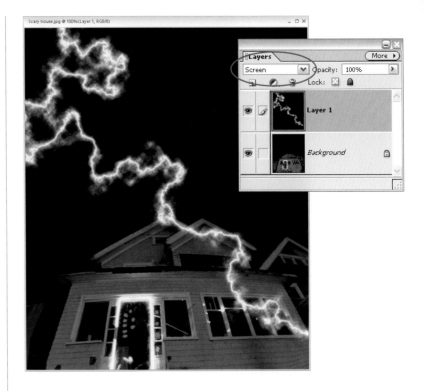

STEP SIX: The lightning goes right over everything in the image, but if you don't want that, you can do this: Press E to switch to the Eraser tool, and in the Options Bar, click on the brush thumbnail to open the Brush Picker. Choose a medium, soft-edged brush, and with the lightning layer active in the Layers palette, erase any lightning areas you don't want to appear on your image, which completes the effect. (*Note:* In this example I pressed V to switch to the Move tool and click-and-dragged the lightning strikes to reposition them in my image.)

Gettin' "Gelly" with Buttons

We're in a "gel design age" thanks to the look of Apple's Aqua interface for Mac OS X and the resulting marketing pieces that sprang forth from it. When we first showed this technique in *Photoshop User* magazine, it took literally twice as many steps, but we've since found a way that makes it so easy, you can create your own aqua-like button in about 60 seconds.

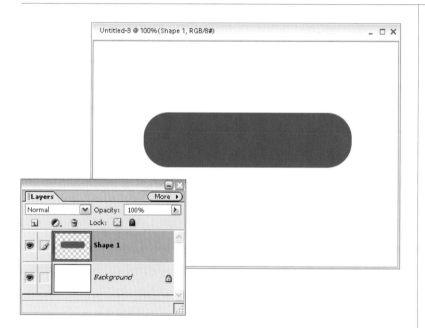

STEP ONE: Create a new document that's in RGB mode set at 72 ppi (the one shown here is 7x5"). Click the Foreground color swatch at the bottom of the Toolbox and choose a light blue in the Color Picker, then press U until the Rounded Rectangle tool appears in the Toolbox. Up in the Options Bar, set the Radius to 40 pixels and drag out your shape, which will appear on its own Shape layer (Shape 1) in the Layers palette. Click the Simplify button in the Options Bar to rasterize the Shape layer into an image layer.

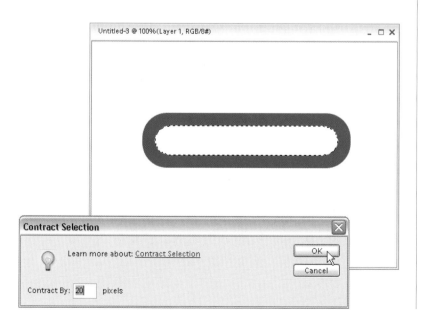

STEP TWO: Control-click on your pill layer (Shape 1) to select it. Click the Create a New Layer icon at the top of the Layers palette to create a blank layer. Then, go under the Select menu, under Modify, and choose Contract. Enter 20 pixels and click OK to contract your selection. (*Note:* How much you contract your selection depends on the size of your original pill shape. If your pill shape is really small, contracting 20 pixels may make the selection completely disappear. So play with the setting until you get a selection that looks like the one shown here.) Press the letter D and then X to set your Foreground color to white. Press Alt-Backspace to fill your contracted selection with white, and then press Control-D to deselect.

Continued

STEP THREE: Go under the Filter menu, under Blur, and choose Gaussian Blur. When the dialog appears, enter 10 pixels and click OK to apply a blur to your white layer. Press V to switch to the Move tool, and drag your blurry white layer down to where its bottom edge touches the bottom of the pill shape.

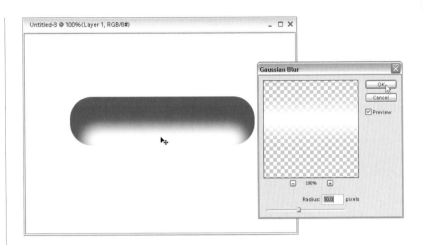

STEP FOUR: Now, Control-click your original pill layer (Shape 1). Create a new blank layer by clicking on the Create a New Layer icon at the top of the Layers palette. Click the Foreground color swatch and choose a darker blue in the Color Picker than the blue that you used for your original pill shape, then fill your selection with this darker blue by pressing Alt-Backspace. Deselect by pressing Control-D.

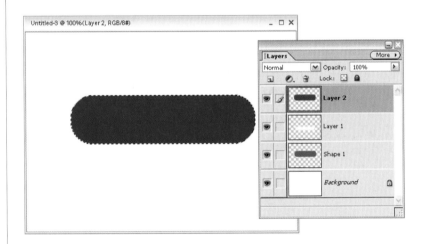

STEP FIVE: In the Layers palette, press-and-hold the Control key and click once on the white blurry layer to put a selection around it (don't change layers, just get the selection in place; the dark blue pill layer should still be active). Now, press the Backspace key to knock a soft hole out of the dark blue pill shape. Don't deselect yet.

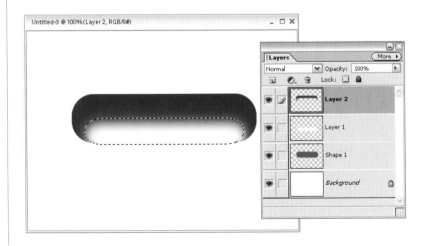

STEP SIX: Press M to switch to the Rectangular Marquee tool, then place your cursor inside the selected area (that you just knocked out) and drag the selection upward a little bit (maybe one-quarter of the way up) and hit Backspace again. Repeat this one or two more times, until you're almost to the top of the pill (make sure you stop just short of the top). Deselect by pressing Control-D.

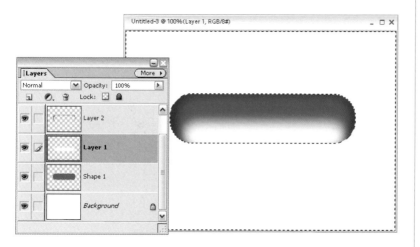

STEP SEVEN: Click on the white blurred layer (Layer 1) in the Layers palette. Press-and-hold the Control key and click once on the original pill layer (Shape 1) to put a selection around the pill (though the white blurry layer is still active). Press Shift-Control-I to inverse your selection, then press Backspace to remove any spillover onto the background from your white blur. Deselect by pressing Control-D.

STEP EIGHT: In the Layers palette, Control-click on your original pill layer (Shape 1) to select it. Click the Create a New Layer icon and drag this new layer (Layer 3) to the top of the layer stack in the Layers palette. Then, go under the Select menu, under Modify, and choose Contract. Enter 20 pixels (or the same number of pixels that you contracted in Step 2) and click OK to contract your selection. Press the letter D and then X to set your Foreground color to white. Now press G to switch to the Gradient tool and press Enter to make the Gradient Picker visible onscreen. Choose the second gradient from the left (Foreground to Transparent) and drag this gradient from the top of your selection to the bottom. Deselect by pressing Control-D.

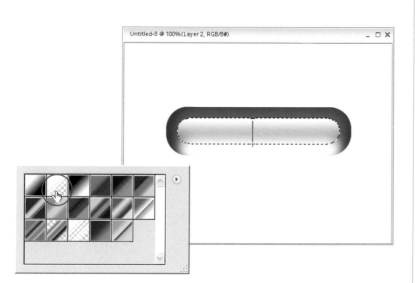

Continued

STEP NINE: Press V to switch to the Move tool, and drag your white gradient layer upward to where it's almost at the top, but leave a gap of dark blue between your white gradient and the top of the pill. This creates the highlight area of the pill.

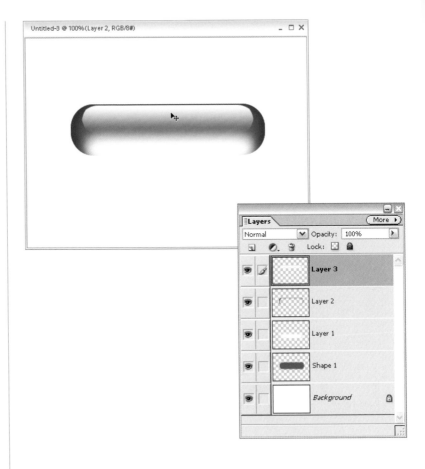

STEP TEN: Press Control-T to bring up Free Transform. Within the bounding box, right-click and choose Perspective in the contextual menu. Then, grab the bottom-left corner point, and click-and-drag to the left just a bit to add a perspective effect to your highlight layer. Press Enter to lock in your transformation.

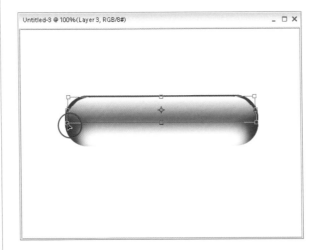

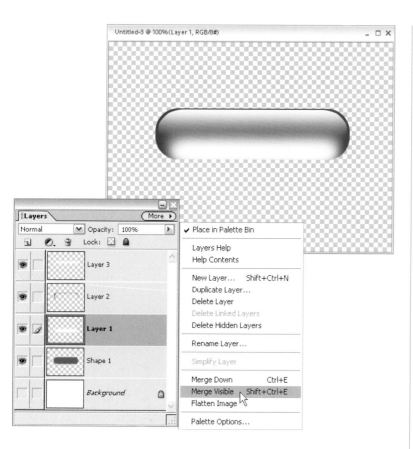

STEP ELEVEN: Hide the Background layer by clicking on the Eye icon to the left of it in the Layers palette, then choose Merge Visible from the palette's flyout menu. This merges all of the layers that make up the pill into one layer.

STEP TWELVE: Click in the empty Eye icon box to the left of the Background layer in the Layers palette to make it visible again. Then, click on the merged pill layer to make it active. Go to the Styles and Effects palette (found under the Window menu), and with Layer Styles selected, choose Drop Shadows from the palette's top-right pop-up menu. Click on the High drop shadow icon. Press T to switch to the Type tool and add any text you'd like (the font here is Minion Pro). To complete the effect, return to the Styles and Effects palette, and with your Type layer active in the Layers palette, click on the Low drop shadow to enhance your type.

Yummy Metal Web Buttons

In this day and age, if you have to make a Web button, it better be pretty slick. Here's a technique for making a yummy-looking, metallic-like, reflecto-looking, plastic thingy that is…well, pretty slick.

STEP ONE: Create a new document in RGB mode at 72 ppi (the example here is 8x6"). Create a new blank layer by clicking on the Create a New Layer icon at the top of the Layers palette. Press M until you have the Elliptical Marquee tool, hold the Shift key, and draw a circular selection. Press D and then X to set your Foreground color to white.

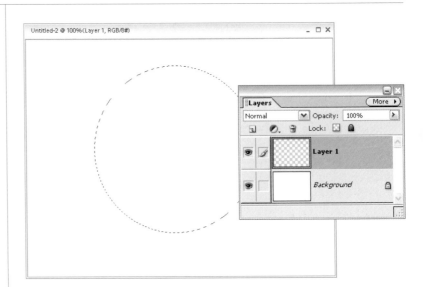

STEP TWO: Press G to switch to the Gradient tool, and then press Enter to open the Gradient Picker onscreen. Choose the Foreground to Background gradient (it's the first one in the Picker). Then in the Options Bar, click on the Radial Gradient icon (it's the second icon in the set of five). Drag a white-to-black gradient from the left center of the selection to about 1/4" past the right edge. Don't deselect yet.

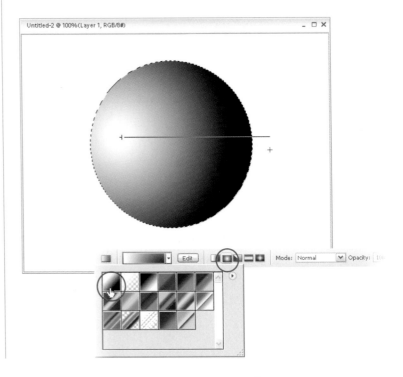

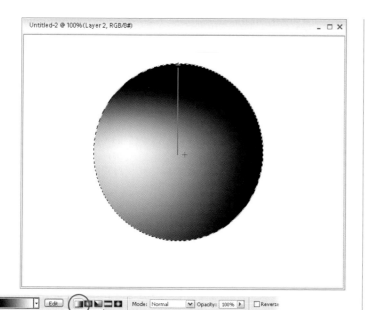

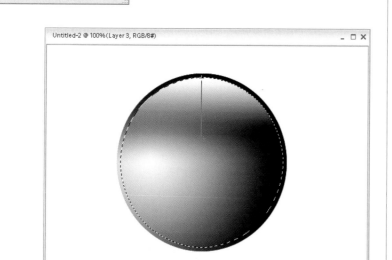

STEP THREE: Click on the Create a New Layer icon at the top of the Layers palette, and then press D to set your Foreground color to black. Press Enter to bring up the Gradient Picker again and choose the Foreground to Transparent gradient (the second one from the left). In the Options Bar, choose the Linear Gradient (the first icon in the set of five). Click the Gradient tool at the top of your selection and drag to the middle to fill the top with black.

STEP FOUR: In the Layers palette, lower the Opacity of this gradient layer to around 75%. With your selection still in place, click on the Create a New Layer icon again. Go under the Select menu, under Modify, and choose Contract. Enter 6 pixels and click OK. Press X to set your Foreground color to white, then click at the top of your new selection with the Gradient tool and drag down through about one-third of your selected area. Press Control-D to deselect.

Continued

STEP FIVE: Go under the Filter menu, under Blur, and choose Gaussian Blur. Enter 3 pixels and click OK. Duplicate your top layer by dragging it to the Create a New Layer icon at the top of the Layers palette. Go under the Image menu, under Rotate, and choose Layer 180°. Press V to switch to the Move tool, press-and-hold the Shift key, and drag this layer straight down almost to the bottom edge of the circle (pressing the Shift key keeps the layer aligned vertically). In the Layers palette, lower the Opacity of this layer to 60%.

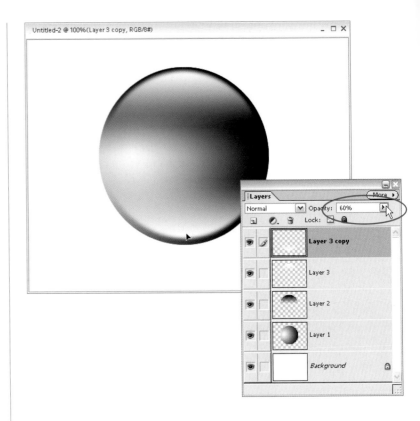

STEP SIX: Click back on Layer 3 (the layer below your current duplicate layer) to make it active and press Control-T to bring up Free Transform. Press-and-hold the Shift key, grab the bottom-right handle, and shrink this white gradient by around 15%. (*Note:* Check out the Width and Height fields in the Options Bar to gauge your percentage.) Press Enter to lock in your transformation.

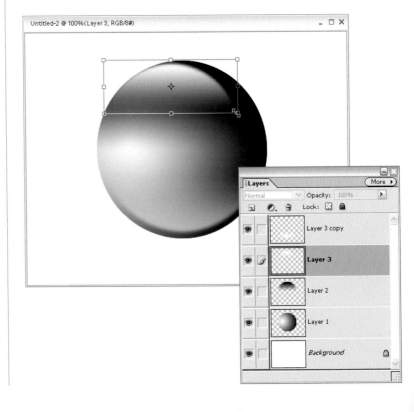

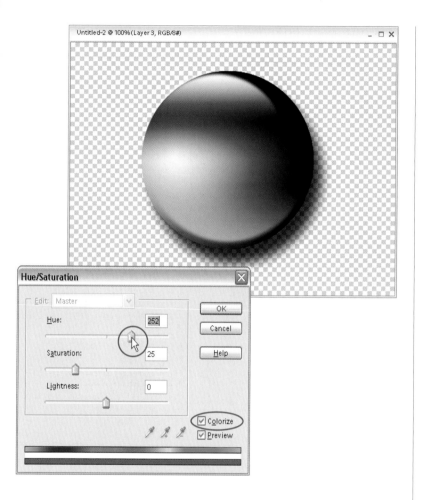

STEP SEVEN: In the Layers palette, click on the Eye icon to the left of the Background layer to hide it, and from the palette's flyout menu choose Merge Visible to merge all of the layers that make up your button into one layer. Then, go to the Styles and Effects palette, and with Layer Styles selected, choose Drop Shadows from the top-right pop-up menu. Click on the High drop shadow icon. You're going to add color to your Web button, so press Control-U to bring up the Hue/Saturation dialog. Click the Colorize checkbox and move the Hue slider to choose a color for your button. When you've found a color you like, click OK.

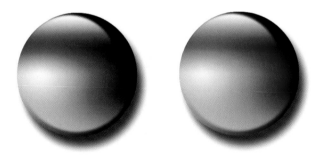

STEP EIGHT: You've just created a Web button that you can use over and over again in any project. Here I clicked on the Background layer to make it active and then dragged my button layer to the Create a New Layer icon at the top of Layers palette to duplicate it. Then I used Hue/Saturation to recolor the duplicate button. Now check out those yummy buttons!

THIS SIDE
TOWARD SCREEN

CHAPTER 8
DOWN & DIRTY TRICKS

THIS SIDE
TOWARD SCREEN

CHAPTER 8
DOWN & DIRTY TRICKS

THIS SIDE
TOWARD SCREEN

CHAPTER 8
DOWN & DIRTY TRICKS

Before you try the techniques in this chapter, it's important to understand what glints, reflections, and shadows are.

Shadows of the Night
Glints, Reflections, and Shadows

Many of you may already have a full understanding, but before you go any further, I think it would be wise (for all parties involved) to test your understanding with a few simple questions. If you're able to answer these three simple queries without a single wrong answer, then this chapter is for you. However, if you miss one or more answers, you might want to skip ahead to the chapter on rainbows, puppies, and cuddly little teddy bears. Ready? Begin:

(1) Which of these is the name of a character in the *Star Trek Enterprise* series? (a) Lt. Shaq, (b) Ensign Puff Daddy, (c) First Officer Eminem, or (d) Sub-commander T'Pol.

(2) On *Star Trek: The Next Generation*, which of these is NOT a real location within the ship? (a) The Holo Deck, (b) the Bridge, (c) Ten-Forward, or (d) Central Perk.

(3) Which *Star Trek TNG* character wound up on *Deep Space Nine* as well? (a) Commander Waffle, (b) First Officer Sausage, (c) Lt. Eggs'n'bacon, or (d) Lt. Worf.

The answers are (and these are so obvious that I hate to even write them): 1: b, 2: a, 3: b. (They're actually all *d* of course, but you have to admit, it made you stop for just a second, didn't it?)

Perspective Cast Shadow

This twist on the classic drop shadow effect adds realism in two ways: (1) It casts a shadow that's more like what an actual light source would cast; and (2) the shadow has a bit of a harder edge near the object but gets softer as it moves away.

STEP ONE: Open the image of an object that you want to give a perspective cast shadow to. Put a selection around the object (here I Shift-clicked the Magic Wand tool [W] on all the white background areas, went under the Select menu, and chose Inverse to select just the two men). With the object selected, go under the Layer menu, under New, and choose Layer via Cut (or press Shift-Control-J).

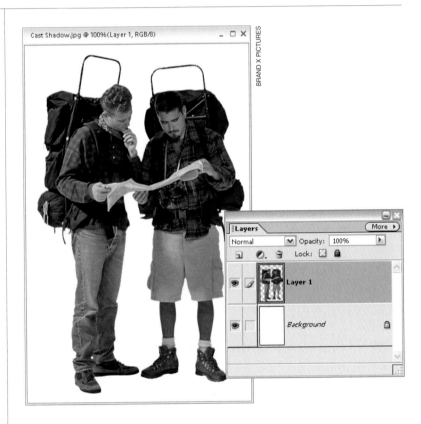

STEP TWO: You'll need to add some canvas area to make room for your cast shadow, so click on the Background layer to make it active. Then, go under the Image menu, under Resize, and choose Canvas Size. In the Canvas Size dialog, enter 4 inches for Width, ensure the Relative checkbox is on, click the right-center square in the Anchor grid, and choose White in the Canvas Extension Color pop-up menu. Click OK to add your white canvas area.

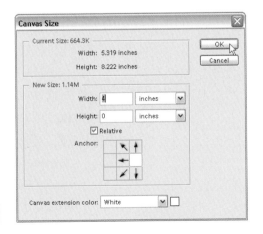

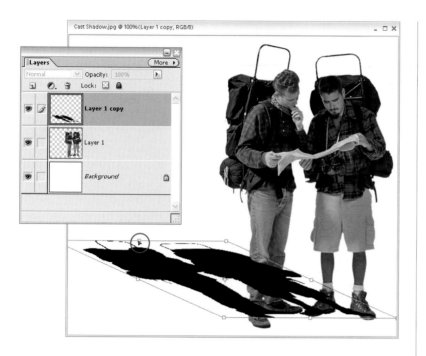

STEP THREE: Make a copy of the object layer by dragging it to the Create a New Layer icon at the top of the Layers palette. Press the letter D to change the Foreground color to black, then press Shift-Alt-Backspace to fill your duplicate object with black (holding Shift fills just the object on the layer and not the entire layer). Now, press Control-T to bring up the Free Transform command. Right-click within the bounding box and choose Distort from the contextual menu. You need to make the copy filled with black lie almost flat in the background, so grab the top-center control point and drag it down and to the left. Press Enter to complete your transformation.

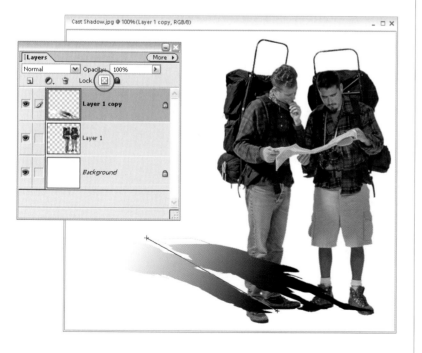

STEP FOUR: Switch to the Gradient tool by pressing the letter G. In the Options Bar, click on the down-facing arrow next to the gradient thumbnail to bring up the Gradient Picker, and choose the Black to White gradient (it's the third one in the Picker). At the top of the Layers palette, click on the Lock Transparent Pixels icon for your shadow layer (it's the first icon after the word "Lock"). Drag the Gradient tool from one end of your shadow to the other. You want the gradient to start with black at the base of your object and change to white as the shadow extends away from the object.

Continued

STEP FIVE: Turn off the Lock Transparent Pixels icon on your shadow layer in the Layers palette. Go under the Filter menu, under Blur, and choose Gaussian Blur. When the dialog appears, enter 2 pixels for Radius, and click OK. (*Note:* For high-res, 300-ppi images, you'll need to use higher settings when applying Gaussian Blurs and feathering selections in this and the following steps.) In the Layers palette, drag Layer 1 copy below Layer 1. This puts the shadow behind your object.

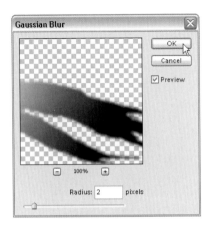

STEP SIX: To add more realism, you can create a perspective blur, where the shadow is less blurry near the object and becomes blurrier the farther away it gets (like in real life). To do this, press M to switch to the Rectangular Marquee tool and draw a rectangular selection that covers the top quarter of your cast shadow. Go under the Select menu and choose Feather. Add a 5-pixel feather to soften the transition. Then, go under the Filter menu, under Blur, and choose Gaussian Blur. Add a 2-pixel blur, and then deselect by pressing Control-D.

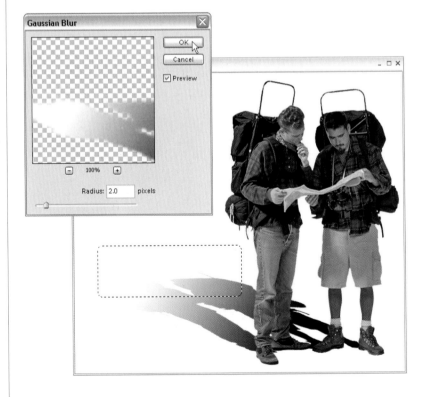

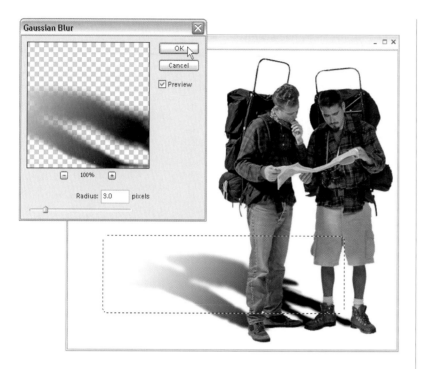

STEP SEVEN: With the Rectangular Marquee tool, draw another selection that covers the top half of your cast shadow. Feather the selection by 5 pixels again, apply a 3-pixel Gaussian Blur, and then deselect (see previous step). Draw a new selection that covers the top three-quarters of your shadow (almost to the base of the object), apply another 5-pixel Feather (from the Select menu), and then press Control-F to apply a 3-pixel Gaussian Blur again.

STEP EIGHT: When you're finished, you'll have created a 10-pixel blur around the farthest areas of the cast shadow, an 8-pixel blur around the three-quarter mark, a 5-pixel blur one-quarter of the distance away from the base, and only a slight 2-pixel blur up close to the object. To finish the effect, lower the Opacity of the shadow layer in the Layers palette to around 45%.

Reverse Cast Shadow

This shadow effect is widely used in print and on the Web to give the impression that the light source is coming from behind the object, rather than from the front or the side, as Photoshop Elements shadows are usually applied. Most notably, I saw it on the logo for the movie *The Talented Mr. Ripley*.

STEP ONE: Create a new document (the one here is 8x6" in RGB mode). Click on the Foreground color swatch at the bottom of the Toolbox and select a color in the Color Picker that you want to use for the background of the image. Press Alt-Backspace to fill the Background layer with the color you chose.

STEP TWO: Press D and then X to set your Foreground color to white. Press T to switch to the Type tool, and enter your type. (*Note:* I used Minion Pro as the typeface, and then on the Background layer, I made a selection with the Rectangular Marquee tool [M] just below the type and filled the selection with a darker color, but it's not necessary for this technique.)

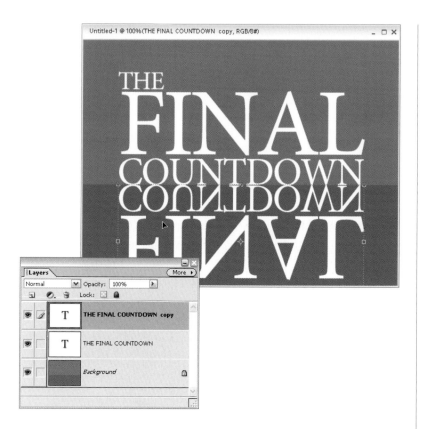

STEP THREE: After you've created your type, go under the Layer menu, under New, and choose Layer via Copy (or press Control-J) to duplicate your Type layer. Go to the Image menu, under Rotate, and choose Flip Layer Vertical. Press V to switch to the Move tool, and while pressing-and-holding the Shift key, drag the flipped layer downward until the bottom of the duplicate text nearly touches the bottom of the original type.

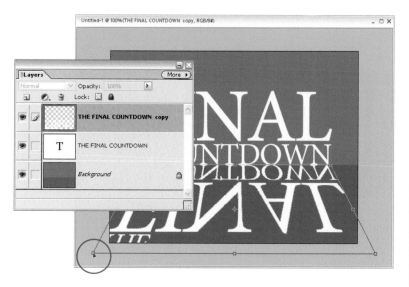

STEP FOUR: From the Layer menu, choose Simplify Layer to rasterize the duplicate Type layer into a regular image layer. Press Control-T to bring up the Free Transform function. Right-click directly inside the Free Transform bounding box and choose Perspective in the contextual menu. Grab either the bottom-left or the bottom-right corner handle of the bounding box and drag outward to create a perspective effect. (*Note:* If you can't see the bounding box, press Control-0 [zero] to resize the image onscreen.) Next, grab either the top-left or the top-right corner handle and drag inward to accentuate the effect, then press Enter to complete the transformation. (To return to the previous view, go under the Window menu, under Images, and choose Cascade.)

Continued

STEP FIVE: With the reflection layer active, press D to set your Foreground to black, and then press Shift-Alt-Backspace to fill the reflection with black (holding Shift fills just the object on the layer instead of the entire layer). Now, go under the Filter menu, under Blur, and choose Gaussian Blur. Add a slight, 1.5-pixel blur to soften the shadow. (*Note:* For high-res, 300-ppi images, you'll need to use higher settings when applying Gaussian Blurs and feathering selections in this and the following steps.)

STEP SIX: Press M to switch to the Rectangular Marquee tool, and drag a rectangular selection around the center of your shadow. Go under the Select menu and choose Feather. In the Feather Selection dialog, choose 10 pixels as your Feather Radius. Click OK to soften the edges of your selected area. Then, return to the Filter menu, under Blur, and choose Gaussian Blur. Apply a 2-pixel blur. Deselect by pressing Control-D.

STEP SEVEN: Draw another rectangular selection at the bottom of your image window, and feather it by 10 pixels again. Press Control-F to apply the 2-pixel Gaussian Blur again. This makes your shadow appear blurrier as it moves away from the base of the type—just like a shadow would in real life.

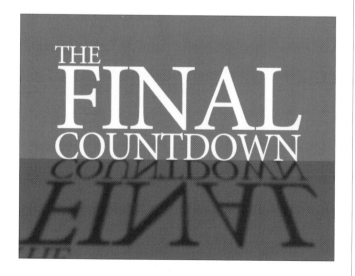

STEP EIGHT: Deselect by pressing Control-D, then go to the Layers palette and lower the Opacity of this shadow layer to around 35% to complete the effect.

Glassy Reflections

This is a nice technique for enhancing a logo or Web button by adding small reflections in a couple of areas to make it appear as if the logo were made of glass. In this tutorial, we start with an elliptical logo, but you can apply a similar effect to a round logo.

STEP ONE: Open the logo (or graphic) to which you want to apply the glass-like highlight reflections. (You can practice with this logo by downloading it from the book's companion website at www.scottkelbybooks.com/ddelements3.) The logo needs to be on its own layer, so if it's not, select the logo with any selection tool (Lasso, Magic Wand, etc.) and go under the Layer menu, under New, and choose Layer via Cut (or press Shift-Control-J) to cut the logo from the Background layer and copy it onto its own layer.

STEP TWO: Press-and-hold the Control key, and in the Layers palette, click on the logo layer to put a selection around it. Go under the Select menu, under Modify, and choose Contract. Enter 12 and click OK. (The goal is to shrink the selection so that it's a couple of pixels inside the inner ellipse. You may have to experiment with the amount of contraction.)

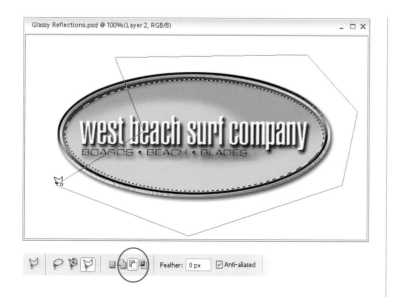

STEP THREE: Press L until the Polygonal Lasso tool appears in the Toolbox. Up in the Options Bar, in the set of four icons, click on the third icon from the left so that when you're using the Polygonal Lasso, it will subtract from the current selection. Start by clicking in the white space just outside the bottom-left side of the logo, then click within the logo about a quarter of the way in from the left, and then click near the top-left side just outside the logo to create a V-shaped selection (that will be the area where the reflection will be added). Continue clicking with the Polygonal Lasso tool all the way around the outside of the logo until you reach the point where you started (remember, you're subtracting from your elliptical selection). When you move the Polygonal Lasso tool over the point where you started, a tiny circle will appear next to your cursor, and when you click on the starting point with your Polygonal Lasso, you'll be left with just the left corner area selected.

STEP FOUR: We need to knock out a thin triangular hole in the middle of our selection for a more-realistic look. Using the Polygonal Lasso tool, draw a straight line that begins just outside the top-left side of your ellipse and goes down at an angle to about three-quarters of the way inside your selection. Continue drawing until you've created a thin rectangle inside your original selection. When you click on the point were you started, that rectangle will be removed from the selection. Next, create a new blank layer by clicking on the Create a New Layer icon at the top of the Layers palette.

Continued

STEP FIVE: Press the letter D and then X to set your Foreground color to white. Press G to switch to the Gradient tool, and press Enter to bring up the Gradient Picker onscreen. Choose the second gradient from the left (Foreground to Transparent). Now, click the Gradient tool at the top-left side of your selection and drag down at an angle just past the right edge of your selection. Deselect by pressing Control-D to complete the left-side reflective highlight. If the reflection seems too intense, you can lower the Opacity of this layer in the Layers palette to around 75%—but that's totally up to you.

STEP SIX: Now on to the lower-right-side reflection: In the Layers palette, click on the Create a New Layer icon, and then press-and-hold the Control key and click on the logo layer to put a selection around it. Return to the Select menu, under Modify, and choose Contract. Enter a number of pixels to shrink the selection to the very edge of the inner ellipse (12 pixels in this example). Press M until you have the Elliptical Marquee tool, and in the set of four icons in the Options Bar, click on the third icon from the left so the tool will subtract from the current selection. Click near the top-left corner of the document and drag out an ellipse that overlaps the current selection so that just a small portion of the original ellipse remains on the lower-right side.

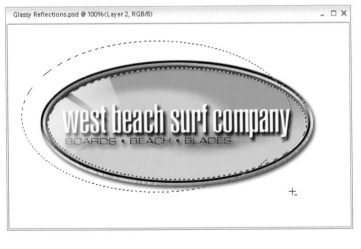

Glassy Reflections.psd @ 100%(Layer 2, RGB/8)

STEP SEVEN: Press G to switch to the Gradient tool (all your settings should still be in place from Step 5), and this time click just outside the bottom-right part of the logo and drag just past the left side of the selection inside the logo. Your selection will fill with the Foreground to Transparent gradient. Press Control-D to deselect.

STEP EIGHT: If needed, lower the Opacity of this reflection layer in the Layers palette to around 85% to complete the effect.

The Fastest Logo Job in Town

This is another popular method for creating a glassy reflection on a logo, but this time, we'll create the logo as well. This method is so quick, you can complete the effect in less than 60 seconds (if you stop at Step 4). If you decide to take it further, it could take you as long as a whopping 90 seconds to get through Step 6. Either way, it's a minute-and-a-half tops.

STEP ONE: Create a new document in RGB mode (the example here is 8x6"). Create a new blank layer by clicking on the Create a New Layer icon at the top of the Layers palette. Press M until you have the Elliptical Marquee tool, and draw an oval selection in the middle of your image area. Click on the Foreground color swatch in the Toolbox, choose a medium blue in the Color Picker, and then fill your oval with blue by pressing Alt-Backspace. Deselect by pressing Control-D.

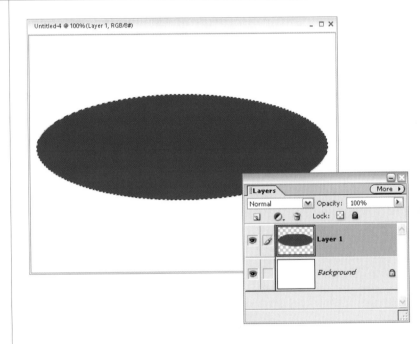

STEP TWO: Press D and then X to set your Foreground color to white, then press the letter T to switch to the Type tool, and create your type (in the example shown here, I used the font Showcard Gothic). Go to the Layers palette and Control-click on the oval layer to put a selection around it. Then, go under the Select menu, under Modify, and choose Contract. When the Contract Selection dialog appears, enter 10 pixels and click OK. (*Note:* For high-res, 300-ppi images, contract by 40 pixels instead.)

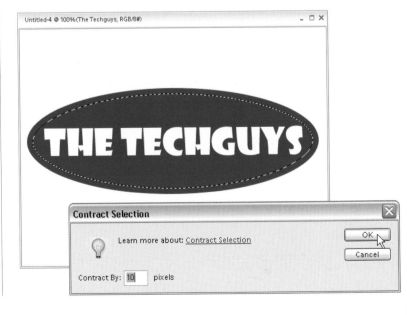

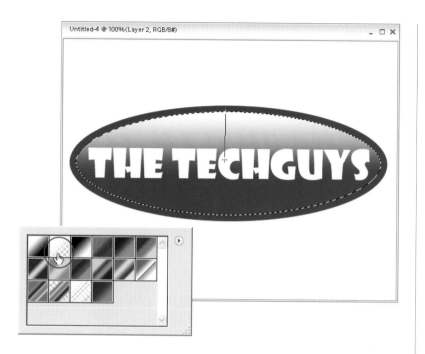

STEP THREE: With white as your Foreground color, create a new blank layer by clicking the Create a New Layer icon at the top of the Layers palette. Press the letter G to switch to the Gradient tool, and press Enter to bring up the Gradient Picker onscreen. Choose the Foreground to Transparent gradient (it's the second gradient in the Picker), ensure that the Linear Gradient icon is selected in the Options Bar, and then drag your gradient from the top of your selection down about halfway through the logo.

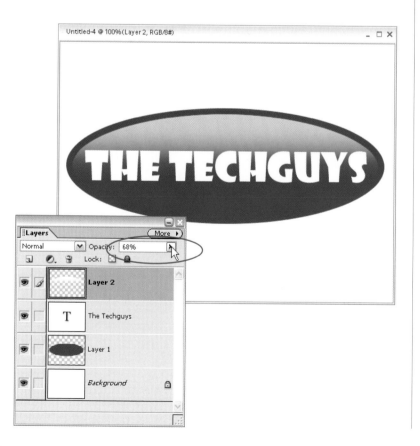

STEP FOUR: Deselect by pressing Control-D. In the Layers palette, lower the Opacity of this layer to around 70%. You could stop at this point and consider the effect complete (and many times I've seen this technique executed only this far), but if you want to add a little more detail (by adding a shadow), go on to the next steps.

Continued

STEP FIVE: In the Layers palette, click the Create a New Layer icon and then Control-click on the oval layer to put a selection around it. Press B to get the Brush tool, click on the brush thumbnail in the Options Bar, and choose a 65-pixel (or larger) soft-edged brush from the Brush Picker. Press D to set your Foreground color to black, then paint a stroke starting at the right side of the oval. Trace along the bottom of your selection, painting down and to the left as you go. Deselect by pressing Control-D.

STEP SIX: After your stroke is drawn, go to the Layers palette and lower the Opacity of this layer to around 50% to complete the effect. (*Note:* This is one of those rare times where I wouldn't add a default drop shadow, because what you just painted acts as a shadow on its own.)

Oscar Starbrights

I call these "Oscar Starbrights" because you see these lens effects used on distant shots of the stage at the Oscar Awards ceremony and a host of other indoor stage events, from boxing matches to rock concerts. The effect is similar to the "star effects" filter used with still cameras.

STEP ONE: Open the image in which you want to apply starbrights. Press the letter D and then X to set your Foreground color to white.

STEP TWO: Press the B key to switch to the Brush tool, and in the Options Bar, click on the brush thumbnail to open the Brush Picker. From the Picker's fly-out menu, choose Load Brushes. In the Load dialog, navigate to the Photoshop Elements 3 folder on your hard drive and under the Presets folder, open the Brushes folder. In that folder, select Assorted Brushes and click the Load button. The Assorted set will load at the bottom of the Brush Picker. Choose the 48-pixel Crosshatch brush (it looks like an "X").

Continued

STEP THREE: Create a new blank layer (Layer 1) by clicking on the Create a New Layer icon at the top of the Layers palette. Now, click your brush on the first spot where you want a starbright to appear (don't paint, just click one time). Click the Create a New Layer icon again (to create Layer 2). Return to the Brush Picker in the Options Bar, and choose the 25-pixel Crosshatch brush (it also looks like an "X"). In the Options Bar, change the Size to 30 pixels and then click on the brush icon to the right of the words "More Options." In the palette that appears, change the Angle to 45°. Click once on the center of your original starbright. Now, go up to the Options Bar and choose the round 27-pixel, soft-edged brush from the Brush Picker. Click the Brush tool once again in the center of your original starbright.

STEP FOUR: Create another blank layer (Layer 3). In the Layers palette, Control-click on the original starbright layer (Layer 1) to put a selection around your starbright. Press G to switch to the Gradient tool, and then go to the Options Bar and click on the down-facing arrow next to the gradient thumbnail to bring up the Gradient Picker. Choose the Spectrum gradient (it's the first one in the third row), click on the Radial Gradient icon in the Options Bar, and then drag the Gradient tool from the center of your starbright to the right, just past the edge of the starbright.

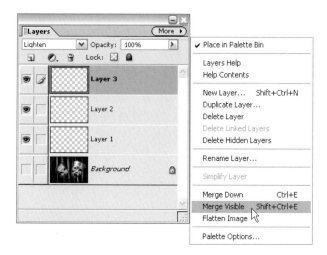

STEP FIVE: Deselect by pressing Control-D. In the Layers palette, change the layer blend mode from Normal to Lighten. Then, click on the Eye icon to the left of the Background layer to hide that layer, and choose Merge Visible from the palette's flyout menu. This merges all of the layers that make up the starbright into a single layer.

STEP SIX: Click on the far-left empty box next to the Background layer to make it visible again. Now you can go under the Layer menu, under New, and choose Layer via Copy (or just press Control-J) a few times to create duplicates of your starbright layer. Press V to switch to the Move tool and click-and-drag the starbrights to other locations in your image, completing the effect.

Adding a Lens Flare

This is a nice way to add some visual interest to an image. The sad part about this technique is that photographers go out of their way to avoid lens flare, and here we're about to show you how to add it. It just ain't flare. ;-)

STEP ONE: Open the photo you want to apply a lens flare effect to, making sure it's set to RGB mode by going to the Image menu, under Mode, and choosing RGB Color. In this example, we're going to apply it to a photo of the sun shining through some trees, but this technique also works well with night images or images that are dark (the photo has to be dark enough for the lens flare effect to be seen). Go to the top of the Layers palette and click on the Create a New Layer icon.

STEP TWO: Press D to set your Foreground color to black, then fill this new layer with black by pressing Alt-Backspace. Under the Filter menu, under Render, choose Lens Flare. When the dialog appears, increase the Brightness to 150% and choose 50-300mm Zoom for Lens Type. We're going to want the lens flare to appear as if it's peeking through the trees, and we'll position it using the Move tool in the next step, but we don't want to have to move the lens flare too much once we've applied it. So while you're still in the Lens Flare dialog, click on the little crosshair in the preview area and drag the center of the lens flare to approximately where you want it located in the final image. When it looks good to you, click OK.

STEP THREE: The black lens flare layer completely covers the photo on the Background layer. So you'll need to go to the Layers palette and change the layer blend mode from Normal to Screen. When you change the layer blend mode, the lens flare will then blend in with your image. Press the letter V to switch to the Move tool, and reposition the center of the flare until it's peeking through the tree branches.

STEP FOUR: That's it—you've completed your lens flare effect. If the flare seems too bright, just lower the lens flare layer's Opacity in the Layers palette.

Instant Star Field

This is one of those "create-something-from-nothing" techniques, because within just a few seconds, you go from a blank document to a star field. This makes a great background for collage projects, or you can add it to existing images. Warning: While replicating this technique, you may feel an uncontrollable urge to say things like, "Make it so!" and "To the Transporter room." This will pass.

STEP ONE: Create a new document (the example here is 8x6") in RGB mode at 72 ppi. Press D to set black as your Foreground color, then press Alt-Backspace to fill your background with black. Next, go under the Filter menu, under Noise, and choose Add Noise. Enter approximately 40% for Amount, choose Gaussian for Distribution, check Monochromatic, and click OK.

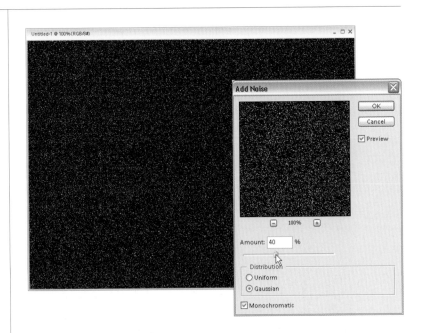

STEP TWO: Return to the Filter menu again, choose Blur, and select Gaussian Blur. For Radius enter 0.5 (half a pixel) and click OK to apply just a slight blur to your noise. To bring out the star field in your noise, go under the Filter menu again, under Adjustments, and choose Threshold. When the Threshold dialog appears, drag the slider to the left until the "stars come out," then click OK. Press Control-F to apply another 0.5-pixel Gaussian Blur to soften the stars.

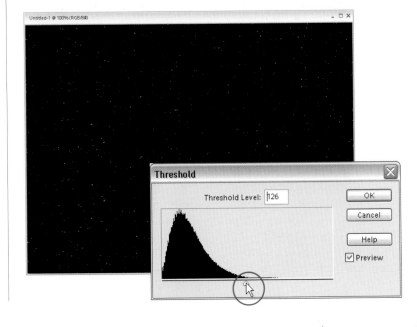

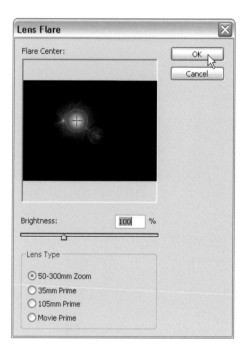

STEP THREE: To enhance the "out-in-space" look, I generally add a Lens Flare effect to the star field. Add a new layer by clicking on the Create a New Layer icon at the top of the Layers palette, and fill this new layer with black by pressing Alt-Backspace. Next, go under the Filter menu, under Render, and choose Lens Flare. Use any Brightness setting or Lens Type you like (I used the defaults settings), and click OK.

STEP FOUR: To bring the Lens Flare into your star field, just change the blend mode of this layer in the Layers palette from Normal to Screen, which completes the effect.

This is the chapter where it all comes together. This is where we dissect some of the most popular product

Show Me the Money
3D and Packaging Effects

and 3D Photoshop Elements effects and expose them for the cheap, tawdry tricks that they are. It's no secret that some big companies spend vast sums of money to find out what motivates people to spend their hard-earned money on a particular product. For example, recent studies have shown that if you use a blue color on the cover of your product, and use a combination of black, blue, and gold on the inside of your product, people will find the product absolutely irresistible, regardless of the content. Further studies have shown that if you're able to work some suggestive words into the name of your product (for example, the word "Dirty"), then overall sales will increase by nearly 32%. If, on top of that, you can somehow apply a grunge effect to the aforementioned word, you'll have a product so compelling that even Hindu priests will abandon their mountaintop spiritual sanctuaries just to buy whatever it is you're selling. This is powerful information. Use it wisely.

3D Magazine Effect

This technique first caught my attention when I saw it in various UK computer magazines (like *Computer Arts*) in their subscription ads, and then it started catching on in the States. It's ideal for giving some depth to a cover design, a page from a newsletter, a magazine, etc.

STEP ONE: Create a new blank document that's slightly larger than the page you're giving depth to (the blank document here is set at 72-ppi in RGB mode, but all you have to make sure of is that your new document is the same resolution as the object to which you want to apply the effect). Then, open your object (in this case, a cover of a newsletter), press V to switch to the Move tool, and click-and-drag the object into your blank document.

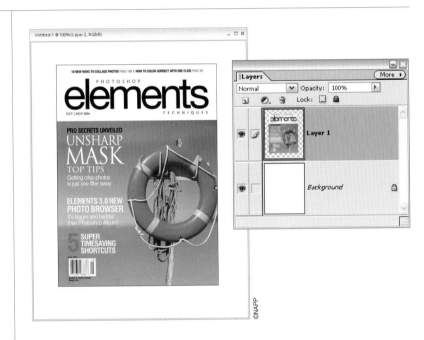

STEP TWO: Press M to switch to the Rectangular Marquee tool, and draw a rectangular selection around the bottom quarter of your cover. Next, create a new blank layer by clicking on the Create a New Layer icon at the top of the Layers palette. Then, go under the File menu, under New, and choose Blank File. When the New dialog appears, enter 1 pixel for Width, 2 pixels for Height, and choose the same resolution and color mode as your original cover document. Click OK to create a very tiny, new document.

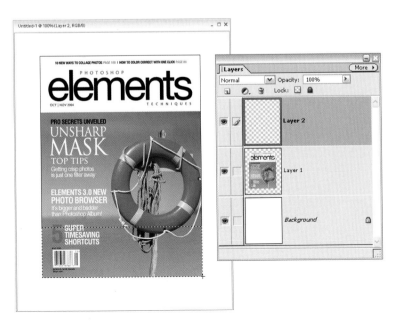

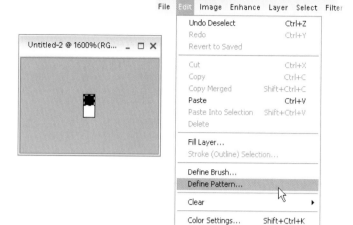

STEP THREE: Press Control-+ (Plus Sign) nine times to zoom in on your document. With the Rectangular Marquee tool, select the top half of your document. Press the D key to set your Foreground color to black, then press Alt-Backspace to fill your selection with black. Press Control-D to deselect. Next, go under the Edit menu and choose Define Pattern. Name your pattern and click OK. Close this document without saving it.

STEP FOUR: Switch back to your original document. Your selection should still be in place, so go under the Edit menu and choose Fill Selection. In the Fill Layer dialog, choose Pattern from the Use pop-up menu. Click on the Custom Pattern thumbnail to bring up the Pattern Picker. Choose the very last pattern in the Picker (it's the one you just created, which is very similar to the TV scan lines effect in Chapter 7, except that we created a smaller scan line). Click OK to fill your selection with horizontal black-and-white lines. Deselect by pressing Control-D.

Continued

STEP FIVE: Press Control-T to bring up the Free Transform bounding box around your black-and-white lines. Drag the top center point downward to shrink your lines. This will act as the book's pages. Next, press-and-hold the Control key, click on the bottom left-hand corner point, and drag upward to pinch the left side of the pages. Press Enter to lock in your changes.

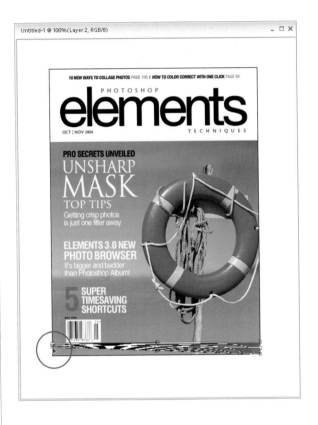

STEP SIX: Press V to switch to the Move tool, and drag the "book pages" down until the top of the pages touches the bottom of your cover. In the Layers palette, drag this layer beneath your cover layer, then click on the cover layer to make it active. Press Control-E to merge the cover with the pages layer directly beneath it.

STEP SEVEN: With the cover layer active in the Layers palette, press Command-T to bring up Free Transform. Move your cursor outside the bounding box and click-and-drag up and to the left to rotate the cover a little. Next, press-and-hold Shift-Alt-Control, grab the top-right corner point and drag inward quite a bit to add a perspective effect. The cover will look pixelated and distorted, but don't sweat it; that will go away once you leave Free Transform. Now, grab the top center point, and drag quite a bit downward to remove the "stretched looked" from the book cover. This works well because it maintains the perspective effect, without all the distorted stretching. Press Enter to lock in your transformation.

STEP EIGHT: Go to the Styles and Effects palette, and with Layer Styles selected, choose Drop Shadows in the palette's top-right pop-up menu. Click on the High drop shadow icon to apply a drop shadow to your cover. Then, in the Layers palette, double-click the Layer Styles icon to the right of the cover layer. In the resulting dialog, lower the Shadow Distance to around 5–10 pixels and click OK to complete the effect.

3D Hardcover Book Effect

This technique for creating the pages and spine of a hardcover book makes great use of what is perhaps the lamest filter in all of Photoshop Elements—3D Transform. Any technique that manages to use this filter has got to be worth something.

STEP ONE: Create a new document in RGB mode at 72 ppi (I created an 8x6" document). Create a new layer by clicking on the Create a New Layer icon at the top of the Layers palette. Then, go under the Filter menu, under Render, and choose 3D Transform. Select the Cube tool from the Toolbox on the left-hand side of the dialog and drag out a cube in the dialog preview window.

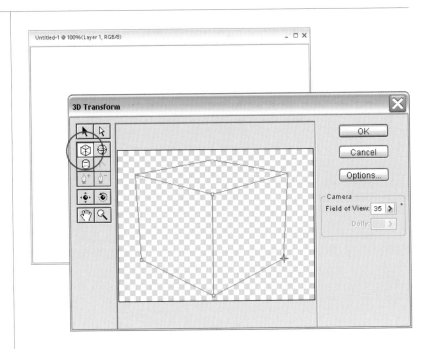

STEP TWO: Press A to switch to the Direct Selection tool (the hollow arrow), click on the back, bottom-right corner of the cube, and drag slightly down and to the left to shrink the depth of your cube, making it look more like a cereal box. Now, click on the front, top-right corner point and drag to the right to tip the box back a bit (don't worry—it'll tip—it's in 3D).

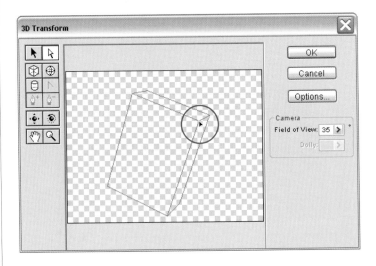

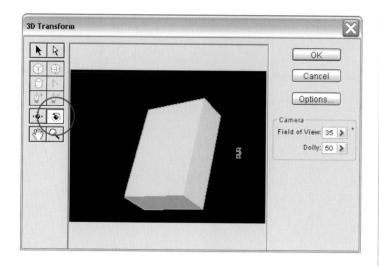

STEP THREE: In the 3D Transform dialog, click on the Options button. In the resulting dialog, ensure the Display Background checkbox is turned off and click OK. While still in the 3D Transform dialog, press R to switch to the Trackball tool (it's right above the Zoom tool in the dialog's Toolbox), click on the left side of the preview window, and drag to the right. Keep dragging until your shape rotates all the way around to reveal the back side (which appears as a solid color). When it looks like the one shown here, click OK and the shape will appear in the document you created in Step 1.

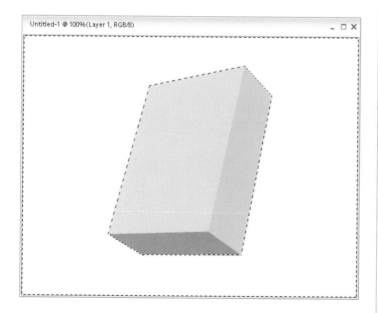

STEP FOUR: In many cases, the edges of your cube will have some fringe or look somewhat jaggy, but that's easy to fix. Press-and-hold the Control key, go to the Layers palette, and click on the cube layer to put a selection around your cube. Then, go under the Select menu, under Modify, and choose Contract. Enter 1 pixel and click OK to shrink your selection slightly. Go under the Select menu and choose Inverse (so now the only thing that's selected on this layer is that 1 pixel, all the way around your cube shape). Press Backspace to remove this 1-pixel edge fringe. Now, you can deselect by pressing Control-D.

Continued

STEP FIVE: Open the image that you've already created for your hardcover book. (The example here is a fictitious book cover, which you can download from this book's companion website, www.scottkelbybooks.com/ddelements3.) Press V to switch to the Move tool, click on this book cover, and drag it into your cube document. In the Layers palette, ensure that this layer appears directly above the cube layer in the layer stack.

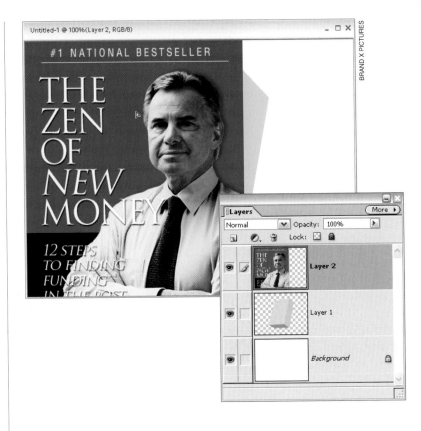

STEP SIX: In the Layers palette, lower the Opacity of the cover layer to 50% so you can see the cube through the cover. Press Control-T to bring up Free Transform. If you can't see the Free Transform handles, press Control-0 (zero) to zoom your image out. Then, press-and-hold the Shift key and drag one of the corner points to scale the photo down until it's just a little larger than the cube. Don't press Enter yet.

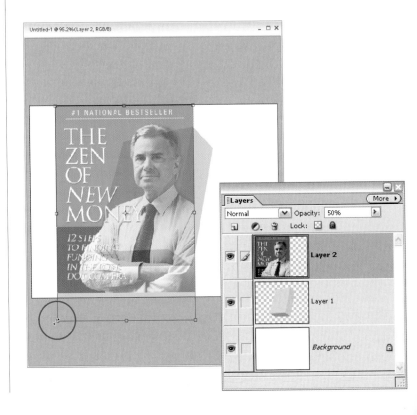

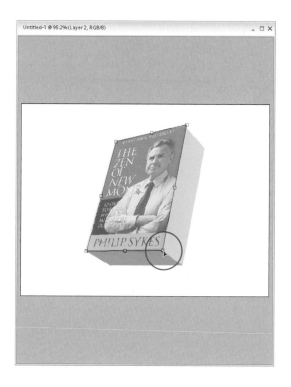

STEP SEVEN: While Free Transform is still active, press-and-hold the Control key, grab the top-left corner point of the cover, and drag it over until it aligns with the top-left corner of the cube. Keep pressing the Control key, grab the bottom-left corner of the cover, and do the same thing—stretch that corner to match the bottom-left corner of the cube. When you're close, drag it down just a tiny bit past the bottom front of the cube, because you want this fake cover to hang below the top part of the pages just a bit. Now do the same to the right side: Grab the top-right corner, align it to the top-right corner of the front face of the cube, and let it extend a little over the edge as well; do the same thing for the bottom-right corner—let a little hang over the edge (like a cover would on a real book). When it looks right, press Enter to lock in your transformation.

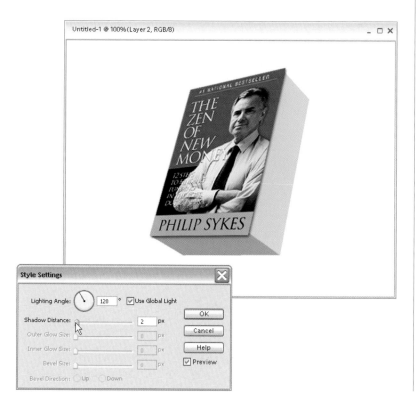

STEP EIGHT: Double-click on the Zoom tool in the Toolbox to return your view to 100%, then go to the Layers palette and raise the Opacity of your cover layer back up to 100%. Now you're going to need a tiny drop shadow between your cover and the pages (your cube), so go to the Styles and Effects palette, and with Layer Styles selected, choose Drop Shadows from the palette's top-right pop-up menu. Click on the Low drop shadow icon, and in the Layers palette, double-click on the Layer Styles icon (it looks like an "ƒ") to the right of the layer. In the Style Settings dialog, lower the Shadow Distance to 2 pixels and click OK.

Continued

STEP NINE: In the Layers palette, click on your pages layer (the cube layer), go under the Layer menu, under New, and choose Layer via Copy (or press Control-J) to duplicate it. Press the letter I to get the Eyedropper tool, and click on a color within your book cover to sample it for the Foreground color (this will become the color of your spine and back cover, which will be slightly visible behind the pages). Then, press Shift-Alt-Backspace to fill your duplicate cube with your chosen color.

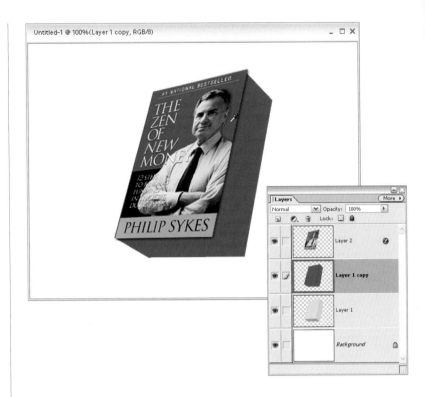

STEP TEN: Go to the Layers palette and drag this layer beneath the original cube layer. Get the Move tool, then press the Down Arrow key on your keyboard two or three times and the Right Arrow key two or three times to reveal the colorized cube, which forms the spine and back cover. To complete the effect, go to the Styles and Effects palette, and with the Drop Shadows section still selected, click on the Soft Edge icon.

Creating 3D Packaging

You can use Photoshop Elements' built-in tools to turn a flat image into an object that has depth (such as product packaging, a video box, etc.). In this tutorial, we'll add perspective to an image using Photoshop Elements' transformation tool, but we'll also add shading and highlights to help "sell" the effect that the image has depth.

STEP ONE: Open the image that you want to use as the cover of your product box. Press Control-A to select the entire image, then go under the Layer menu, under New, and choose Layer via Cut (or press Shift-Control-J) to cut your cover shot from the Background layer and copy it onto its own layer. In the Layers palette, double-click directly on this layer's name to highlight it, and rename it "Front."

STEP TWO: Go under the Image menu, under Resize, and choose Canvas Size. Ensure the Relative checkbox is turned on, and enter 4 inches in both the Width and Height fields. In the Canvas Extension Color pop-up menu choose White, and then click OK. This gives some needed work area around the image. Press the letter V to switch to the Move tool, and click-and-drag your image to the right side of the document window.

Continued

STEP THREE: To build the spine, create a new layer by clicking on the Create a New Layer icon at the top of the Layers palette. Double-click on this layer's name and rename it "Spine." Press M to switch to the Rectangular Marquee tool and draw a vertical rectangular selection to the left of your box front that's the same height as the box front. Click on the Foreground color swatch at the bottom of the Toolbox, and in the resulting Color Picker, choose a color that will complement the colors in your box front. (*Note:* While the Color Picker is open, move your cursor outside the dialog, and when your cursor turns into the Eyedropper tool, click within your image to sample a color.) Fill this selection with your chosen color by pressing Alt-Backspace, and then press Control-D to deselect. Press D to set your Foreground color to black, and with the Rectangular Marquee tool, select the top part of the spine. Press Alt-Backspace to fill the selection with black, and then press Control-D to deselect.

STEP FOUR: Click on the Front layer in the Layers palette to make it active. With the Rectangular Marquee tool, draw a long narrow rectangle across the top of the Front layer that's roughly the same height as the one you drew at the top of the spine in Step 3. Press Alt-Backspace to fill this rectangle with black, and then press Control-D to deselect.

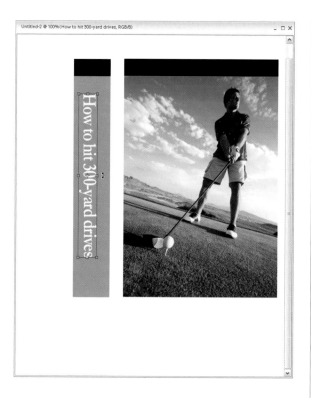

STEP FIVE: I recommend adding some text to the spine to help sell the 3D effect, so press D and then X to set your Foreground color to white, and then press T to switch to the Type tool. Enter your white type (I used the typeface Adobe Garamond Pro). Once you've entered your type, press Control-T to bring up Free Transform. Click outside the bounding box and drag to rotate the type 90° to the right to make it vertical, then click within the bounding box to position your type in the center of the spine. To enlarge your text, grab a corner point and drag outward slightly. When it looks good to you, press Enter.

STEP SIX: You need to merge your Type layer with the Spine layer beneath it, so with the Type layer active in the Layers palette, press Control-E to merge the layers together. Now, click on the merged Spine layer and press Control-T to bring up Free Transform again. Press-and-hold Shift-Alt-Control, then click-and-drag the top-right corner point of the bounding box straight upward about ½" higher than the top of the box front (you'll see the spine stretch both up and down on the right side as you do this). Release the keys, grab the middle-left handle, and drag inward about the same amount as you dragged the top-right corner point to remove the distortion caused by the stretching. Press Enter when it looks good to you.

Continued

STEP SEVEN: Switch to the Type tool again and enter any text that you want on your cover. The title is set in the font Garamond and the golfer's name is in the font Adobe Garamond Pro, while the production company and tagline are set in Myriad Pro. For the title, I went to the Styles and Effects palette (found under the Window menu), and with Layer Styles selected, I chose Drop Shadows from the top-right pop-up menu, and then clicked on the Soft Edge icon. Add any logos (such as the DVD logo I used here) as well. When you've added all the items you want on your cover, go to the Layers palette, click on the Front layer to make it active, and then click on the second empty box to the left of those Type and logo layers to link them all together. Choose Merge Linked from the Layers palette's flyout menu to merge all of the cover elements into one layer.

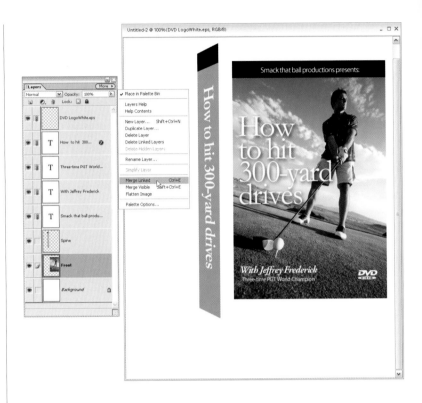

STEP EIGHT: Make sure you still have the Front layer active and press Control-T to bring up Free Transform. Press-and-hold Shift-Control and grab the upper-left corner point and drag straight upward until it matches the height of the spine. Then, grab the lower-left corner point and drag straight downward until it lines up with the bottom of the spine. Release the keys and drag the middle-right handle inward about 1". Press Enter to lock in your transformation.

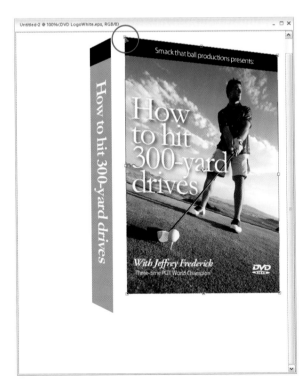

STEP NINE: Click on the Spine layer in the Layers palette to make it active. Press V to switch to the Move tool, and drag the spine to the right until it touches the left edge of the box. (*Note:* If a corner doesn't align, press Control-T, press-and-hold Shift-Control, grab a corner point, and align it to the front corner. Press Enter when you're done.) Press Control-L to bring up Levels. Move the highlight Output Levels slider to the left a bit to darken the spine, and then click OK.

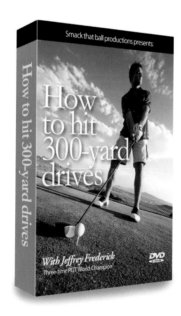

STEP TEN: Next, click on the Front layer in the Layers palette, then press B to switch to the Brush tool. In the Options Bar, lower the Opacity of the Brush tool to 20%, click on the Airbrush icon (it's to the right of the Opacity field), and then click on the brush thumbnail. In the resulting Brush Picker, choose a very small, hard-edged brush. Press D and then X to set your Foreground color to white. Press-and-hold the Shift key and click at the top corner where the spine and cover meet, and drag down between the box front and the spine to add a highlight along the edge. Now, click on the Background layer in the Layers palette, and press D to set your Foreground color to black. In the Options Bar, lower the Opacity of the Brush tool to around 40%, then click on the brush thumbnail, and in the resulting Brush Picker, choose a very large, soft-edged brush. Paint a soft drop shadow below the box with one smooth stroke. That's it!

Creating a DVD Effect

This is a simple version of how to create a DVD. I've seen different gradients used for this effect, but the rainbow one I'm showing here seems to be the most popular. I've seen this technique used mostly on products in which the disc appears as if it's protruding from some DVD packaging, because everybody wants to make it clear that the package contains a DVD, not a VHS tape.

STEP ONE: Create a new document in RGB mode (the one here is 8x8"). Then, create a new blank layer by clicking on the Create a New Layer icon at the top of the Layers palette. Press M until you get the Elliptical Marquee tool, press-and-hold the Shift key, and drag out a circular selection for your disc.

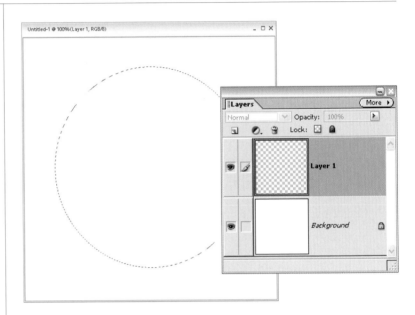

STEP TWO: Press G to switch to the Gradient tool, then up in the Options Bar click on the Edit button to bring up the Gradient Editor. In the Gradient Editor, you'll create a gradient that goes from a medium gray to white to medium gray. Start by clicking on the Orange to Yellow to Orange gradient (it's the last one in the top row of Presets), and under the gradient ramp, double-click on the far-left color stop. Choose a medium gray in the Color Picker. Then, double-click the center color stop and choose white in the Color Picker. Finally, double-click the right color stop and choose a medium gray in the Color Picker. Name this gradient "gray," click the New button, and then click OK.

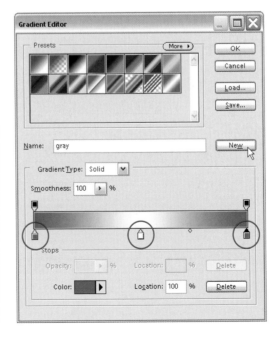

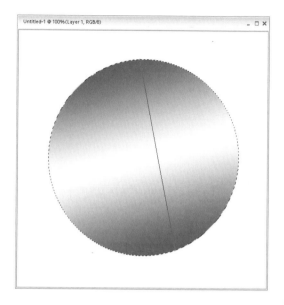

STEP THREE: Click the Gradient tool at the top of the selection and drag downward, at a slight angle to the right, through the circular selection. Don't deselect yet. Click on the Create a New Layer icon in the Layers palette, then go under the Select menu, under Modify, and choose Contract. When the Contract dialog appears, enter 4 pixels and click OK to shrink your selection.

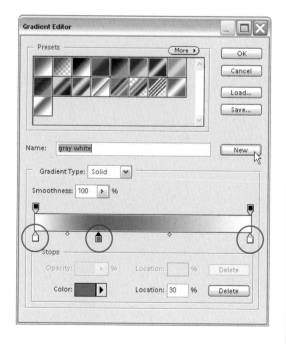

STEP FOUR: You'll build a different gradient for this layer, so get the Gradient tool again, click on the Edit button in the Options Bar to bring up the Gradient Editor, and edit the existing gradient. Double-click the far-left color stop and choose white in the Color Picker. Then, double-click the center color stop, choose a dark gray in the Picker, and drag this color stop closer to the far-left white color stop. Finally, double-click the far-right color stop and choose white in the Picker. Name this gradient "gray white," click the New button, and then click OK.

Continued

STEP FIVE: Click the Gradient tool at the top of the selection and drag downward at a slight angle to the right. The gradient only affects the area within the selected area, and because you contracted the selection by 4 pixels, you can still see part of the original gradient around the edge of the circle just outside of the current selection.

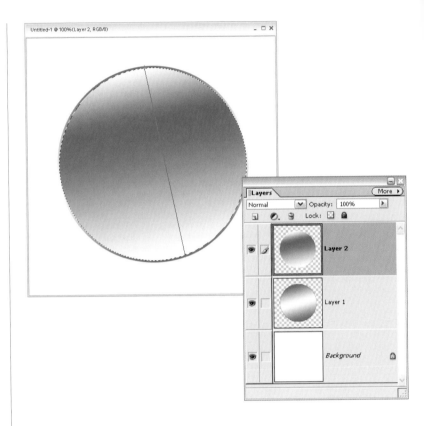

STEP SIX: Choose Stroke (Outline) Selection from the Edit menu. When the Stroke dialog appears, change the Width to 1 pixel, set the Location to Outside, click on the Color swatch and choose black in the Color Picker, lower the Opacity to 50%, and then click OK to put a thin black stroke around your inner circle gradient. Press Control-D to deselect. In the Layers palette, click on the original circle layer (Layer 1), go under the Edit menu, choose Stroke (Outline) Selection again, and just click OK (the settings should be the same as before) to apply the same stroke to the original, larger gradient circle layer.

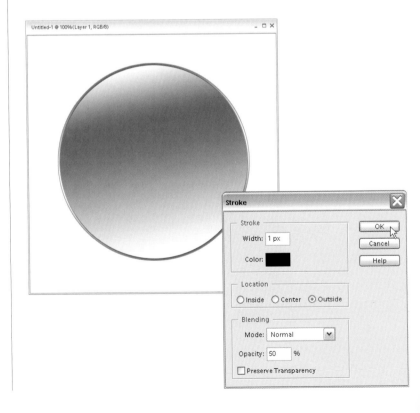

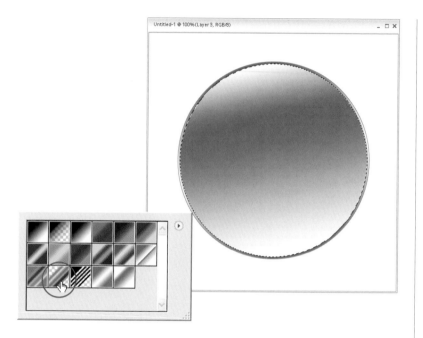

STEP SEVEN: In the Layers palette, Control-click the smaller circle layer to put a selection around it, then click the Create a New Layer icon. Drag this new blank layer to the top of the layer stack, making it the topmost layer. Get the Gradient tool again and press Enter to bring up the Gradient Picker onscreen. Choose the Transparent Rainbow gradient (it's the second gradient in the bottom row).

STEP EIGHT: Click-and-drag this rainbow gradient through the center of your selection, but don't drag from the top of the selection to the bottom—start just above the middle and drag downward to just below the middle, at a slight angle to the right. Don't deselect yet.

Continued

STEP NINE: With the rainbow gradient layer active in the Layers palette, go under the Filter menu, under Distort, and choose Pinch. Enter 100% for Amount and click OK. Now, go under the Filter menu again, under Blur, and choose Radial Blur. Enter 40 for Amount, choose Spin for Blur Method, Good for Quality, and click OK. Press Control-D to deselect.

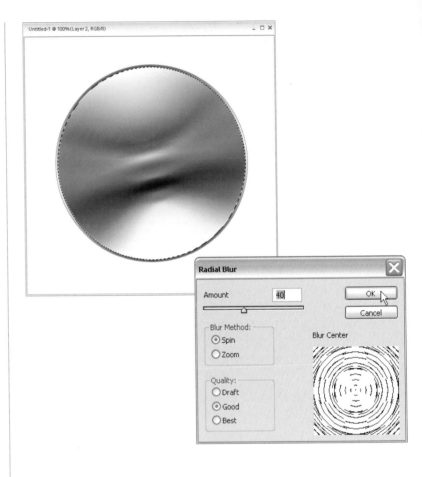

STEP TEN: Press-and-hold the Shift key, then with the Elliptical Marquee tool, draw a smaller circular selection in the center of the disc. (*Note:* Press-and-hold the Spacebar as you drag out your selection to reposition it if needed. When you have it where you want it, just release the Spacebar and continue dragging out the selection.) With your selection in place, go under the Select menu and choose Feather. In the Feather Selection dialog, enter 20 pixels for the Radius and click OK to soften the center selection. Press Backspace to knock a soft hole out of the rainbow effect, then press Control-D to deselect.

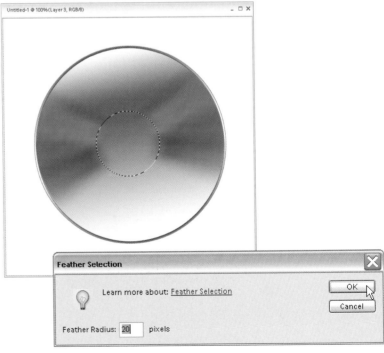

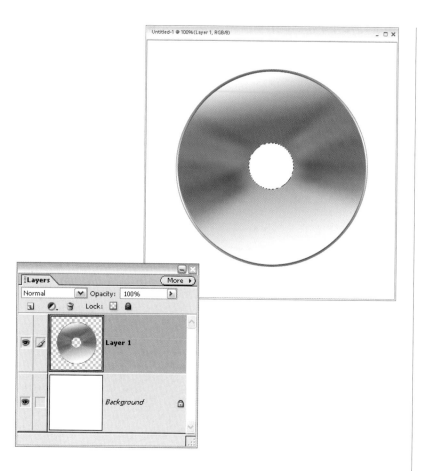

STEP ELEVEN: In the Layers palette, ensure that the top rainbow layer is active and press Control-E two times to merge the three gradient layers into one disc layer. Using the Elliptical Marquee tool, press-and-hold the Shift key, and create another small circular selection in the center of your DVD (this circular selection should be smaller than the one you created in the previous step). Press Backspace to knock out a hole on this disc layer, and then press Control-D to deselect, which completes the DVD effect. But if you want to see your DVD in action, see the option below.

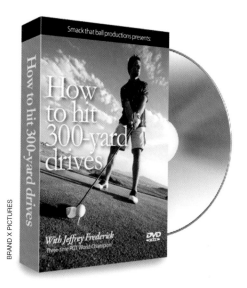

OPTION: You can make your DVD appear to be popping out of a package if you like. Just open your DVD package (this is the one we created earlier in this chapter), and make sure the package is on its own layer (you can click the Magic Wand tool [W] on the white background, go under the Select menu and choose Inverse, then press Shift-Control-J to cut the package from the Background layer and copy it onto its own layer). Switch to your DVD document, press V to switch to the Move tool, and drag-and-drop your disc onto the package document. Drag the disc layer below the package layer in the Layers palette, then press Control-T to bring up Free Transform. Right-click in the bounding box and choose Perspective in the contextual menu. Then grab the bottom-left corner point and drag downward to give the disc the same perspective as the package. Press Enter and you're done!

3D Photo Cubes

I've seen people create these photo cubes before, but it's always been such a long and laborious process that I usually ended up going in a different direction. However, using the 3D Transform filter, it suddenly becomes really simple. Don't let the number of steps fool you—this is a very easy project.

STEP ONE: Create a new document in RGB mode (the one here is 8x8"). Start by creating a new blank layer by clicking on the Create a New Layer icon at the top of the Layers palette. We'll use this layer to create a 3D cube that we'll use as our guide.

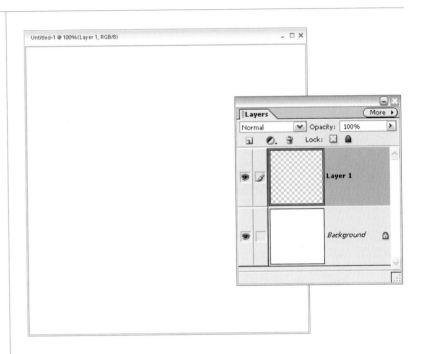

STEP TWO: Go under the Filter menu, under Render, and choose 3D Transform. When the 3D Transform dialog appears, click on the Cube tool in the Toolbox on the left and drag out a cube shape in the preview window. Click on the Options button, and in the resulting dialog, turn off the Display Background checkbox and click OK. While still in the 3D Transform dialog, press R to switch to the Trackball tool, click within your preview area, and drag to the right. As you drag, the cube will rotate, exposing its back side, which includes shading on all three sides. (*Note:* You'll have to click-and-drag quite a ways to the right—in fact, your cursor will actually extend outside the 3D Transform dialog as you drag.) When it looks good to you, click OK and your shaded cube will appear on your blank layer.

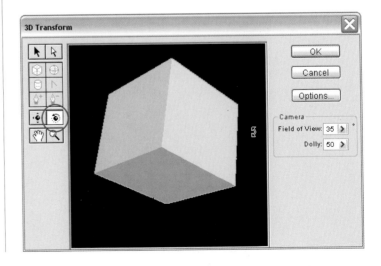

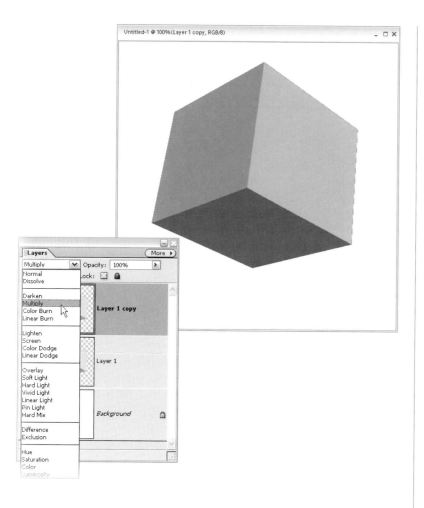

STEP THREE: The shading is somewhat subtle, so to intensify it, duplicate the cube layer by going under the Layer menu, under New, and choosing Layer via Copy (or by pressing Control-J). Then, change the layer blend mode in the Layers palette for this duplicate layer to Multiply. This has a multiplying effect and makes the shading on the cube more pronounced. Now, press Control-E to merge the Multiply cube layer permanently with the original cube layer below (creating just one layer).

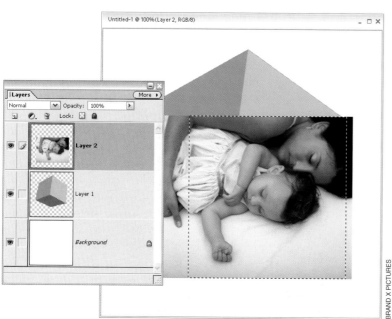

STEP FOUR: Open the first photo you want to use on your photo cube. Press V to switch to the Move tool, and click-and-drag this photo over to your cube document. It will appear on its own layer above your cube layer. (*Note:* If needed, press Control-T to bring up Free Transform, press-and-hold the Shift key, grab a corner point, and resize your image so it fits onscreen.) The cube has perfectly square sides, so to keep from distorting your photos as you place them into the cube shape, you'll need to make them perfectly square as well. To do that, press M to switch to the Rectangular Marquee tool, press-and-hold the Shift key, and drag out a square selection over your photo. If you need to reposition your square once it's in place, just click the Rectangular Marquee tool within your selection and drag just the selection.

Continued

STEP FIVE: When your square selection is positioned correctly, go under the Select menu and choose Inverse. This inverses the selection. Press Backspace, and everything on that layer inside your selection is erased, leaving you with a perfectly square photo. Press Control-D to deselect.

STEP SIX: In the Layers palette, lower the Opacity of this layer to 20% so you can see the cube below (the cube is your guide, so being able to see it is critical). Now, press Control-T to bring up Free Transform. Press-and-hold the Control key, grab the top-left corner of the bounding box, and drag it until it aligns with the top-left corner of the right face of the cube. Because you lowered the opacity of your photo layer, this is very easy. By the way, holding the Control key as you drag invokes Free Transform's Distort feature.

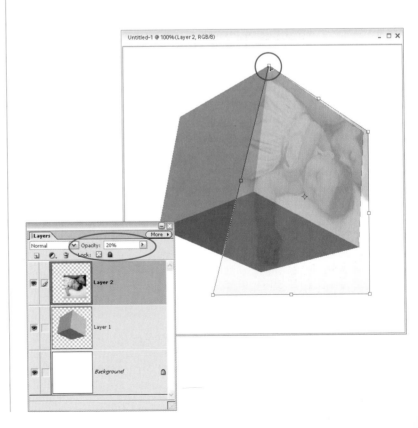

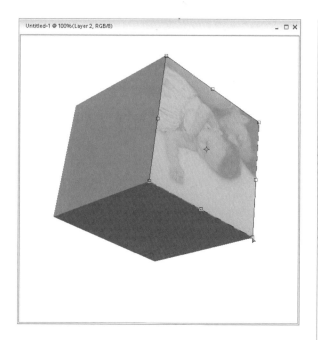

STEP SEVEN: Next, while still holding the Control key, grab the top-right Free Transform point and drag it until it aligns with the top-right corner of the cube. You'll do this for all four corners: Press-and-hold the Control key, grab a corner of your photo's bounding box, and align it with the corresponding corner of your cube face until all four sides match the cube. Then, press Enter to lock in your transformation on the right side of the cube.

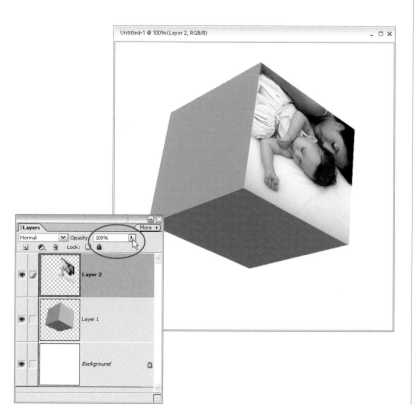

STEP EIGHT: Remember how you lowered the opacity of this layer earlier? Well, now that the photo's aligned to the cube, you can go to the Layers palette and raise the Opacity of your photo layer back up to 100%.

Continued

STEP NINE: Now you're going to repeat the process (Steps 4–8) for the left and bottom faces of the cube: Open a photo, drag it over into your cube document, put a square selection around the most important part of the photo, inverse your selection, press Backspace, lower the Opacity of the layer to 20%, bring up Free Transform, hold the Control key, align the corner points to the cube, press Enter to lock in your transformation, and raise the Opacity back to 100%.

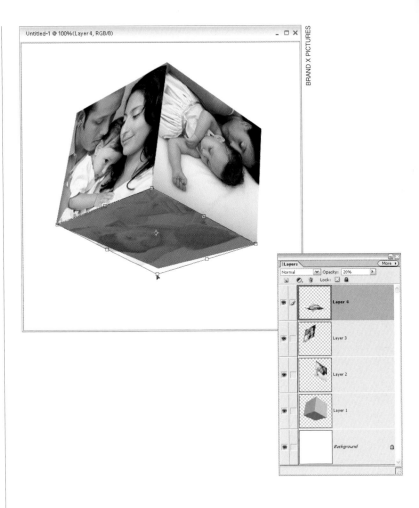

STEP TEN: Once you align all three photos and raise their Opacity settings back to 100%, you'll see the photo cube take shape. The only problem is, we've covered up all the shading from the cube (the photo on the bottom isn't darker, the right side isn't lighter, etc.). So go to the Layers palette, and with the top layer active, press Control-E twice to merge the three photo layers into just one layer, right above the cube layer (don't merge the cube layer with the photo layers).

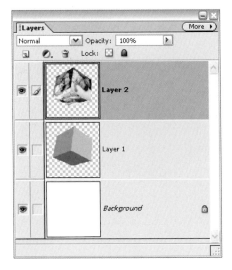

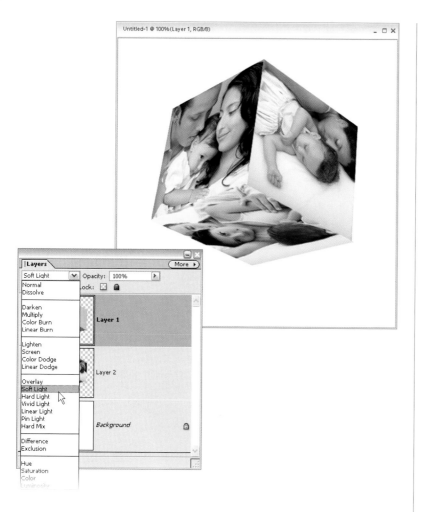

STEP ELEVEN: Now you're going to use the cube itself to add the shading to your photos. In the Layers palette, drag the cube layer above your photo layer, then change the layer blend mode of this cube layer to Soft Light. When you do this, your photo cube will appear subtly shaded, with the bottom photo becoming darker, the right photo lighter, and the left side not as light.

BRAND X PICTURES

OPTION: The effect is essentially complete, but I thought I'd put it on a background just to show you the final effect. Open a photo you want to use as a background (I opened a photo of some clouds for my background). Now, return to your photo cube layer and press Control-E to merge your shaded cube and photo cube together permanently. Switch to the Move tool and click-and-drag this cube over onto the clouds background to complete the effect. (Notice how the bottom of the cube now appears darker?) This is just one way to use this effect—try creating multiple cubes, with other photos, and slightly rotate each for a different effect.

This is where it all pays off. These are the edge effects that you can use when it's time to present your work

Photo Finish
Edge Effects

to the client. This is where you'll learn how to add those little extras that make you and your photos stand out from the crowd. This is where your "click-click" turns into "bling-bling!"; where your "tap-tap" turns into "cha-ching"; where your "pipp-pipp" turns into your "ace-deuce." Okay, I should've stopped with bling-bling. These are the kinds of effects that can transform you from a scrappy kid in the streets, struggling along with some off-brand megapixel point-and-shoot, and turn you into a real playa, poppin' Cristal corks at one of P. Diddy's parties and cranking off shots with your Nikon D2X. That is, provided you actually are a scrappy kid in the streets. If you're not, and instead you're a middle-aged wedding photographer from Grand Rapids, I don't think you'll make it past the bouncers where P. Diddy hangs. But it's certainly worth a try. It's all gravy.

Filmstrip Templates

Photographers use this technique for a host of reasons: displaying client photos (especially modeling shots), high school senior portraits, travel shots, and shots used in online portfolios. There's one great thing about this technique—once you've created one filmstrip, you can save it as a template and apply it to any photo in seconds. Here's how it's done:

STEP ONE: Create a new document in RGB mode at a resolution of 300 ppi (the example here is 6x4"). Click on the Create a New Layer icon at the top of the Layers palette to create a new blank layer. Press D to set your Foreground color to black, then press M to switch to the Rectangular Marquee tool. Create a large rectangular selection, fill it with black by pressing Alt-Backspace, and then deselect by pressing Control-D.

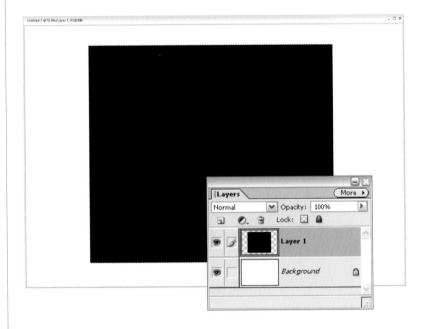

STEP TWO: Inside your black rectangle, draw a smaller rectangular selection with the Rectangular Marquee tool. You're going to need this smaller rectangular selection later in this project, so save it by going under the Select menu and choosing Save Selection. When the dialog appears, enter a name and click OK. Now, press the Backspace key to knock the smaller rectangular selection out of the larger black rectangle. Deselect by pressing Control-D.

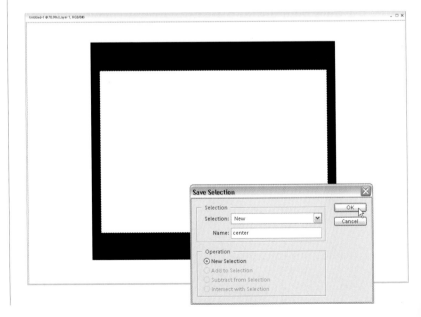

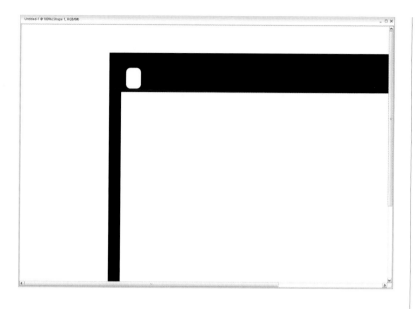

STEP THREE: Press the letter X to set white as your Foreground color. Next, go to the Layers palette and create a new blank layer. You'll need to zoom in close for this step, so press Alt-Control-+ (Plus Sign) to zoom in without changing your window size. Press-and-hold the Spacebar key to temporarily access the Hand tool, and click-and-drag within your image area until you're viewing the top-left corner of your black rectangle. Release the Spacebar, then press the U key until you have the Rounded Rectangle tool in the Toolbox. Now, up in the Options Bar, enter 15 pixels in the Radius field (the higher the number, the rounder the corners). On this new layer, draw a small rounded corner shape in the top black border area (you're actually creating the first hole along the top of the filmstrip). Then, click the Simplify button in the Options Bar to convert this Shape layer into an image layer.

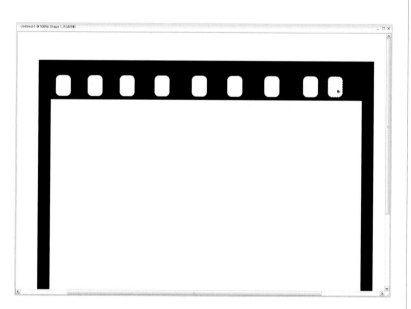

STEP FOUR: Once you've got your first shape drawn, press the letter V to switch to the Move tool, then go to the Layers palette and Control-click on this layer to put a selection around your shape. Press-and-hold Shift-Alt, then click-and-drag the shape to the right to create a dupli-cate of your shape (the Shift key keeps your dragged copy aligned horizontally, and the selection ensures that the dupli-cate shape is drawn on the same layer as the original shape instead of a new layer being created for it). Continue dragging copies until you have a whole row across the top, then press Control-D to deselect.

Continued

STEP FIVE: Press Control-0 (zero) to fit your entire filmstrip onscreen. Go back to the Layers palette and Control-click on the "row-of-rounded-rectangles" layer (Shape 1) to select all of the rectangles. Press-and-hold Shift-Alt again, but this time drag straight down to the bottom border to duplicate this row of rectangles, creating the holes along the bottom of the filmstrip. Press Control-D to deselect.

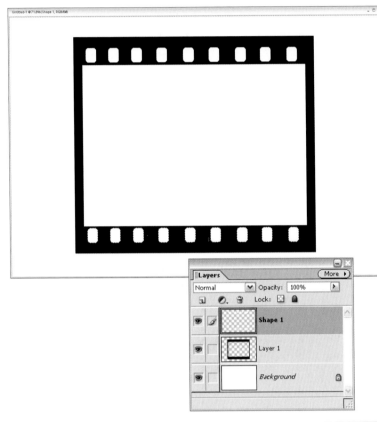

STEP SIX: Return to the Layers palette and Control-click on the little rectangles layer (Shape 1) to put a selection around all the white rounded rectangles at the top and bottom of the filmstrip. Once the selection appears, you can drag-and-drop this layer onto the Trash icon at the top of the Layers palette to delete it (you don't need it anymore—you only needed it to create the selection). In the Layers palette, click on the black rectangle layer (your selection should still be in place) and press Backspace to knock that selection out of your black rectangle. Press Control-D to deselect (we'll now refer to this as our "filmstrip layer").

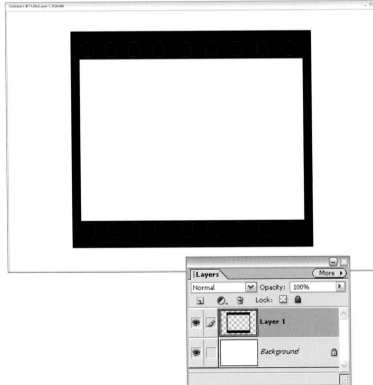

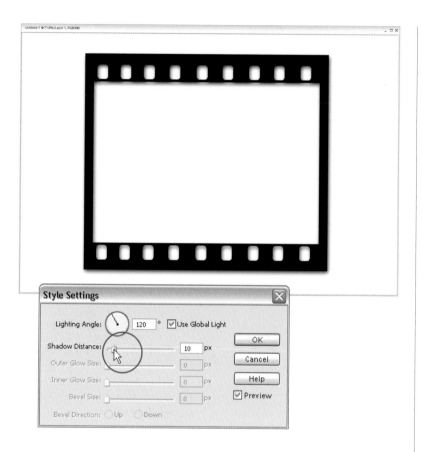

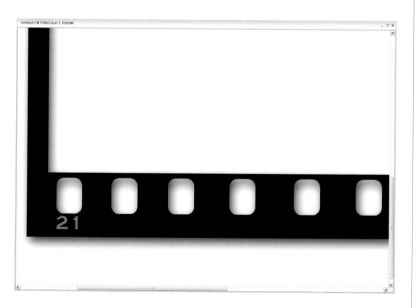

STEP SEVEN: Click on the filmstrip layer to make it active in the Layers palette. Then, go to the Styles and Effects palette (found under the Window menu), and with Layer Styles selected, choose Drop Shadows from the palette's top-right pop-up menu. Click on the Low drop shadow icon, then return to the Layers palette and double-click on the Layer Styles icon (it looks like an "ƒ") to the right of the filmstrip layer. In the resulting Style Settings dialog, decrease the Shadow Distance to 10 pixels and click OK.

STEP EIGHT: Click on the Foreground color swatch at the bottom of the Toolbox, and when the Color Picker appears, choose an olive color (I used R: 141, G: 162, and B: 68) and click OK. Now press Z to switch to the Zoom tool, and zoom into the lower left-hand corner of the filmstrip. Press the letter T to switch to the Type tool, and type the number "21" (as if this were the 21st frame on the roll). I used Adobe's font Copperplate Gothic Bold set at 9 points in the example shown here.

Continued

STEP NINE: Now, create a new blank layer by clicking on the Create a New Layer icon at the top of the Layers palette. Then, press L until you have the Polygonal Lasso tool from the Toolbox. You're going to draw a thin triangle at the bottom of the filmstrip, so click once and drag upward or downward to create a straight vertical line for the left side of your triangle. Click again to the right where you want the point of the triangle to be, then click back where you started (or double-click) to close the selection. Now, go under the Edit menu and choose Stroke (Outline) Selection. When the Stroke dialog appears, for Width choose 3 pixels and click OK to stroke your triangular selection with the olive green color that you chose earlier. Deselect by pressing Control-D. Now, switch back to the Type tool and enter "21A" to the right of your triangle (hold the Alt key and click with the Zoom tool to zoom out if you need to). We're adding this type and the triangle to make the filmstrip look more realistic.

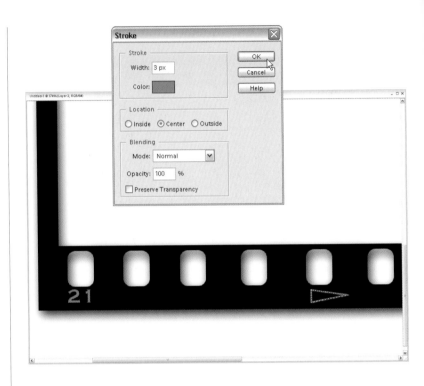

STEP TEN: Open the photo that you want to appear within your filmstrip. Switch to the Move tool and click-and-drag this photo directly into your filmstrip document. In the Layers palette, drag this image layer down in the layer stack until the photo appears directly below your filmstrip layer. If you need to resize the photo, press Control-T to bring up Free Transform, press-and-hold the Shift key, grab any corner point, and resize the photo so that the part that you want to keep appears within the center of the filmstrip. When it looks good to you, press Enter.

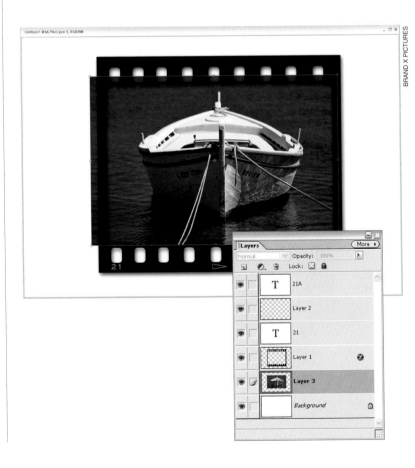

BRAND X PICTURES

STEP ELEVEN: Remember that selection we saved back in Step 2? Well, Bunky, now you need it. With your image layer active in the Layers palette, go under the Select menu and choose Load Selection. Your selection should appear in the dialog (if not, click on the down-facing arrow to open the Selection pop-up menu and choose your selection from the list). Click OK in the Load Selection dialog. Now you're going to remove the excess parts of the image so the image appears completely within the filmstrip. To do that, go under the Select menu again and choose Inverse (or just press Shift-Control-I) to select everything on this layer but the photo in the center (in other words, all the excess photo is selected). Press Backspace to erase those areas. Now, you can deselect by pressing Control-D. Go under the File menu and choose Duplicate, then choose Save As from the File menu to save this "template" as a PSD file with all of its layers intact.

STEP TWELVE: Back in your original filmstrip document, you'll need to link together all the layers that make up your filmstrip in the Layers palette, so click once in the second column of the filmstrip layer, each Type layer, the triangle layer, and your photo layer to link them together. Now press Control-T to bring up Free Transform. Move your cursor outside the bounding box, and click-and-drag to rotate your filmstrip. Press Enter to lock in your rotation, completing the effect. (*Note*: Remember how you saved the file back at Step 11, before the rotation? You did that because it can now act as a template. To use this effect again on a different photo, simply open your saved filmstrip document, trash the photo layer, open a different photo, drag it in, load your saved selection, inverse the selection, delete the excess photo areas, link the layers, rotate, and you're done!)

Photo Mount Effect

Here's a handy technique for creating visual interest by adding photo mounts to the corners of your images. This is popular with wedding and travel photographers, as well as photo retouchers. What's nice about this is that once you've created one set of mounts, you can save the layered file and use them again and again. Plus, at the end of the effect, there's a pretty cool background texture you create from scratch.

STEP ONE: Create a new document in RGB mode (the one here is 6x4"). Create a new blank layer by clicking on the Create a New Layer icon at the top of the Layers palette. Press the letter M to switch to the Rectangular Marquee tool, press-and-hold the Shift key, and draw a square selection in the middle of your image area. Press D to set your Foreground color to black, then fill your square with black by pressing Alt-Backspace. Deselect by pressing Control-D.

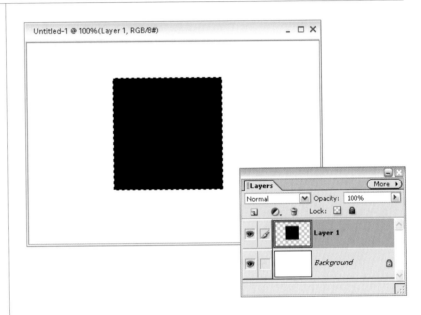

STEP TWO: Press L until you have the Polygonal Lasso tool. You're going to first draw a diagonal line through the center of your square, so click the tool just outside the square's bottom-left corner, drag diagonally beyond the square's top-right corner, and click again. Now, drag to the left beyond the top-left corner of the square and click, and then return to the bottom-left corner where you started and click one last time to complete your selection. Press Backspace to remove that area of the square, then press Control-D to deselect. You'll be left with a black triangle.

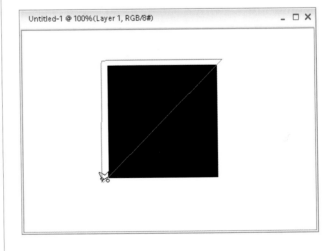

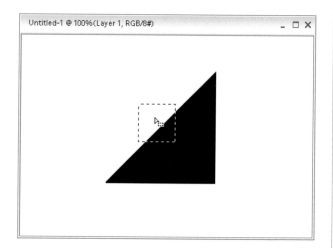

STEP THREE: Switch to the Rectangular Marquee tool again, press-and-hold the Shift key, and drag out a small square selection that's quite a bit smaller than your black triangle. With the Rectangular Marquee tool, click inside the selection and drag it so it overlaps a small section in the center of the black triangle's left side. Press the Backspace key to knock a little triangular chunk out of your black triangle. Deselect by pressing Control-D.

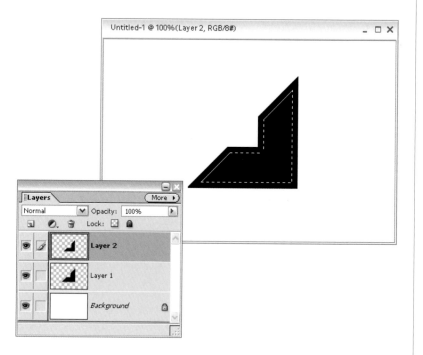

STEP FOUR: Next, press-and-hold the Control key, go to the Layers palette, and click on your shape's layer. This puts a selection around your entire shape. You'll need to shrink your selection, so go under the Select menu, under Modify, and choose Contract. When the Contract Selection dialog appears, enter 8 pixels, then click OK to shrink your selection (depending on the size and resolution of your shape, you may need to experiment with the number of pixels that you contract by). Create a new blank layer by clicking on the Create a New Layer icon at the top of the Layers palette. Fill your selection with black by pressing Alt-Backspace. Deselect by pressing Control-D.

Continued

STEP FIVE: With your new shape layer active in the Layers palette, go to the Styles and Effects palette (found under the Window menu), and with Layer Styles selected, choose Bevels from the palette's top-right pop-up menu. Click on the Simple Pillow Emboss icon, then go to the Layers palette and double-click on the Layer Styles icon (it looks like an "*f*") to the right of the top shape layer. In the resulting Style Settings dialog, decrease the Bevel Size to around 3 pixels. When you click OK, some soft highlights and shadows are added inside your contracted shape, which help make it appear embedded into the larger shape.

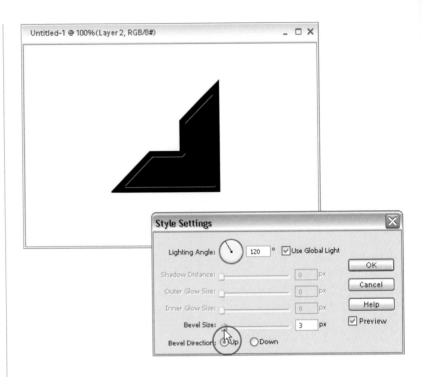

STEP SIX: In the Layers palette, click on the larger black shape layer (Layer 1), then return to the Styles and Effects palette. With Bevels still selected in the palette's top-right pop-up menu, click on the Simple Inner icon. Then, from the Styles and Effects palette's top-right pop-up menu, choose Drop Shadows and click on the Soft Edge icon. In the Layers palette, double-click on the Layer Styles icon to the right of the larger shape layer. In the resulting dialog, change the Lighting Angle to -30°, lower the Bevel Size to around 3 pixels, and click OK. In the following steps, we'll add this mount to the four corners of a photograph.

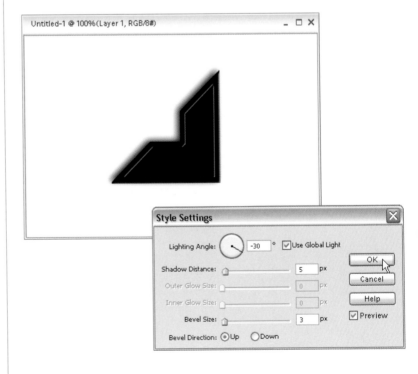

BRAND X PICTURES

STEP SEVEN: Open the photo you want to apply the effect to. Then, create a new, larger blank document in RGB mode (the document must be larger than your image). Press V to switch to the Move tool, and then click-and-drag your photo onto this new document. Your photo will show up on its own separate layer. Use the Move tool to center your photo within the image area.

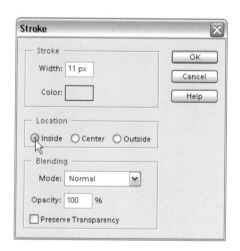

STEP EIGHT: You're going to add a border around your photo, so choose Stroke (Outline) Selection from the Edit menu. In the Stroke dialog, enter 11 pixels for Width, choose Inside for Location, and then click on the Color swatch and choose a light gray in the Color Picker. When you click OK, a Polaroid-like border appears around your photo (which can be seen in the capture in the following step).

Continued

STEP NINE: Go back to your photo mount document and merge your two shape layers together by clicking on the top layer in the Layers palette and pressing Control-E. Then, choose Simplify Layer from the Layer menu. Switch to the Move tool, click on the photo frame mount, and drag-and-drop it onto your photo document. It'll probably be too big, so you'll need to scale it down to size: Press Control-T to bring up Free Transform. Press-and-hold the Shift key, grab a corner point, and drag inward to scale the photo mount down to size. When the size looks right, move your cursor within the bounding box, and click-and-drag it into position at the bottom-right corner of your image. Press Enter to lock in your transformation.

STEP TEN: Duplicate your photo frame mount by going under the Layer menu, under New, and choosing Layer via Copy (or by pressing Control-J). Then, go under the Image menu, under Rotate, and choose Flip Layer Horizontal to flip your duplicate layer (this will become your bottom-left mount). Using the Move tool, click-and-drag to position this mount in the bottom-left corner of the image. Now, you'll need to repeat this process for the other two corners: Duplicate the bottom-left mount layer, choose Layer 90° Right from the Rotate submenu, and position it in the top left-hand corner. Then, duplicate that mount layer, choose Flip Layer Horizontal, and position it in the top right-hand corner.

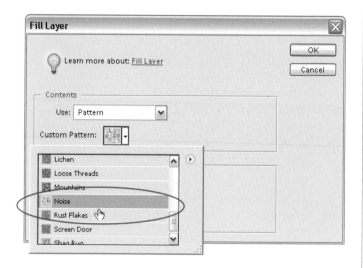

STEP ELEVEN: Now you're going to add a background texture. In the Layers palette, click on the Background layer and press Control-J to duplicate it. Choose Fill Layer from the Edit menu. In the Fill Layer dialog, choose Pattern from the Use pop-up menu, and then click on the Custom Pattern thumbnail to bring up the Pattern Picker. Click on the Pattern Picker's flyout menu and choose Texture Fill to load that set of texture patterns. Return to the flyout menu again and choose Small List so you can see the patterns by name. Choose the pattern named Noise, but don't click OK yet.

STEP TWELVE: In the Fill Layer dialog, lower the Opacity amount to 29% and click OK to apply this texture to the Background copy layer. Press Control-L to bring up Levels. In the Levels dialog, grab the highlight Output Levels slider and drag it to the left a little to darken the pattern and make it look a bit like marble. Click OK in the Levels dialog and the effect is complete.

Quick Slide Mounts

Several years ago, I wrote a Photoshop tutorial on how to make your own digital slide mounts. The end result looked authentic, but getting there was pretty brutal, because creating rounded corners for your slide took a series of blurs, Levels adjustments, and a host of other "pain-in-the-butt" steps. The original effect took 10 to 15 minutes to create. Now it's down to 60 seconds—thanks to features in Photoshop Elements—and that's good because displaying your photos in slide mounts (for online portfolios, wedding shots, etc.) is becoming popular once again.

STEP ONE: Create a new document in RGB mode at whatever size and resolution you'd like. Click on your Foreground color swatch at the bottom of the Toolbox and choose a light gray in the Color Picker (I used R: 212, G: 212, and B: 212). Press U until you have the Rounded Rectangle tool from the Toolbox. Up in the Options Bar, the Radius setting should be set to 10 pixels by default, which is fine for low-res, 72-ppi images (but enter 40 pixels for 300-ppi, high-res images). Click-and-drag out a rounded rectangle that has the same proportions as a typical slide. You'll notice Elements automatically creates a Shape layer for this rectangle in the Layers palette, but we want this layer to be a pixel-based layer, so in the Options Bar, click on the Simplify button.

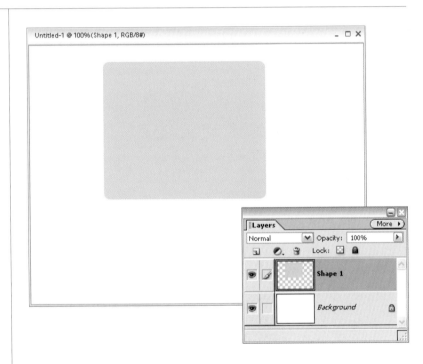

STEP TWO: Press M to switch to the Rectangular Marquee tool and drag out a horizontal selection within the center of the gray, round-cornered rectangle. Once your selection is in place, just press Backspace to knock a hole out of your slide, which creates the basic slide shape. Deselect by pressing Control-D.

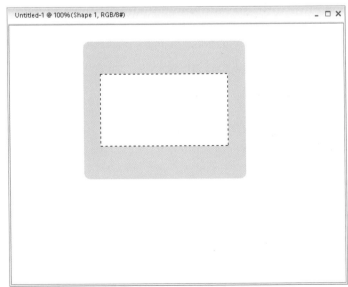

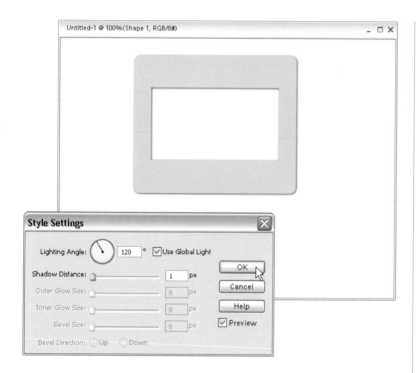

STEP THREE: Go to the Styles and Effects palette (found under the Window menu), and with Layer Styles selected, choose Drop Shadows from the palette's top-right pop-up menu. Click on the Low drop shadow icon. Now, go under the Layer menu, under Layer Style, and choose Style Settings. In the Style Settings dialog, decrease the Shadow Distance to 1 pixel and click OK. This shadow will cast onto the photo that you'll place on the layer beneath the slide in the last two steps of this technique, making the photo appear as if it's inside the mount itself.

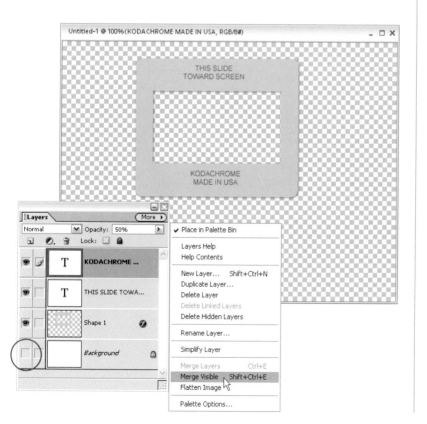

STEP FOUR: To finish off our slide template, we'll add some text for added realism (I call it a template, because once you've built this one slide, you can use it as a template to create as many slides as you'd like). Press D to set your Foreground color to black, then press the letter T to switch to the Type tool. Add your type (the font used here is Arial in all caps with the Center Text icon selected in the Options Bar). Now, lower the Opacity setting for your Type layers to 50% in the Layers palette to help them blend in with the slide. Then, click on the Eye icon next to the Background layer to hide it, and choose Merge Visible from the Layers palette's flyout menu. This leaves you with a single layer with the completed slide on it. Click on the far-left empty box next to the Background layer to make it visible again.

Continued

STEP FIVE: Now for the fun part: Open a photo you want to appear within your slide, press V to switch to the Move tool, and click-and-drag the image into your slide template. In the Layers palette, drag the photo layer below your slide layer. To get your photo small enough to fit inside the slide window, press Control-T to bring up Free Transform. Press-and-hold the Shift key, grab a corner point, and drag inward to shrink it until it's just slightly larger than the center opening of the slide. Press Enter to lock in your resize.

STEP SIX: Merge the photo layer and the slide layer together by clicking on the top slide layer and pressing Control-E. Then click within the document window and drag your completed slide into a new document. Now you can go back to your template and create more slides: Just press Control-Z to undo the merge, drag the photo layer to the Trash icon at the top of the Layers palette, repeat Step 5 using a different photo, and then repeat this step. In this final piece, I made four slides and rotated each in a different direction using Free Transform.

Painted Edges Technique

This technique, where you essentially hide the photo and then paint it back in, is particularly popular for landscape and portrait photographers; but it works so well, for so many different styles of photos, that you'll be amazed at how many other uses you'll find for it.

STEP ONE: Open the photo you want to apply the effect to.

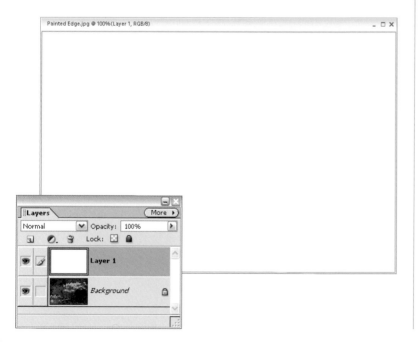

STEP TWO: Create a new blank layer by clicking on the Create a New Layer icon at the top of the Layers palette. Press D and then X to set your Foreground color to white, then fill this new layer with white by pressing Alt-Backspace (your image will disappear, but we'll get it back in a minute).

Continued

STEP THREE: Press the E key to switch to the Eraser tool. Go up to the Options Bar, and bring up the Brush Picker by clicking on the brush thumbnail. You're going to load a set of brushes, so click on the Brush Picker's flyout menu (it's the right-facing black triangle in the top-right corner of the Picker) and choose Load Brushes. In the Load dialog, click on the Thick Heavy Brushes set and click Load. (*Note:* You may need to navigate on your hard drive to find the brushes. If so, find the Photoshop Elements 3 folder, open the Presets folder, then open the Brushes folder, and the presets will appear.) These brushes will automatically be added to the end of the Brush Picker, so scroll down near the end of the Picker and click on the first Thick Heavy Brush, the 111-pixel Flat Bristle brush.

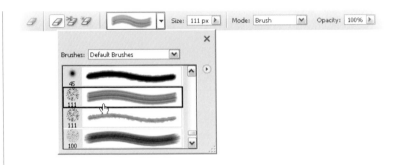

STEP FOUR: To help you see what you want to paint back in, lower the Opacity of the top white layer to around 50% in the Layers palette. Now you can paint over the areas you want to be visible. Start painting a few strokes with this brush from left to right across your image area. As you do, the original photo will paint back in. One of the cool things about this brush is that it has some gaps in it (like painting with a real dry brush), which helps give it a realistic, painted look. Take a look at the bottom stroke in particular and you can see the gaps (some upper areas don't have as many gaps because I painted more than one stroke over those areas).

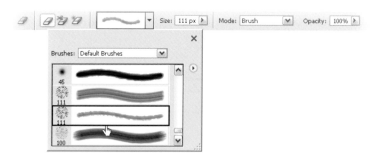

STEP FIVE: Go back to the Brush Picker in the Options Bar and choose the next 111-pixel brush (the Rough Flat Bristle brush) in the Picker. Paint a stroke along the top of the painted effect with only a very small portion of this brush tip extending over the top of the already painted areas. This adds a more random, spattered look along the top edge. Do the same along the bottom. Raise the Opacity of this white layer in the Layers palette back to 100% so you can see your painting effect.

STEP SIX: For the finished piece, you can add a line of text. Press D to set your Foreground color to black, then press T to switch to the Type tool and enter your text (the typeface used here is Minion).

Distressed Edge Effect

For years now, we've all been doing a cheesy "Diffuse filter version" of this technique to create edge effects, but generally, the pros have never used it (instead they've always used third-party frame plug-ins and other stock photo sources for a more realistic edge effect). Well, I came up with a way to create edges that look like the ones the pros use, and although it takes a little more effort than the "Diffuse cheesy version," it looks vastly better.

STEP ONE: Open the photo you want to use in this effect, and press D to set your Background color to white. Press Control-A to select the entire photo, then go under the Layer menu, under New, and choose Layer via Cut (or press Shift-Control-J) to cut the photo from the Background layer and copy it onto its own separate layer (Layer 1).

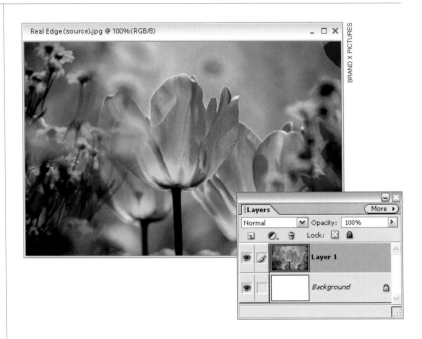

STEP TWO: To create an edge, you'll need to add a little breathing room around your photo, so go under the Image menu, under Resize, and choose Canvas Size. When the dialog appears, ensure the Relative checkbox is on, enter 2 inches in both the Width and Height fields, choose White from the Canvas Extension Color pop-up menu, and click OK to add some white space around your photo (which can be seen in the following step).

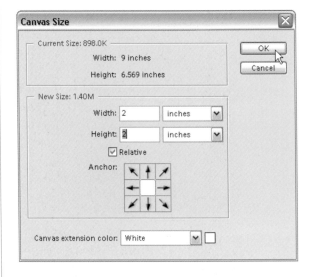

STEP THREE: Now that you've got that white space, you'll need to add a thick black stroke around your photo. Choose Stroke (Outline) Selection from the Edit menu. In the Stroke dialog, set the Width to 10 pixels, set the Location to Inside (to give your stroke straight corners rather than the default rounded corners), and click on the Color swatch and choose black in the Color Picker. Click OK to apply the black stroke around your photo.

STEP FOUR: We're going to use different photos to help us create our edges, so open a photo that you'd like to use for one of your four distressed edges. Photos that have objects with visible straight edges in them (such as buildings) work best. The lines don't have to be perfectly horizontal or vertical, because you can always rotate it once it's in place.

Continued

STEP FIVE: Go under the Enhance menu, under Adjust Color, and choose Remove Color (or just press Shift-Control-U) to remove the color from your photo. Then, go under the Enhance menu, under Adjust Lighting, and choose Brightness/ Contrast. You're going to adjust the Contrast to create an ultra-high-con- trast image that's just short of looking bitmapped. In this instance, moving the Contrast slider all the way to the right gives us a good messy edge; but adjust yours until you've created an edge within your image that you like. Now, drag the Brightness slider to the right to remove even more black from the image. When it looks good to you, click OK.

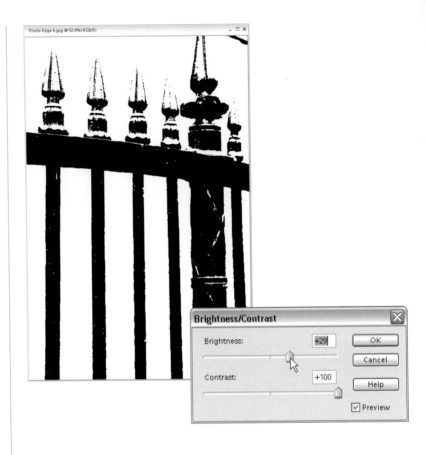

STEP SIX: Switch to any selection tool you're comfortable with (I used the Rectangular Marquee tool in this case, but you could just as easily use the Polygonal Lasso tool) and select the edge you want to use in your main image. Press V to switch to the Move tool, then click within your selection and drag it over into your original photo document, which puts this edge piece on its own separate layer in the Layers palette.

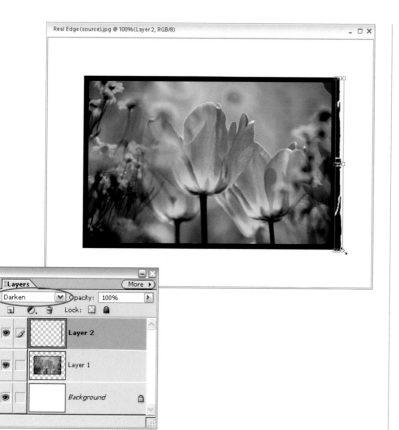

STEP SEVEN: Most likely the edge is too large, so press Control-T to bring up Free Transform. Press-and-hold the Shift key, grab a corner point, and drag inward to scale it down until it fits. (*Note:* If you can't see the corner points of the Free Transform bounding box, press Control-0 [zero] to zoom out.) Click within the bounding box and position the edge on a side of your photo. You may need to click outside the bounding box and drag to rotate the edge, especially when applying it to the left or right side of the photo. When it looks good to you, press Enter to lock in your transformation. In the Layers palette, change the layer blend mode from Normal to Darken (this makes it easier to align the edge and blends it in with the black stroke around your photo).

STEP EIGHT: You'll repeat Steps 4–7 until you've created new edges for the other three sides of your photo: Open a new image, remove the color (Shift-Control-U), bring up Brightness/Contrast, adjust the sliders in the dialog until it looks good to you, select your edge, drag it into your photo, size and position the edge using Free Transform (Control-T), and change the layer blend mode to Darken. Once all the pieces are in place you may need to "clean up" some of the edges, so press the letter E to switch to the Eraser tool, go to the Layers palette and click on the edge layer that you want to erase from, then erase over any chunks along the side that you don't want in the image, which completes the effect.

Ripped Edge Technique

While working on another book, I showed some color proofs to a friend and he asked how we had created the ripped edge effect that we had used on long menus and the Options Bar (we had "ripped" away parts of menus and the Options Bar when they were too long to fit on the page). He thought I should include the technique in a book, so here it is.

STEP ONE: Open the image you want to rip. Press D and then X to set your Background color to white. You need the image cut from the Background layer, so press Control-A to select your image, then go under the Layer menu, under New, and choose Layer via Cut (or press Shift-Control-J) to put the image on its own layer (Layer 1).

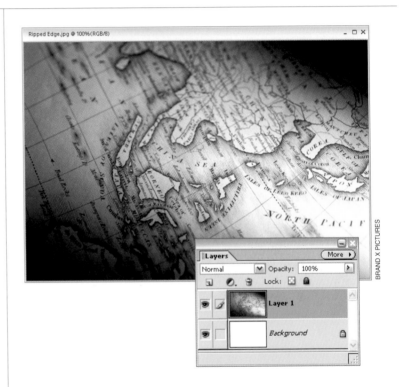

STEP TWO: Press L to switch to the Lasso tool, and draw a selection around the part of the image that you want to keep. I started by drawing a jaggy line through the document from top to bottom (this will be the part of the image that's torn), then I dragged outside the image window, going all the way around to the point where I started making my selection. (*Note:* To add to your selection, press-and-hold the Shift key while using the Lasso tool, or to subtract from your selection, press-and-hold the Alt key.)

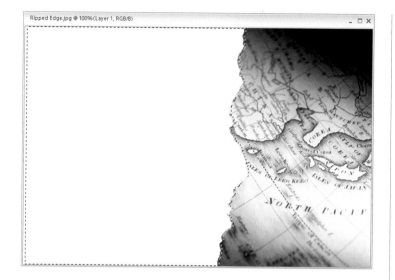

STEP THREE: Go under the Select menu and choose Inverse (or press Shift-Control-I) to inverse your selection, selecting the part of your image that you no longer want visible. Press Backspace to delete this area. Then, press the Right Arrow key (or whichever arrow key matches the direction your tear is in) about four times to nudge your selection over about 4 pixels into your image.

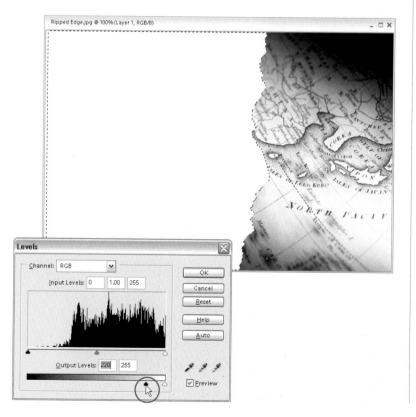

STEP FOUR: Press Control-L to bring up the Levels dialog. At the bottom of the dialog, drag the shadow Output Levels slider to the right until it reads 220, and then click OK. This lightens the 4-pixel selected area to almost white. Press Control-D to deselect.

Continued

STEP FIVE: Go to the Styles and Effects palette (found under the Window menu), and with Layer Styles selected, choose Drop Shadows from the palette's top-right pop-up menu. Click on the Soft Edge icon, then in the Layers palette, double-click on the Layer Styles icon to the right of the image layer. In the resulting dialog, decrease the Shadow Distance to 0 pixels, change the Lighting Angle to 179°, and click OK.

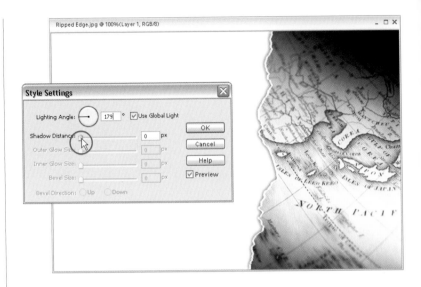

STEP SIX: Now just press T to switch to the Type tool and add any type you'd like to complete the effect. (The typeface used here is Gill Sans Light.)

220 EPC SSO

4X5 FILM

11

This chapter is actually much cooler than its subtitle implies; it's just that I couldn't come up with a cooler

Different Strokes
Artistic Effects

sounding name than "Artistic Effects," so don't hold that against the effects themselves—it's not their fault. I was afraid the name might scare some people away, because they might think, "Oh, that's painting and working with brushes, and I can't paint, so I'll just skip over this chapter and head on over to 'Advertising Effects.'" I don't think the Gary Coleman reference in the chapter head helped sell this chapter much either, but there's a trick in here for taking a photograph and making it look like you really can paint. It's called "The Evil Deceit Trick." Not really, but I bet if it were, that's the first one you'd turn to. Yes, you would. Oh come on, you act like I hardly know you.

Faking Hand-Drawn Silhouette Illustrations

The inspiration for this technique came from a T-shirt I saw for a zoo. You start with objects or people in photographs and convert them into silhouettes, and the final effect looks as if you drew the figures in Adobe Illustrator. In this project, we're going to build a design for a golf competition by converting a photo into a drawing.

STEP ONE: Start by opening the photo that you want to change into a drawing. Use any selection tool you'd like to put a selection around the object (I used the Magnetic Lasso tool). As usual, the Magnetic Lasso tool didn't do a perfect job all by itself, so after it was done, I had to add in some areas to the selection by pressing L until I had the Lasso tool, pressing-and-holding the Shift key, and clicking-and-dragging to select the additional areas. (*Note:* To subtract from your selection, press-and-hold the Alt key while using the Lasso.)

STEP TWO: Once the object is fully selected, go under the Layer menu, under New, and choose Layer via Copy (or press Control-J) to copy the selection onto its own separate layer (Layer 1) above the Background layer.

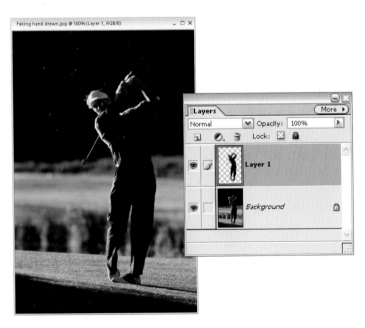

BRAND X PICTURES

STEP THREE: Open the photo that will serve as a background for the object (in this case, it's a photo of a sunset). Go to the Layers palette and click on the Create a New Layer icon to create a new blank layer. Then, press M to switch to the Rectangular Marquee tool and draw a rectangular selection across the bottom quarter of your photo. Press D to set your Foreground color to black, then press Alt-Backspace to fill this rectangle with black. Press Control-D to deselect.

STEP FOUR: Switch back to the original photo, and with your object's duplicate layer active in the Layers palette, press the letter V to switch to the Move tool. Click on the object and drag it over onto your sunset background. Once it's in your sunset document, you'll probably need to scale it down in size, so press Control-T to bring up Free Transform. Press-and-hold the Shift key, grab a corner point, and drag inward to shrink the object. When it's the size you want, press Enter to lock in your transformation.

Continued

STEP FIVE: Your Foreground color should still be black, so all you have to do is press Shift-Alt-Backspace to fill the object with black, creating a hand-drawn silhouette effect (holding the Shift key fills just the object with black and not the entire layer).

STEP SIX: The final step is simply to add some type with the Type tool (I used the font Copperplate Regular), which completes the effect.

Colorizing Line Art

Colorizing line art is really very simple: Start out by switching to RGB color mode, create selections inside your line art, and then colorize the selections on layers. Sounds easy enough, so let's get started.

STEP ONE: Scan your line art image into Photoshop Elements in RGB mode if possible, because your image has to be in a color mode if you're going to add color to it. If your line art image is already in Grayscale mode, you can simply go under the Image menu, under Mode, and choose RGB Color.

STEP TWO: Your scanned image will appear on the Background layer, but we need to convert it to a regular layer. In the Layers palette, double-click directly on the name "Background" and a dialog will appear in which you can name your new layer. Name it "Lines" and click OK to convert your Background layer into a regular editable layer.

Continued

STEP THREE: Create a new blank layer by clicking on the Create a New Layer icon at the top of the Layers palette. Then, go under the Layer menu, under New, and choose Background From Layer. This converts your just-created blank layer into a Background layer (we need this empty Background layer because it provides a white backdrop to work upon).

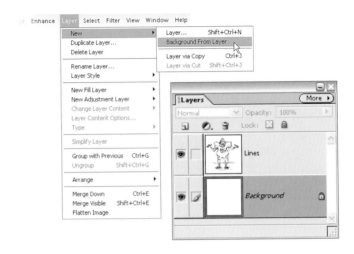

STEP FOUR: In the Layers palette, click on your Lines layer to make it active. Change its layer blend mode from Normal to Multiply. This makes the white areas of your Lines layer transparent, leaving only the black lines visible (you can't see this onscreen because of your white Background layer below, but it will all become very "clear" soon—sorry, couldn't help myself). Press W to switch to the Magic Wand tool. Click once inside an area you want to colorize and the Magic Wand tool will select that area. In this example, I clicked on the football player's jersey. (*Note:* You can use any selection tool you'd like: Lasso, Selection Brush, etc. Also, you can press-and-hold the Shift key to add to your selection, or press-and-hold the Alt key to subtract from your selection. Both shortcuts work with most selection tools.)

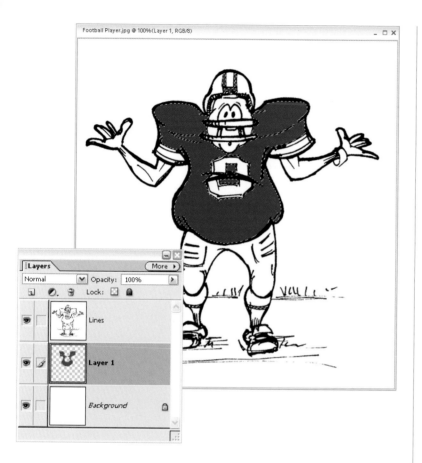

STEP FIVE: Press-and-hold the Control key and click on the Create a New Layer icon. This creates a new layer directly beneath your Lines layer, and this is where you'll add your color for the jersey. Click on the Foreground color at the bottom of the Toolbox, choose your color in the resulting Color Picker, then press Alt-Backspace to fill your selected area with color. Because your Lines layer is in Multiply mode, you can see the color through the white areas on that layer. Press Control-D to deselect.

STEP SIX: You'll continue this same process to colorize the rest of the image—just repeat Steps 4 and 5 to complete the effect. You put each color on its own layer because if you later want to change colors, you can just Control-click on that color layer in the Layers palette, choose your new color from the Foreground color swatch, and fill the selection with the new color. (For the final image here, I pressed B to switch to the Brush tool, chose green as my Foreground color, and on a new layer, I painted in some grass with a medium, hard-edged brush.)

From Photo to Oil Painting

I had heard that Ted LoCascio (our former Senior Associate Designer at *Photoshop User* magazine) had come up with a pretty amazing technique for turning any photo into an oil painting, and as soon as he showed it to me, I asked him (okay, I begged him) to let me share it here in the book. It's without a doubt one of the best-looking, easiest oil techniques I've ever seen.

STEP ONE: Open the photo you want to apply the effect to.

STEP TWO: Go under the Enhance menu, under Adjust Color, and choose Hue/Saturation (or just press Control-U). When the dialog appears, increase the Saturation to 50 and click OK to make your photo's colors more vivid.

STEP THREE: Go under the Filter menu and choose Filter Gallery. In the middle column of the Filter Gallery dialog, click on the Distort set to expand its set of filters, and then click on the Glass thumbnail. Set the Distortion amount to 3, set the Smoothness to 3, choose Canvas from the Texture pop-up menu, and set the Scaling to 79%. Don't click OK yet.

STEP FOUR: Click on the New Effect Layer icon in the bottom-right corner of the dialog (right next to the Trash icon). Click on the Artistic set, and then click on the Paint Daubs thumbnail. Set the Brush Size to 4, set Sharpness to 1, and choose Simple in the Brush Type pop-up menu. Don't click OK just yet....

Continued

STEP FIVE: Click on the New Effect Layer icon again at the bottom of the dialog. Click on the Brush Strokes set, and then click on the Angled Strokes thumbnail. Set the Direction Balance to 46, Stroke Length to 3, and Sharpness to 1. No, don't click OK yet.

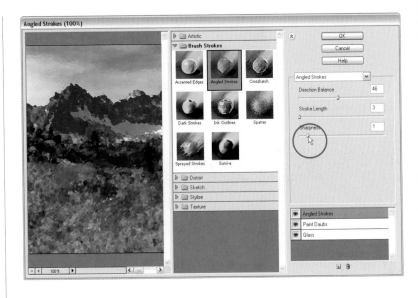

STEP SIX: Click on the New Effect Layer icon one last time at the bottom of the dialog. To add a canvas-like texture, click on the Texture set, then click on the Texturizer thumbnail. Choose Canvas in the Texture pop-up menu, set the Scaling to 65%, set Relief to 2, and choose Top Left for Light. *Now* you can click OK to apply all four filters to your photo.

STEP SEVEN: Duplicate this filter layer by going under the Layer menu, under New, and choosing Layer via Copy (or by pressing Control-J). Then, go under the Enhance menu, under Adjust Color, and choose Remove Color (or press Shift-Control-U) to remove all the color from this layer. In the Layers palette, change the layer blend mode of this layer from Normal to Overlay.

STEP EIGHT: Go under the Filter menu, under Stylize, and choose Emboss. When the Emboss dialog appears, set the Angle to 135°, the Height to 1 pixel, and the Amount to 500%, and click OK. Then, go to the Layers palette and lower the Opacity of this layer to 40%, to give the oil painting effect.

Instant Woodcut Effect

This is a quick effect that allows you to instantly transform a color RGB image into that drawn woodcut effect that's popping up everywhere. We see this effect on the Web quite often where a woodcut object is used as an icon, but the effect works just as well in other projects.

STEP ONE: Open the image that you want to turn into a woodcut, then double-click on the Background layer. In the resulting dialog, just click OK and your Background layer will become a regular layer (named Layer 0 by default). Make a copy of this layer by dragging it to the Create a New Layer icon at the top of the Layers palette.

BRAND X PICTURES

STEP TWO: Go under the Filter menu, under Other, and choose High Pass. In the High Pass dialog, enter a Radius of 2.5 pixels and click OK. Now, go under the Enhance menu, under Adjust Color, and choose Remove Color (or press Shift-Control-U) to remove all the color from your duplicate layer.

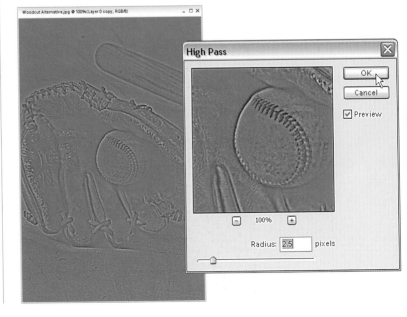

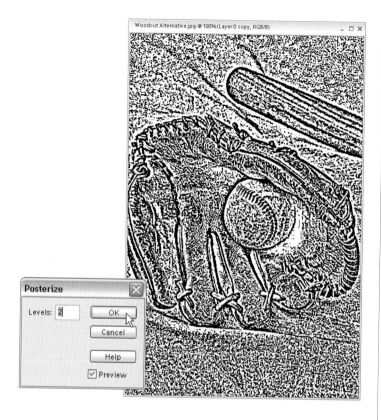

STEP THREE: Go to the Filter menu, under Adjustments, and choose Posterize. When the dialog appears, enter 2 in the Levels field and click OK.

STEP FOUR: To see the effect take shape, change the layer blend mode in the Layers palette from Normal to Multiply. Next, click on Layer 0 (the bottom layer) in the Layers palette to make it active and lower the Opacity of this layer to 60% to complete the effect. (You'll have to use your own judgment, but somewhere between 60–70% opacity usually looks about right.)

Photo to Line Art Morph

This is a great little trick that morphs a photograph into line art. I've seen this used numerous times, most recently in a backlit ad on the terminal wall at LAX. Those who remember the award-winning video for the song "Take On Me," by the group a-ha, will experience a momentary 80s flashback when they try this technique.

STEP ONE: Open the image you want to morph into a line drawing. Go under the Layer menu, under New, and choose Layer via Copy (or press Control-J) to create a duplicate of your Background layer.

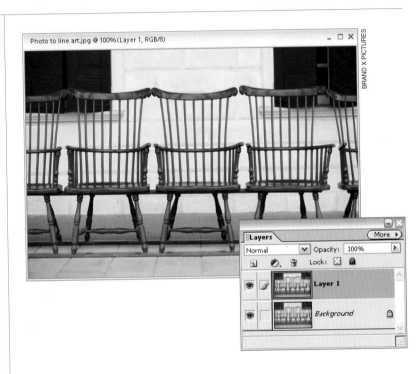

STEP TWO: While on this duplicate layer, go under the Filter menu, under Stylize, and choose Find Edges (don't worry, there are no dialog options here—Photoshop Elements automatically finds the edges within your document). Then, go under the Enhance menu, under Adjust Color, and choose Remove Color (or press Shift-Control-U) to remove all the color from the duplicate layer. (Note: Applying the Find Edges filter introduces lots of highly saturated patches of color, so removing the color is a must.)

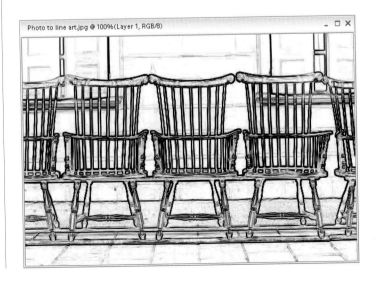

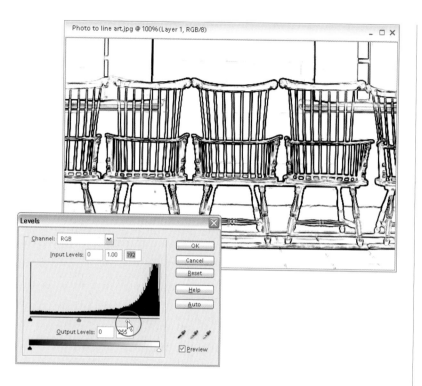

STEP THREE: Now that the color is gone, we need to remove some of the leftover "noise" and unnecessary detail created by the Find Edges filter. Press Control-L to bring up the Levels dialog. Drag the highlight Input Levels slider to the left to "blow out" the extra detail, leaving just the most substantial lines. When it looks good to you, click OK.

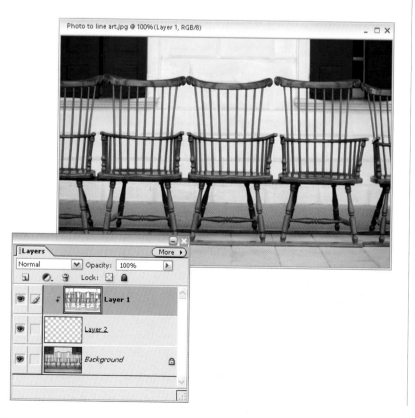

STEP FOUR: In the Layers palette, ensure your black-and-white line layer is active, then Control-click on the Create a New Layer icon at the top of the palette to create a new blank layer beneath your line layer. Click back on your line layer to make it active and choose Group with Previous from the Layer menu (or press Control-G) to group this line layer with the blank layer below it, which will hide the line layer onscreen.

Continued

STEP FIVE: Press D to set your Fore-ground color to black. Switch to the Gradient tool by pressing the G key, and then press Enter to bring up the Gradient Picker. Click on the Foreground to Transparent gradient (it's the second one in the Picker). Now, go to the Layers palette and click on the empty layer below your line layer to make it active. With the Gradient tool, click on the right side of your image and drag to the left. After you drag out your gradient, the left side of the top layer will become transparent, revealing the original photo on the layer below, and it will smoothly blend into the line art version of your image on the right.

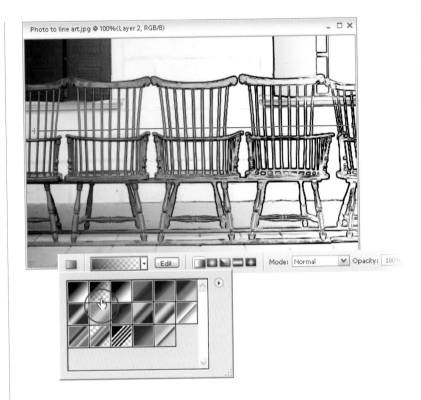

STEP SIX: If you want to add a little color to your line art, change the layer blend mode of your gradient layer in the Layers palette to Lighten (which I used here), Vivid Light, or (for a lot of color) Overlay; this completes the effect.

30-second portrait, 12
3D and packaging effects, 203–229
    3D hardcover book effect, 208–212
    3D magazine effect, 204–207
    3D photo cubes, 224–229
    creating 3D packaging, 213–217
    creating DVD effect, 218–223
3D hardcover book effect, 208–212
3D magazine effect, 204–207
3D packaging, creating, 213–217
3D photo cubes, 224–229
3D Transform filter, 208, 224
3D type, instant, 108–110

A
Academy Awards. *See* Oscar Awards
ad-libbing, 79–105
Adams, Ansel, 6
adding
    captions to photos, 139
    drop shadows, 46
    highlights, 213
    lens flare, 198–199
    motion effects, 34–37
    objects behind existing objects, 22–25
    persons into existing images, 22
    perspective to images, 213
    photo mounts to corners of
        images, 238
    shading, 213
    small reflections, 188
Adobe Illustrator, 260
ads
    classified, 94–97
    Levi's print, 122
    magazine, 88
    print, 14, 17, 28, 51, 64, 70, 94
advertising effects, 79–105
    backlit photo backgrounds, 80–83
    classified ad effect, 94–97
    credit cards from photos, 98–99
    fade-away reflection, 91–93
    high-tech transparent info boxes,
        100–103
    quick elegant product background,
        84–87
    quick product shot background,
        88–90
    turning logos into brushes, 104–105
age, gel design, 169
airbrush artist, chrome effect created by
        traditional, 156
American Express, 98
American Life, 17

Apple's Aqua interface, 169
Apple's iLife product box, 148
Aqua interface, Apple's, 169
aqua-like button, 169
art
    colorizing line, 263–265
    line, 272–274
artistic effects, 259–274
    colorizing line art, 263–265
    faking hand-drawn silhouette
        illustrations, 260–262
    instant woodcut effect, 270–271
    photo to line art morph, 272–274
    from photo to oil painting, 266–269
artists, chrome effects created by
        traditional airbrush, 156
attention, focusing, 43–61
    backscreening, 44–45
    magnifying glass trick, 58–61
    popping out images, 51–53
    snapshot focus effect, 54–57
    vignetting attention, 48–50
attention, vignetting, 48–50
Awards, Oscar, 195

B
background image, very busy or very
        dark, 44
background objects, moving in front of
        type, 120–121
background textures, creating, 238
backgrounds
    backlit photo, 80–83
    blurred, 2–3
    for portraits, 88
    product shot, 12
    products displayed on white, 91
    quick elegant product, 84–87
    quick product shot, 88–90
    selecting and enlarging part of, 58
    soft-edged portrait, 12–13
backlit photo backgrounds, 80–83
backscreen area, 139
backscreening, 44–45
    popular effect in print and
        multimedia, 44
badges, convention, 98
Bar, Options, 104, 254
billboards, 26, 136
black-and-white images, colorizing,
        67–69
black-and-white photos, 6
blank pages, starting, 21
blowout look, trendy fashion, 17–19

blur, zoom, 34
blurred background, 2–3
blurring copy of photo, 2
book cover, 136
book effect, 3D hardcover, 208–212
border technique, soft, 48
boxes
    Apple's iLife product, 148
    high-tech transparent info, 100–103
    video, 213
brands, store, 126
Brush Picker, 104
brushed metal, 152–153
brushes, turning logos into, 104–105
burned-in effect around edges of
        images, 12
burned-in edge effect, 14
burning in portraits, 14–16
buttons
    aqua-like, 169
    gettin' gelly with, 169–173
    yummy metal Web, 174–177

C
captions, adding to photos, 139
cards
    credit, 98–99
    frequent flyer, 98
    frequent shopper, 98
    phone, 98
    slot club, 98
carved in stone, 129–131
carved type effects, 129
cast shadow
    perspective, 180–183
    reverse, 184–187
catalog shots, 88
CD covers, 17
CD-ROMs, Photoshop training, 100
chrome effect created by traditional
        airbrush artists, 156
chrome gradient, reflective, 156–160
circles, type on, 114–116
classified ad effect, 94–97
client logos, 104
client photos, displaying, 232
Clipping Group, 117
clothing, 126
club cards, slot, 98
Coleman, Gary, 259
collage projects, background for, 200
collages, blending images for instant,
        32–33
color, in living, 63–77

colorizing black-and-white images, 67–69
instant stock photo effect, 64–66
painting away color, 70–71
photo tinting, 76–77
sepia tone effect, 74–75
visual color change, 72–73
color, painting away, 70–71
color change, visual, 72–73
color effects, 63–77
  colorizing black-and-white images, 67–69
  instant stock photo effect, 64–66
  painting away color, 70–71
  photo tinting, 76–77
  sepia tone effect, 74–75
  visual color change, 72–73
color mode, RGB, 263
color photos, tinting, 76
color RGB image, transforming into woodcut effect, 270
color effect, wild, 64
colorizing
  black-and-white images, 67–69
  grayscale images, 67
  line art, 263–265
colors, changing in product shots, 72
commands, Hue/Saturation, 67
company, fictitious tennis racket, 91
Computer Arts magazine, 204
computer magazines, UK, 204
contrasty grayscale conversion, 74
convention badges, 98
conversion, contrasty grayscale, 74
converting photos into drawing, 260
Cool American Color Effects, 63
cool type effects, 107–133
  carved in stone, 129–131
  distressed type, 126–128
  grunge type, 122–125
  instant 3D type, 108–110
  moving background objects in front of type, 120–121
  perspective type logo, 111–113
  putting images into type, 117–119
  transparent TV type, 132–133
  type on circles, 114–116
cover design, 204
covers
  book, 136
  CD, 17
  magazine, 14, 136
Cradle 2 the Grave (Li), 17
create-it-from-scratch-in-60-second effects, 84

create-something-from-nothing techniques, 200
credit cards from photos, 98–99
cubes, 3D photo, 224–229

D

damaged type, 126
depth, create, 108
depth and focus, creating, 46
depth-of-field effect, 4–5
design, cover, 204
design age, gel, 169
designing credit cards, 98
different strokes, 259–274
diffuse filter version, 250
digital pixel effect, 136–138
digital slide mounts, 244
Dirty Dancing (movie), 43
Displace filter, 144
Displacement Map technique, 144
Distort feature, Free Transform's, 111
distressed edge effect, 250–253
distressed type, 126–128
drawings, converting photos into, 260
drop shadow effects, 180
drop shadows, adding, 46
DVD
  interface, 100
  packaging, 218
DVD effect, creating, 218–223

E

edge effects, 231–256
  burned-in, 14
  distressed, 250–253
  distressed edge effect, 250–253
  filmstrip templates, 232–237
  painted edges technique, 247–249
  photo mount effect, 238–243
  quick slide mounts, 244–246
  ripped edge technique, 254–256
edge technique, ripped, 254–256
edges, softening, 48
edges technique, painted, 247–249
editorial purposes, photos taken for, 34
effects
  3D hardcover book, 208–212
  3D magazine, 204–207
  adding motion, 34–37
  burned in, 12
  burned-in edge, 14
  carved type, 129
  chrome, 156
  classified ad, 94–97

create-it-from-scratch-in-60-second, 84
creating DVD, 218–223
depth-of-field, 4–5
digital pixel, 136–138
distressed edge, 250–253
drop shadow, 180–183
hand-tinted, 67
instant stock photo, 64–66
instant woodcut, 270–271
lens, 195
lightning, 166–168
one-point perspective, 111
photo mount, 238–243
photographic special, 1
sepia tone, 74–75
shadow, 184
snapshot focus, 54–57
transforming color RGB images into woodcut, 270
wild color, 64
effects, 3D and packaging, 203–229
  3D hardcover book effect, 208–212
  3D magazine effect, 204–207
  3D photo cubes, 224–229
  creating 3D packaging, 213–217
  creating DVD effect, 218–223
effects, advertising, 79–105
  backlit photo that grounds, 80–83
  classified ad effect, 94–97
  credit cards from photos, 98–99
  fade-away reflection, 91–93
  high-tech transparent info boxes, 100–103
  quick elegant product background, 84–87
  quick product shot background, 88–90
  turning logos into brushes, 104–105
effects, artistic, 259–274
  colorizing line art, 263–265
  faking hand-drawn silhouette illustrations, 260–262
  instant woodcut effect, 270–271
  photo to line art morph, 272–274
  from photo to oil painting, 266–269
effects, color, 63–77
  colorizing black-and-white images, 67–69
  instant stock photo effect, 64–66
  painting away color, 70–71
  photo tinting, 76–77
  sepia tone effect, 74–75
  visual color change, 72–73

effects, cool type, 107–133
  carved in stone, 129–131
  distressed type, 126–128
  grunge type, 122–125
  instant 3D type, 108–110
  moving background objects in front of type, 120–121
  perspective type logo, 111–113
  putting images into type, 117–119
  transparent TV type, 132–133
  type on circles, 114–116
effects, edge, 231–256
  distressed edge effect, 250–253
  filmstrip templates, 232–237
  painted edges technique, 247–249
  photo mount effect, 238–243
  quick slide mounts, 244–246
  ripped edge technique, 254–256
effects, photographic, 21–37
  blending images for instant collages, 32–33
  montage from one image, 28–31
  putting images in monitors, 26–27
effects, portrait and studio, 1–19
  blurred background, 2–3
  burning in portraits, 14–16
  creating gallery prints, 6–11
  depth-of-field effect, 4–5
  sharp foreground, 2–3
  soft-edged portrait background, 12–13
  trendy fashion blowout look, 17–19
effects, special, 135–177
  attaching notes to photos, 139–143
  brushed metal, 152–153
  building video walls, 161–165
  digital pixel effect, 136–138
  dividing photos into puzzle pieces, 148–151
  gettin' gelly with buttons, 169–173
  lightning effect, 166–168
  mapping textures to persons, 144–147
  reflective chrome gradient, 156–160
  TV scan lines, 154–155
  yummy metal Web buttons, 174–177
effects filter, star, 195
effects, photographic
  adding motion effects, 34–37
  adding objects behind existing objects, 22–25
elliptical logo, 188
Entertainment Weekly, 28
ESPN, 100

events, sports, 100
existing images, adding persons into, 22
existing objects, adding objects behind, 22–25
exposure, maximum, 21–37

F
fade-away reflection, 91–93
fake classified ad, 94
fashion, trendy, 17–19
features
  cool Warp Text, 114
  Free Transform's Distort, 111
field, instant star, 200–201
filmstrip templates, 232–237
filters
  3D Transform, 208, 224
  diffuse, 250
  Displace, 144
  lamest, 208
  star effects, 195
flare, adding lens, 198–199
flyer cards, frequent, 98
focus effect, snapshot, 54–57
focus, creating depth and, 46
focusing attention, 43–61
  backscreening, 44–45
  magnifying glass trick, 58–61
  popping out images, 51–53
  snapshot focus effect, 54–57
  vignetting attention, 48–50
Fonzarelli, Arthur, 107
foreground, sharp, 2–3
four puzzle shapes, 148
Fox Sports, 100
frames, Polaroid snapshot, 54
Free Transform, 26, 111
frequent flyer cards, 98
frequent shopper cards, 98

G
gallery prints, creating, 6–11
gel design age, 169
glass trick, magnifying, 58–61
glassy reflections, 188–191
  creating, 192
glints, reflections, and shadows, 179–201
  adding lens flare, 198–199
  fastest logo job in town, 192–194
  glassy reflections, 188–191
  instant star field, 200–201
  Oscar Starbrights, 195–197
  perspective cast shadow, 180–183

reverse cast shadow, 184–187
glow, creating outer, 28
gradients
  rainbow, 218
  reflective chrome, 156–160
grayscale, converting images to, 74
grayscale images, colorizing, 67
grayscale conversion, contrasty, 74
ground and sky, reflection of, 156
Group, Clipping, 117
grunge type, 122–125

H
hand-drawn silhouette illustrations, faking, 260–262
hand-tinted effect, 67
Happy Days, 107
hardcover book effect, 3D, 208–212
high school senior portraits, 232
highlights, adding, 213
high-tech transparent info boxes, 100–103
Hollywood movie titles, 122
houses, windows of, 26
Hue/Saturation command, 67

I
iLife product box, Apple's, 148
illustrations, faking hand-drawn silhouette, 260–262
images
  adding persons into existing, 22
  adding perspective to, 213
  adding photo mounts to corners of, 238
  blending for instant collages, 32–33
  burned in effect around edges of, 12
  color rising grayscale, 67
  colorizing black-and-white, 67–69
  converting to grayscale, 74
  depth of, 213
  fitting into miscellaneous spaces, 26
  going out of focus, 4
  montage from one, 28–31
  popping out, 51–53
  putting in monitors, 26–27
  putting into type, 117–119
  RGB color, 270
  turning into pixels, 136
in living color, 63–77
  colorizing black-and-white images, 67–69
  instant stock photo effect, 64–66
  painting away color 70-71, 70–71

photo tinting, 76–77
sepia tone effect, 74–75
visual color change, 72–73
info boxes, high-tech transparent, 100–103
instant 3D type, 108–110
instant collages, blending images for, 32–33
instant star field, 200–201
instant stock photo effect, 64–66
instant woodcut effect, 270–271
interfaces
Apple's Aqua, 169
DVD, 100

J

jealous type, 107–133
jewelery, 84

L

lamest filter, 208
landscape photographer, 247
Las Vegas nightclub, 70
lens effects, 195
lens flare, adding, 198–199
Levi's print ad, 122
Li, Jet, 17
light source, impression of coming from
behind, 184
lightning effect, 166–168
line art, colorizing, 263–265
line art morph, photo to, 272–274
lines, TV scan, 154–155
living color, in, 63–77
colorizing black-and-white images,
67–69
instant stock photo effect, 64–66
painting away color, 70–71
photo tinting, 76–77
sepia tone effect, 74–75
visual color change, 72–73
LoCascio, Ted, 266
logo job in town, fastest, 192–194
logos
client, 104
creating glassy reflections on, 192
elliptical, 188
network, 132
perspective type, 111–113
round, 188
turning into brushes, 104–105
look
shot-in-the-studio, 84
trendy fashion blowout, 17–19

M

Mac OS X, 169
Madonna, 17
magazines, 64
3D, 204–207
ads, 88
Computer Arts, 204
covers, 14, 136
page from, 204
Photoshop User, 169, 266
Sports Illustrated, 46
spreads, 136
UK computer, 204
Map techniques, Displacement, 144
MasterCard, 98
maximum exposure, 21–37
metal, brushed, 152–153
metal Web buttons, yummy, 174–177
MGM Grand, 70
modeling shots, 232
modes, RGB color, 263
money, show me the, 203–229
monitors
putting images in, 26–27
wall made on the TV, 161
montage from one image, 28–31
morph, photo to line art, 272–274
motion effects, adding, 34–37
mount effect, photo, 238–243
mounts, slide, 244–246
movie poster layout, 122
movie posters, 17, 126
movie titles, Hollywood, 122
movies
Dirty Dancing, 43
VH1 original, 28
multimedia, 44
multiple images, collage, 32

N

network, UPN TV, 111
network logos in lower right-hand of
TV screens, 132
newspaper, page from, 204
night, shadows of the, 179–201
nightclub, Las Vegas, 70
notes, attaching to photos, 139–143

O

objects
adding, 22–25
adding objects behind existing, 22–25
moving background, 120–121

oil painting, from photo to, 266–269
Olive Garden restaurant, 48
one hour photo, 1–19
one image, montage from, 28–31
one-point perspective effect, 111
online portfolios, 244
shots used in, 232
options, Outer Glow, 28
Options Bar, 104, 254
original movie, VH1, 28
Oscar Awards, distant shots of stage
at, 195
Oscar Starbrights, 195–197
Outer Glow option, 28

P

packaging
creating 3D, 213–217
DVD, 218
product, 213
packaging effects, 3D and, 203–229
3D hardcover book effect, 208–212
3D magazine effect, 204–207
3D photo cubes, 224–229
creating 3D packaging, 213–217
creating DVD effect, 218–223
pages
from magazines, 204
from newspapers, 204
starting blank, 21
painted edges technique, 247–249
painting
away color, 70–71
from photo to oil, 266–269
park, SeaWorld theme, 54
persons
adding, 22
mapping textures to, 144–147
perspective, adding to images, 213
perspective cast shadow, 180–183
perspective transformation, applying
to type, 108
perspective type logo, 111–113
phone cards, 98
photo
blurring copy of, 2
finish, 231–256
to line art morph, 272–274
mount effect, 238–243
one hour, 1–19
retouchers, 238
tinting, 76–77
photo background, backlit, 80–83
photo cubes, 3D, 224–229

photo effect, instant stock, 64–66
photo sources, stock, 250
photo to oil painting, from, 266–269
photographers
    landscape, 247
    portrait, 247
    travel, 238
    wedding, 238
photographic effects, 21–37
    adding motion effects, 34–37
    adding objects behind existing
        objects, 22–25
    blending images for instant collages,
        32–33
    montage from one image, 28–31
    putting images in monitors, 26–27
photographic special effects, 1
photos. See also Shots
    adding captions to, 139
    attaching notes to, 139–143
    black-and-white, 6
    converting into drawings, 260
    credit cards from, 98–99
    displaying client, 232
    dividing into puzzle pieces, 148–151
    grunging, 122
    images extending out from, 51
    road of the three stock, 64
    starting each project with, 21
    taken for editorial purposes, 34
Photoshop training CD-ROMs, 100
Photoshop User magazine, 169, 266
Picker, Brush, 104
pictures. See Photos; Shots
pieces, dividing photos into puzzle,
    148–151
pixel effect, digital, 136–138
pixels, images turning into, 136
Polaroid snapshot frame, 54
popping out images, 51–53
portfolios
    online, 244
    shots used in online, 232
portrait and studio effects, 1–19
    blurred background, 2–3
    burning in portraits, 14–16
    creating gallery prints, 6–11
    depth-of-field effect, 4–5
    sharp foreground, 2–3
    soft-edged portrait background,
        12–13
    trendy fashion blowout look, 17–19
portrait background, soft-edged, 12–13
portrait photographers, 247

portraits
    30-second, 12
    background for, 88
    burning in, 14–16
    high school senior, 232
poster layout, movie, 122
posters, movie, 17, 126
print, 44, 100, 154, 184
print ads, 14, 17, 28, 51, 64, 70, 94
    Levi's, 122
prints, creating gallery, 6–11
product background, quick elegant,
    84–87
product box, Apple's iLife, 148
product packaging, 213
product shots
    of all kinds, 88
    background, 12
    changing colors in, 72
product shot background, quick,
    88–90
products
    displayed on white background, 91
    purchasing, 79
projects
    background for collage, 200
    starting each with photographs, 21
prospective effect, one-point, 111
purchasing products, 79
puzzle pieces, dividing photos into,
    148–151
puzzle shapes, four, 148

Q

quick slide mounts, 244–246
quick product shot background, 88–90

R

racket, tennis, 91
rainbow gradient, 218
reflections
    adding small, 188
    creating glassy, 192
    fade-away, 91–93
    glassy, 188–191
    of ground and sky, 156
reflections, shadows, and glints,
    179–201
    adding lens flare, 198–199
    fastest logo job in town, 192–194
    glassy reflections, 188–191
    instant star field, 200–201
    Oscar Starbrights, 195–197

perspective cast shadow, 180–183
    reverse cast shadow, 184–187
reflective chrome gradient, 156–160
restaurant, Olive Garden, 48
retouchers, photo, 238
reverse cast shadow, 184–187
reverse type, creating, 139
RGB color mode, 263
RGB image, color, 270
ripped edge technique, 254–256
round logo, 188
royalty-free stock photos, 64

S

Saturation command. See Hue/
    Saturation command
Saturday night special, 135–177
scan lines, TV, 154–155
scores, displaying, 100
screening. See Backscreening
screens
    network logos in lower right-hand of
        TV, 132
    TV, 26
Seabiscuit, Ryan, 63
SeaWorld theme park (Orlando,
    Florida), 54
senior portraits, high school, 232
sepia tone effect, 74–75
shading, adding, 213
shadow effect, drop, 180–183
shadows
    adding drop, 46
    of the night, 179–201
    perspective cast, 180–183
    reverse cast, 184–187
shadows, glints, and reflections, 179–20
    adding lens flare, 198–199
    fastest logo job in town, 192–194
    glassy reflections, 188–191
    instant star field, 200–201
    Oscar Starbrights, 195–197
    perspective cast shadow, 180–183
    reverse cast shadow, 184–187
shapes, four puzzle, 148
sharp foreground, 2–3
shopper cards, frequent, 98
shot-in-the-studio look, 84
shots
    catalog, 88
    changing colors in product, 72
    modeling, 232
    product, 88
    travel, 232

used in online portfolios, 232
wedding, 244
how me the money, 203–229
ilhouette illustrations, faking hand-drawn, 260–262
ky, reflection of ground and, 156
lide mounts, quick, 244–246
ot club cards, 98
mall reflections, adding, 188
napshot focus effect, 54–57
napshot frame, Polaroid, 54
oft border technique, 48
oft spotlight, 84
oft-edged portrait background, 12–13
oftening edges, 48
paces, fitting images into miscellaneous, 26
pecial, Saturday night, 135–177
pecial effects, 135–177
  attaching notes to photos, 139–143
  brushed metal, 152–153
  building video walls, 161–165
  digital pixel effect, 136–138
  dividing photos into puzzle pieces, 148–151
  gettin' gelly with buttons, 169–173
  lightning effect, 166–168
  mapping textures to persons, 144–147
  photographic, 1
  reflective chrome gradient, 156–160
  TV scan lines, 154–155
  yummy metal Web buttons, 174–177
ports, Fox, 100
ports events, 100
ports Illustrated magazine, 46
potlight, soft, 84
pread, magazine, 136
tar effects filter, 195
tar field, instant, 200–201
tar Trek Enterprise series, 179
tar Trek: The Next Generation, 179
tarbrights, Oscar, 195–197
tats, displaying, 100
tock photo effect, instant, 64–66
tock photo sources, 250
tock photos, royalty-free, 64
tone, carved in, 129–131
tore brands, 126
trokes, different, 259–274
tudio 54, 70
tudio effects, portrait and, 1–19
  blurred background, 2–3
  burning in portraits, 14–16
  creating gallery prints, 6–11
  depth-of-field effect, 4–5

sharp foreground, 2–3
soft-edged portrait background, 12–13
trendy fashion blowout look, 17–19
Swayze, Patrick, 43

T

Talented Mr. Ripley, The, 184
team info, displaying, 100
techniques
  create-something-from-nothing, 200
  Displacement Map, 144
  painted edges, 247–249
  ripped edge, 254–256
  soft border, 48
television. See TV
templates, filmstrip, 232–237
tennis racket company, fictitious, 91
Text, Warp, 114
textures
  creating background, 238
  mapping to persons, 144–147
theme park, SeaWorld, 54
tinting, photo, 76–77
titles, Hollywood movie, 122
tone, sepia, 74–75
Transform, Free, 26
Transform filter, 3D, 224
transformation, perspective, 108
transparent info boxes, high-tech, 100–103
transparent TV type, 132–133
travel photographers, 238
travel shots, 232
trendy fashion blowout look, 17–19
trick, magnifying glass, 58–61
Tuscadero, Pinky, 107
TV, 70, 94, 154
TV monitors, wall made out of, 161
TV network, UPN, 111
TV scan lines, 154–155
TV screens, 26
  network logos in lower right-hand of, 132
TV type, transparent, 132–133
type
  applying perspective transformation to, 108
  on circles, 114–116
  creating reverse, 139
  damaged, 126
  distressed, 126–128
  grunge, 122–125
  instant 3D, 108–110

jealous, 107–133
moving background objects in front of, 120–121
putting images into, 117–119
transparent TV, 132–133
wrapping around, 51
type effects
  carved, 129
  cool, 107–133
type logo, perspective, 111–113

U

UK computer magazines, 204
UPN TV network, 111

V

version, diffuse filter, 250
VH1 original movie, 28
video, 100
  box, 213
  Dirty Dancing, 43
video walls, building, 161–165
vignetting attention, 48–50
Visa, 98
visual color change, 72–73

W

wall made out of TV monitors, 161
walls, building video, 161–165
Warp Text feature, cool, 114
watches, 84
Way She Moves, The, 28
Web, 14, 64, 154, 184
Web buttons, yummy metal, 174–177
wedding photographers, 238
wedding shots, 244
white background, products displayed on, 91
wild color effect, 64
windows of houses, 26
woodcut effects
  instant, 270–271
  transforming RGB image into, 270

Z

zoom blur, 34

COLOPHON

The book was produced by a design team using all Macintosh computers, including a Power Mac G4 733-MHz, a Power Mac G4 Dual Processor 1.25-GHz, a Power Mac G5 1.8-GHz, and a Power Mac G5 Dual Processor 2-GHz. We use Apple, LaCie, and Sony monitors.

Page layout was done using InDesign CS. The headers for each technique are set in 20-point CronosMM700 Bold with the Horizontal Scaling set to 95%. Body copy is set using CronosMM408 Regular at 10 points on 13-point leading, with the Horizontal Scaling set to 95%.

Screen captures were taken with TechSmith SnagIt 7.1.1 on a Dell Precision M60 and a Dell Precision Workstation 650, and were placed and sized within InDesign CS. The book was output at 150-line screen, and all in-house proofing was done using a Tektronix Phaser 7700 by Xerox.

ADDITIONAL RESOURCES

ScottKelbyBooks.com
For information on Scott's other books, visit his book site. For background info on Scott, visit www.scottkelby.com.

http://www.scottkelbybooks.com

Photoshop Elements Techniques
Photoshop Elements Techniques is a newsletter packed with practical, real-world tips and techniques from some of the leading Photoshop Elements gurus, including Dave Cross, Jan Kabili, Dave Huss, and Scott Kelby. Every issue will be a valuable resource for Photoshop Elements users. Visit the website to view subscription information.

http://www.photoshopelementsuser.com

Photoshop Elements Techniques Website
The ultimate source for Photoshop Elements users features tutorials, downloads, forums, and much more! The site also contains up-to-date Elements news, tips and tricks, and contests.

http://www.photoshopelementsuser.com

KW Computer Training Videos
Scott Kelby and Dave Cross are featured in a series of Adobe Photoshop and Adobe Photoshop Elements training DVDs, each on a particular Photoshop

or Elements topic, available from KW Computer Training. Visit the website or call 813-433-5000 for orders or more information.

http://www.photoshopvideos.com

The Photoshop Elements 3 Book for Digital Photographers
This book gives you the inside tips and tricks of the trade for correcting, editing, sharpening, retouching, and presenting your photos like a pro. You'll be absolutely amazed at how easy and effective these techniques are—once you know the secrets.

http://www.scottkelbybooks.com

National Association of Photoshop Professionals (NAPP)
The industry trade association for Adobe® Photoshop® users and the world's leading resource for Photoshop training, education, and news.

http://www.photoshopuser.com

Adobe Photoshop Seminar Tour
See Scott live at the Adobe Photoshop Seminar Tour, the nation's most popular Photoshop seminars. For upcoming tour dates and class schedules, visit the tour website.

http://www.photoshopseminars.com

Photoshop World Conference & Expo
The convention for Adobe Photoshop users has now become the largest Photoshop-only event in the world. Scott Kelby is technical chair and education director for the event, as well as one of the instructors.

http://www.photoshopworld.com

PlanetPhotoshop.com
"The Ultimate Photoshop Site" features Photoshop news, tutorials, reviews, and articles posted daily. The site also contains the Web's most up-to-date resources on other Photoshop-related websites and information

http://www.planetphotoshop.com

Mac Design Magazine
Scott is Editor-in-Chief of *Mac Design Magazine*, "The Graphics Magazine for Macintosh Users." It's a tutorial-based print magazine with how-to columns on Photoshop, Illustrator, InDesign, Dreamweaver, Final Cut Pro, and more. It's also packed with tips and shortcuts for your favorite graphics applications.

http://www.macdesignonline.com

You've seen our images in this book, now search the entire collection online at BrandX.com

You'll find objects with clipping paths, people, backgrounds, textures, abstracts, locations, concepts and more. Unique royalty-free images from Brand X Pictures are perfect for all your Photoshop® projects. Ready to manipulate or composite, they offer a world of possibilities. Best of all, Brand X Pictures are available online right now.

Unique Royalty-Free Images

The Ultimate Photoshop Elements 3 Resources
FROM THE EDITOR-IN-CHIEF OF *PHOTOSHOP USER* MAGAZINE

PHOTOSHOP ELEMENTS 3 FOR BEGINNERS DVD *By Scott Kelby*

Join Scott Kelby for a detailed introduction on the power and features of Photoshop Elements 3. If you want to get up and running quickly, this DVD offers an excellent way to focus on the essential tools and techniques you need to know. Scott concentrates on real-world, practical information that you can start using right away, to use Photoshop Elements 3 more effectively and efficiently.

PHOTOSHOP ELEMENTS 3 FOR BEGINNERS DVD | **BY SCOTT KELBY** | **$39.95** PLUS S&H

PHOTOSHOP ELEMENTS 3 FOR PHOTOGRAPHERS *By Scott Kelby*

Aimed specifically at photographers, this DVD walks you through the essential tools and key features of Photoshop Elements 3 that photographers use most. Scott Kelby, best-selling author and Editor of *Photoshop User* magazine, shows you how to make the most out of Photoshop Elements 3 so you can spend less time on your images and still get award winning results. If you're a photographer looking to get the most out of Photoshop Elements 3, grab this DVD and start transforming your photographs today!

PHOTOSHOP ELEMENTS 3 FOR PHOTOGRAPHERS DVD | **BY SCOTT KELBY** | **$39.95** PLUS S&H

PHOTOSHOP ELEMENTS 3 BOOK FOR DIGITAL PHOTOGRAPHERS *By Scott Kelby*

If you're ready for an Elements book that breaks all the rules, this is it, because it does something for digital photographers that's never been done before--it cuts through the bull and shows you exactly "how to do it." It tells you, flat-out, which settings to use, when to use them, and why. It's all Elements, step-by-step, cover-to-cover in the only book of its kind, and you're gonna love it!

PHOTOSHOP ELEMENTS 3 BOOK FOR DIGITAL PHOTOGRAPHERS | **BY SCOTT KELBY** | **$31.99** PLUS S&H

order your copy call 800-738-8513 or 813-433-5006
visit www.scottkelbybooks.com

...hop is a registered trademark of Adobe Systems, Inc.

The Basic Elements for Digital Photography

B&H

PHOTO - VIDEO - PRO AUDIO